NO ORDINARY MEN

NO ORDINARY MEN

Special Operations Forces Missions in Afghanistan

COLONEL BERND HORN

Foreword by General T.J. Lawson (Ret.),
Former Chief of the Defence Staff

DUNDURN
TORONTO

Editor: Dominic Farrell
Design: Laura Boyle and Jennifer Gallinger
Cover Design: Jennifer Gallinger
Printer: Webcom

Library and Archives Canada Cataloguing in Publication

Horn, Bernd, 1959- , author

    No ordinary men : Special Operations Forces missions in Afghanistan / by Bernd Horn ; foreword by General T.J. Lawson.

Includes index. Issued in print and electronic formats.

ISBN 978-1-45972-410-5 (paperback).--ISBN 978-1-45972-413-6 (pdf).--
ISBN 978-1-45972-414-3 (epub)

1. Canada. Canadian Armed Forces. Joint Task Force Two. 2. Special operations (Military science)--Afghanistan. 3. Afghan War, 2001- --Participation, Canadian. 4. Canada--Armed Forces--Afghanistan. I. Title.

DS371.412.H67 2009   958.104'7   C2009-902990-1
                                                  C2015-906890-8

1 2 3 4 5   20 19 18 17 16

We acknowledge the support of the **Canada Council for the Arts** and the **Ontario Arts Council** for our publishing program. We also acknowledge the financial support of the **Government of Canada** through the **Canada Book Fund** and **Livres Canada Books,** and the **Government of Ontario** through the **Ontario Book Publishing Tax Credit** and the **Ontario Media Development Corporation.**

Care has been taken to trace the ownership of copyright material used in this book. The author and the publisher welcome any information enabling them to rectify any references or credits in subsequent editions.

— *J. Kirk Howard, President*

The publisher is not responsible for websites or their content unless they are owned by the publisher.

Printed and bound in Canada.

VISIT US AT
Dundurn.com | @dundurnpress | Facebook.com/dundurnpress | Pinterest.com/dundurnpress

Dundurn
3 Church Street, Suite 500
Toronto, Ontario, Canada
M5E 1M2

DISCLAIMER

Names of individuals and operations used in this book, unless they are already part of the public/historical record, are pseudonyms, used to protect the identities of individuals or specifics of operational names.

TABLE OF CONTENTS

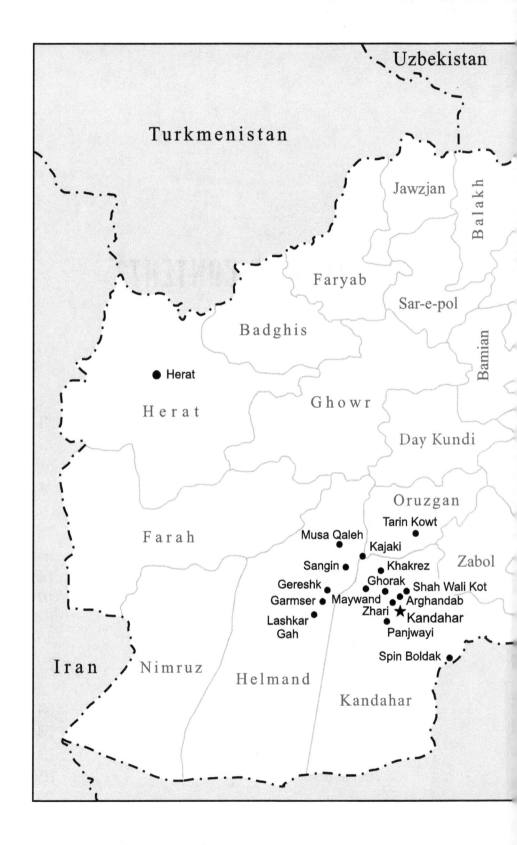

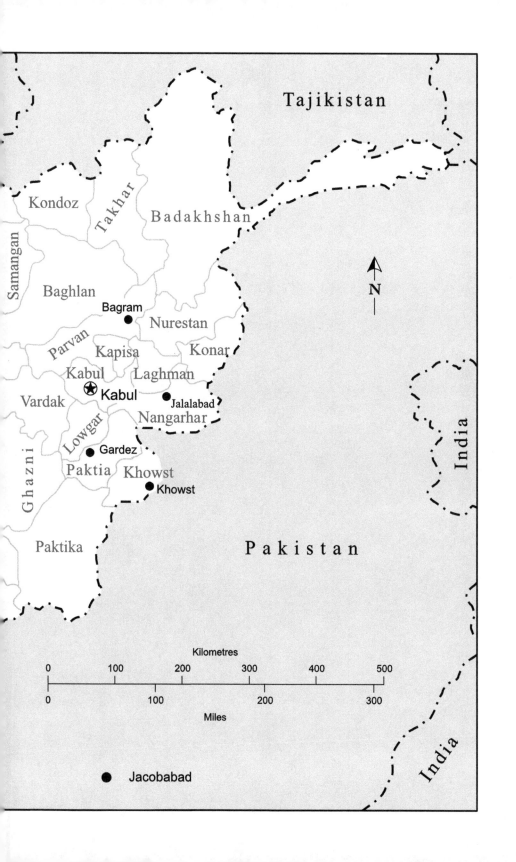

FOREWORD

I am delighted to have the opportunity to introduce *No Ordinary Men: Special Operations Forces Missions in Afghanistan*. Our special operations forces (SOF) have certainly proven their worth during the past twenty years, in war zones from Africa to Bosnia to Afghanistan. I was fortunate enough to have the opportunity to get to know many of the men and women who make up the Canadian special operations forces (CANSOF) community and I found them among the best the nation has to offer. Highly skilled, intelligent, and exceedingly professional, these warrior-diplomats consistently do Canada proud. In fact, their highly regarded skill sets, their ability to adapt to changing situations and circumstances, as well as their mental agility and knack for innovation, have earned them the respect of our allies to the point that our CANSOF capability is in high demand in the many struggles ongoing in the current security environment.

Nowhere was this more evident than in Afghanistan. The outstanding performance of CANSOF's special operations task force, which was deployed in support of the American special operation Enduring Freedom from December 2001 to November 2002, set a mark for excellence and served as a clear demonstration to our allies of what exactly our SOF are capable of achieving. Their re-introduction into the Afghan theatre as a special operations task force, where they served from 2005 until the end of Canadian combat operations in 2011, has simply reinforced perception of their ability and value.

Quite simply, as a direct result of their thoroughly planned missions and their courageous and tenacious execution of them, CANSOF operators have carved a name for themselves in the dangerous, inhospitable, and complex environment that is Afghanistan. It should be no surprise to anyone, as it was publicly announced on numerous occasions that CANSOF conducted myriad missions that disrupted and removed Taliban leadership, IED (improvised explosive device) facilitators, bomb-makers, as well as insurgent gunfighters. By the spring of 2007, CANSOF had removed an entire generation of Taliban leadership in the Kandahar area. This was achieved at great risk, but the payoff was huge. They not only removed many of those responsible for the deaths of Canadian service men and women, but by disrupting Taliban planning and operations, they provided our conventional forces, as well as those of our allies and the Government of Afghanistan, the necessary time and space to advance programs of reconstruction and governance. They continued this significant contribution right until the end of combat operations in 2011.

Telling the stories of such heroes, however, always presents a quandary. Although it is important to share CANSOF success with other members of the Canadian Armed Forces and Canadians at large, there is always a delicate balance between the desire for transparency and the need for operational security. Clearly, our number one priority is the safety of the men and women who serve in harm's way. As such, it is sometimes essential to keep certain details and events secret, to avoid providing the enemy with any advantage that might put Canadian, allied, or coalition lives or missions at risk. However, I am confident we can now release this book and tell some exciting stories that provide a glimpse of the courage and capability of your CANSOF operators. Undoubtedly, you will shortly realize that they are no ordinary men.

General T.J. Lawson (Ret.)
Former Chief of the Defence Staff

INTRODUCTION

Rounds snapped through the air and whacked into the thick mud walls as two Joint Task Force 2 (JTF 2) special operators scrambled onto the roof of a nearby building. The dark Afghan sky became the backdrop for a dynamic light show. Red and green tracers arced through the night, and the sky was punctuated by brilliant orange flashes of light as rocket-propelled grenades (RPGs) and artillery rounds impacted into the ground and walls of the surrounding compounds.

A JTF 2 assault force had been dropped off just moments earlier by large lumbering CH-47 Chinook helicopters. The soldiers stepped immediately into a hailstorm of fire. A relatively simple raid in theory, to capture a Taliban leader, had turned drastically complex in execution. Instead of only five Taliban fighters being present, in accordance with the intelligence assessment they were given prior to departure, in reality the JTF 2 troops were met by what seemed to be hundreds of enemy swarming around the target location.

Unruffled by the sea of belligerents surging around them, two of the JTF 2 operators surveyed their surroundings through their night vision goggles (NVGs) and picked up a number of insurgents working their way through a wadi (valley) system on the flank of the special operations forces (SOF) assault element. The operators trained their infrared (IR) laser sights on the approaching enemy. Seen through their goggles, the lasers cut through the dark night air with a bright red beam that connected the weapon system to the target like the hand of god. Invisible to the naked eye, the red beam was a virtual sentence of death.

The JTF 2 operators took up the slack in their triggers and then squeezed off successive shots, repositioning their lasers in quick succession. The muffled "thup, thup, thup" of their silenced weapons went unrecognized in the din of explosions and the exchange of automatic rifle fire that filled the air all around them. The only clues that betrayed the presence of the two SOF operators on the roof were the dead insurgents that now lay lifeless on the hard, unforgiving Afghan soil.

Despite the death and destruction being wreaked on the Taliban, they kept up the pressure on the outnumbered JTF 2 soldiers. The fight became one for survival. Even the aerial arsenal being unleashed by the protective AC-130 Spectre gunship overhead could not stop the wave of insurgents intent on crashing over the SOF assault force.

The desperate action waged between Canadian troops and Taliban insurgents that warm night in a remote district of Afghanistan is not one that is widely known. The fact that it was conducted by Canada's elite CANSOF forces — or that the nation even had SOF operators — was equally little known. In fact, most Canadians have no understanding of what special operations forces actually are, much less that Canada has a considerable history with SOF and SOF-like organizations.

SOF are traditionally defined as forces that are "specially selected, specially trained, specially equipped, and given special missions and support."[1] However, in the more contemporary security environment, particularly since the terrorist attacks on the Twin Towers of the World Trade Center in New York on September 11, 2001 (9/11), special operation forces have become the force of choice due to their agility, high readiness, and unique capabilities. Not surprisingly, the definition of SOF has also evolved to better reflect their true nature. As a consequence, SOF are now defined as below:

organizations containing specially selected personnel that are organized, equipped, and trained to conduct high-risk, high-value, special operations to achieve military, political, economic, or informational objectives by using special and unique operational methodologies in hostile, denied, or politically sensitive areas to achieve desired tactical, operational, and/or strategic effects in times of peace, conflict, or war.[2]

Within the Canadian context, CANSOF units and personnel are organized, trained, and equipped to accomplish operational tasks, including but not be limited to the following core tasks:

- counterterrorism;
- maritime special operations;
  - maritime counterterrorism;
  - boarding operations;
- direct action (DA);
- special recovery operations;
  - personnel recovery operations;
  - hostage rescue operations;
  - noncombatant evacuation operations;
  - material recovery operations;
- special protection operations;
  - close personal protection;
  - special force protection;
- sensitive site exploitation (SSE);
- special reconnaissance;
- irregular warfare;
  - military assistance;
  - stability activities;
  - counterinsurgency;
- special aerospace warfare;
  - special operations air-land integration;

- airborne reconnaissance and surveillance; and
- airborne fire support.

Tasks set aside, it must be understood that the key component of SOF success is its people. SOF selection is a rigorous process that specifically seeks those that demonstrate a number of key attributes. Specifically, SOF looks for individuals who are:

1. *Risk Accepting* – Individuals who are not reckless, but rather carefully consider all options and consequences and balance the risk of acting versus the failure to act. They possess the moral and physical courage to make decisions and take action within the commander's intent and their legal parameters of action to achieve mission success regardless of possible career consequences.
2. *Creative* – Individuals who are capable of assessing a situation and devising innovative solutions, kinetic or non-kinetic, to best resolve a particular circumstance. In essence, they have the intellectual and experiential ability to immediately change the combat process.
3. *Agile Thinkers* – Individuals who are able to transition between tasks quickly and effortlessly. They can perform multiple tasks at the same time — in the same place, with the same forces. They can seamlessly transition from kinetic to non-kinetic modes, or vice versa, employing the entire spectrum of military, political, social, and economic solutions to complex problems to achieve the desired outcomes. They can react quickly to rapidly changing situations, transitioning between widely different activities to ensure they position themselves to exploit fleeting opportunities. Moreover, they can work effectively within flexible rules of engagement (ROE) in volatile, ambiguous, and complex threat environments and use the appropriate levels of force.
4. *Adaptive* – Individuals who respond effectively to changing situations and tasks as they arise. They do not fear the

unknown but embrace change as an inherent and important dynamic element in the evolution of organizations, warfare, and society.

5. *Self-Reliant* – Individuals who exercise professional military judgment and disciplined initiative to achieve the commander's intent without the necessity of constant supervision, support, or encouragement. They accept that neither rank nor appointment solely defines responsibility for mission success. They can function cohesively as part of a team, but are also able to perform superbly as individuals. They will continue to carry on with a task until it is impossible to do so. They take control of their own professional development, personal affairs, and destiny, and strive to become the best possible military professional achievable. They demonstrate constant dedication, initiative, and discipline, and maintain the highest standards of personal conduct. They understand that they are responsible and accountable for their actions at all times, and always make the correct moral decisions, regardless of situation or circumstance.

6. *Seeking Challenge* – Individuals who have an unconquerable desire to fight and win. They have an unflinching acceptance of risk and a mindset that accepts that no challenge is too great. They are tenacious, and unyielding in their pursuit of mission success.

7. *Consistently Pursuing Excellence* – Individuals who consistently demonstrate an uncompromising, persistent effort to excel at absolutely everything they do. Their driving focus is to attain the highest standards of personal, professional, and technical expertise, competence, and integrity. They have an unremitting emphasis on continually adapting, innovating, and learning to achieve the highest possible standards of personal, tactical, and operational proficiency and effectiveness.

8. *Relentlessly Pursuing Mission Success* – Individuals who

embody a belief that, first and foremost, the demand of service to country before self is fundamental to SOF and is practised to a higher level and order of magnitude that is normally practised in military organizations. They have an unwavering dedication to mission success and an acceptance of hardship and sacrifice. They strive to achieve mission success at all costs, yet within full compliance of legal mandates, civil law and the law of armed conflict.

9. *Culturally Attuned* – Individuals who are warrior-diplomats, who are comfortable fighting but attempt to find non-kinetic solutions to problems. They are capable of operating individually, in small teams, or larger organizations, integrally, or with allies and coalition partners. They are comfortable and adept at dealing with civilians, other governmental departments (OGD), and international organizations, as well as non-governmental organizations (NGOs). They are culturally attuned and understand that it is important to "see reality" through the eyes of the other culture. They understand that it is not the message that was intended that is important, but rather the message that was received. They strive to be empathetic, understanding, and respectful at all times when dealing with others. They comprehend that respect and understanding build trust, credibility, and mission success.[3]

This pursuit of specific individuals who embody these attributes and characteristics has been the key to SOF efficacy throughout its history. After all, it is the specially trained and equipped operators who are capable and empowered to proactively, as well as reactively, take the necessary decisions and actions that ensure mission success. It is their courage, innovation, agility of thought, and individual and team capability that have always provided the secret behind SOF effectiveness. This record of excellence has generated five internationally accepted and espoused SOF "Truths" that speak to the nature of SOF and special operations.

1. *Humans are more important than hardware.* The SOF operator is the "core system" and the reason for mission success. In essence, SOF equips and enables the man; it does not man the equipment.

2. *Quality is better than quantity.* This truth is self-explanatory. In the end, effectiveness and special operations mission success are normally more dependent on the presence of qualified, specially trained, and experienced operators — agile in thought and action, culturally attuned, and adaptive, and creative in their response to changing, complex, or ambiguous situations — than on the number of actual boots on the ground.

3. *SOF cannot be mass produced.* The special selection and subsequent training, education, and experience that accumulate over time through the necessary practice, exercise, and operations to create the fully mature, insightful, reflective, and capable SOF operator take time, as well as dedicated resources and mentorship. There are no short cuts or easy methodologies for increasing output.

4. *Competent SOF cannot be created rapidly after emergencies occur.* A solid SOF capability, with depth of personnel and capacity, requires a consistent, well-resourced structure that continually nurtures and grows that capability and looks to the future to ensure constant evolution in order to not only be capable of reacting to and defeating the next threat but also of pre-empting and disrupting it. SOF must always stay ahead of a nation's adversaries. Without this consistent long-range outlook, the ability to quickly generate the necessary SOF capability, or increased capacity, is impossible in the immediate aftermath of a crisis. It will take time to create/develop/grow the necessary SOF response after the fact if it has not been anticipated, supported, or resourced prior to the emergency.

5. *Most special operations require non-SOF assistance.*[4] Despite SOF's attributes and characteristics, SOF relies on

conventional forces to assist in most of its mission sets, either troops in supporting functions, particularly combat enablers that are not already integrated into standing task forces (e.g., airlift, fires, intelligence, surveillance, reconnaissance (ISR)), or combat forces (e.g., cordon and/or follow-on forces).[5]

But it must also be understood that selecting the right individuals and training them to perform precision drills in ambiguous, complex, and very dangerous environments is not enough. SOF also inculcates its members with an ethos that shapes the community and all those in it. The CANSOF ethos is captured through the expression of its core values:

1. ***Internalization of Canadian Armed Forces (CAF) Core Values*** – this entails understanding, accepting, and internalizing the four core values of the CAF, which are fundamental to CANSOFCOM members as Canadians and practitioners of the profession of arms. Specifically the CAF values as interpreted by SOF are:

    a. **Duty** – First and foremost: service to country before self; unwavering dedication to mission success; acceptance of hardship and sacrifice; compliance with law and adherence to the law of armed conflict; maintenance of the highest levels of tactical and technical competence; audacity in accepting personal risk for mission accomplishment; the relentless pursuit of excellence in the execution of all tasks; constant dedication, initiative, and discipline; maintenance of the highest standards of personal conduct; being responsible and accountable for one's actions at all times; and always making the correct moral decisions regardless of situation or circumstance;

b. **Loyalty** – Unquestioned allegiance to country and faithfulness to comrades; dedicated support of the intentions of superiors and obedience to lawful direction and commands; the strength to question and challenge decisions and directives when required (truth to power); and the adherence to the two moral imperatives of mission success and the safety and well-being of one's subordinates;

c. **Integrity** – Unconditional and steadfast commitment to a principled approach to meeting obligations; trustworthiness in the context of handling the nation's most sensitive missions and information; maintaining the nation's values; operating to the highest moral standards and always being responsible and accountable for one's actions regardless of situation or circumstance. It requires transparency in actions and honesty in word and deed within the constraints of operational security and the tenet of "need to know"; and

d. **Courage** – Willpower and the resolve not to quit; an uncompromising and unrelenting drive to overcome all obstacles and achieve mission success; an overwhelming desire to fight and win; willingness to disregard the cost of an action in terms of physical difficulty, risk, discomfort, advancement, or popularity; and ability to make the right choices among difficult alternatives. SOF demands uncompromising moral and physical courage under all conditions.

2. *Relentless Pursuit Of Excellence* – An uncompromising, persistent effort to excel at absolutely everything; a

consistent and driving focus at attaining the highest standards of personal, professional, and technical expertise, competence, and integrity; an unremitting emphasis on continually adapting, innovating, and learning to achieve the highest possible standards of personal, tactical, and operational proficiency and effectiveness.

3. *Indomitable Spirit* – The unconquerable desire to fight and win; the acceptance of risk; a mindset that accepts that no challenge is too great; a tenacious, unyielding and unremitting pursuit of mission success; and a disregard for discomfort.

4. *Shared Responsibility* – The exercising of professional military judgment and disciplined initiative to achieve the commander's intent; an acceptance that neither rank nor appointment define sole responsibility for mission success; the requirement for everyone to contribute to the plan, conduct and execution of a task through collaborative planning, innovative ideas, feedback, the sharing of expertise and competence; and the unwavering loyalty and support of those entrusted with a task or command. This includes the responsibility of "Truth to Power," that is the requirement to address shortcomings in ability, experience or training whether it is found in subordinates, peers, or superiors.

5. *Creativity* – The realization that innovation, agility of thought and action, as well as inventive and unconventional solutions to unexpected problems are the only response to a battle space that is complex and chaotic, as well as rife with ambiguity, uncertainty, and change; the rejection of risk aversion or a reliance on status quo traditional responses to new, unique, or changing circumstances.

6. *Humility* – An adherence and dedication to quiet professionalism; a personal commitment to the highest standards of professionalism; and a focus on serving a higher authority — the nation and the people of Canada.[6]

In sum, the term *SOF* is more than an official descriptor; it applies to more than a suite of equipment and is more than a unit designation. It signifies a mindset and philosophical approach to war as much as it does an organizational capability. It is the agility, courage, and cognitive capacity, as well as tenacity and the relentless pursuit of mission success embodied in its practitioners that truly form a nation's SOF core capability. It is the spirit that strives for perfection and is undaunted by any challenge, regardless of how formidable it may seem. It is an ethos that accepts nothing short of mission success. This book captures that spirit and outlines Canada's SOF legacy. But more specifically, it provides insight into six Canadian SOF operations in Afghanistan from 2005 to 2011 that clearly demonstrate that the nation's SOF operators are no ordinary men.

CHAPTER 1

THE CANADIAN SOF LEGACY[1]

The general public has become more attuned to SOF as a result of 9/11 and the war in Afghanistan. For many, though, the existence of an elite Canadian counterterrorist unit only became known as a result of a media disclosure that they were deploying to Afghanistan in support of the American effort. However, the nation's SOF legacy goes far deeper than that. In fact, Canada has a long history and association with SOF.

After all, nothing embodies the idea of daring special operations more than the practice of *la petite guerre* by the French Canadian raiders during the struggle for colonial North America. Facing a harsh climate, unforgiving terrain, and intractable and savage enemies, the intrepid Canadian warriors personified boldness, courage, cunning, and tenacity. Their fearless forays and daring raids behind enemy lines struck terror in the hearts of their Native antagonists, as well as the British and American colonists and soldiers. In fact, for an extended period of time, these tactical actions had a strategic effect on the bitter struggle for North America.

Schooled in the bitter war of annihilation with the Iroquois in the seventeenth century, the French Canadians developed a class of fighters who were able to adapt to the new style of warfare required in the

New World.[2] Moreover, they demonstrated an intellectual and tactical agility that made them unsurpassed in "raiding" and what would later be dubbed commando operations. Their emphasis on stealth, speed, violence of action, physical fitness, and courage, as well as their ability to mount joint operations with indigenous allies created a force that successfully wreaked havoc on their enemy.

This capability, much to the misery of the English, was consistently displayed as the two competing European powers increasingly fought for control of North America. Quite simply, the French consistently relied on the outnumbered Canadians to hold onto French territory through their proficient execution of their distinct Canadian way of war, specifically small parties of experienced *coureur de bois* and partisans who conducted dangerous scouts, ambushes, and raids in English territory.[3] Raids against the English in Hudson Bay in 1686, the Seneca in New York in 1687, the Iroquois in 1693 and 1696, and a number of devastating strikes against English settlements such as Casco, Deersfield, Haverhill, Salmon Falls, and Schenectady during a succession of wars from 1688 to 1761, provided proof of the effectiveness of the French Canadian raiders who specialized in the conduct of lightning strikes behind enemy lines.

Many French and Canadian leaders, particularly those with extended exposure to the North American manner of war, or those born and raised in Canada, came to reject the conventional European manner of making war. Rather, they believed that the optimum war-fighting technique was achieved by a mixed force — regulars, with their military strengths (e.g., courage, discipline, tactical acumen), and volunteers and Natives, with their strengths (e.g., endurance, familiarity with wilderness navigation and travel, marksmanship) — who relied more on initiative, independent action and small unit tactics than on rigid military practices and drills. The effectiveness of the Canadians was evidenced in the fear they created in their enemies. British generals and numerous contemporary English accounts conceded that the Canadian raiders "are well known to be the most dangerous enemy of any ... reckoned equal, if not superior in that part of the world to veteran troops."[4]

The impact of the French Canadian raiders was immense. One British colonel confided, "I am ashamed that they have succeeded in all their scouting parties and that we never have any success in ours."[5] This state of affairs continually blinded the British command and deprived them of intelligence of French preparations or plans. Understandably, this often led to poor and untimely decisions, which in turn led to unfortunate consequences, whether the ambush of a British column or the loss of a strategic fort.[6] Moreover, the constant depredations, ambushes, and raids of the Canadians and their Native allies caused a constant material and economic drain on the British. But equally important, they created an overwhelming blow against the morale of the Anglo-American colonies. The British forces seemed unable to strike back. It was a constant series of defeats, thwarted campaigns, and offensives, all of which devastated the Anglo-American colonies. Everywhere, the Canadians and Natives would appear as phantoms in hit-and-run attacks, leaving in their wake smouldering ruins and the mutilated bodies of the dead and dying. Despite their small numbers, they consistently inflicted a disproportionately high number of casualties on the enemy. The end result was an utterly paralyzing effect on the English combatants and colonists alike.[7]

The unmitigated success of the French Canadians raiders forced the British to develop a similar capability of their own. One of the first efforts was in 1744, in the North American theatre of operations, as part of the larger War of the Austrian Succession (1740–1748). During this conflict, the British presence in the Maritimes was once again prey to the marauding Abenakis and Mi'kmaq war parties that were aligned with the French. As a result, an "independent corps of rangers," also known as the corps of New England Rangers, was raised. Two companies were recruited and deployed to Annapolis, Nova Scotia, in July 1744 to reinforce the garrison. In September, a third company arrived, led by Captain John Goreham.

Goreham's command composed of sixty Mohawk and Metis warriors. Familiar with the Native way of war, they swiftly engaged the French and their Native allies. Massachusetts governor William Shirley commended Goreham and his Rangers for their success, stating that "the garrison is now entirely free from alarms."[8] The majority of the companies later returned to Massachusetts, where they originated, leaving Captain Goreham and his company to patrol Nova Scotia alone from 1746 to 1748. Their success was such that Shirley wrote, "the great service which Lieutenant-Colonel

Gorham's Company of Rangers has been to the Garrison at Annapolis Royal is a demonstration of the Usefulness of such a Corps."⁹

Goreham's Rangers continued to serve on the volatile frontier. Prior to the onset of the French and Indian War, also known in its global context as the Seven Years' War (1756–1763), Goreham's Rangers were used to protect the British settlements in Nova Scotia against Native raids. However, with the official outbreak of the war, they became increasingly involved in military operations, specifically because of their expertise at irregular warfare.¹⁰

Despite their prior success, Goreham's Rangers were eclipsed in the war by a British creation aimed at matching the effectiveness of the French Canadian raiders in the strategically important Lake Champlain theatre of operations. What the British eventually created was the legendary Rogers' Rangers. In the early stages of the war, when fortunes seemed to be against the British, Robert Rogers's knowledge and experience with the "haunts and passes of the enemy and the Indian method of fighting" soon brought him to the attention of his superior, Major-General William Johnson.¹¹ By the fall of 1755, Rogers was conducting dangerous scouts deep behind enemy lines. Rogers's efforts soon earned him an overwhelming reputation. These efforts also led Major-General William Shirley, then the commander-in-chief of the British Army in North America, to argue:

> It is absolutely necessary for his Majesty's Service, that one Company at least of Rangers should be constantly employ'd in different Parties upon Lake George and Lake Iroquois [Lake Champlain], and the Wood Creek and Lands adjacent ... to make Discoveries of the proper Routes for our own Troops, procure Intelligence of the Enemy's Strength and Motions, destroy their out Magazines and Settlements, pick up small Parties of their Battoes upon the Lakes, and keep them under continual Alarm.¹²

By the winter of 1756, Rogers's bold forays with his small band of unofficial rangers behind enemy French lines were regularly reported in newspapers throughout the colonies. They provided a tonic to a belea- guered English frontier. In March 1756, Major-General Shirley, ordered Rogers to raise a sixty-man independent ranger company that was sep- arate from both the provincial and regular units. As such, it was titled His Majesty's Independent Company (later Companies) of American Rangers. His unit was directed to scout and gain intelligence in the Lake Champlain theatre, as well as "distress the French and their allies by sacking, burning, and destroying their houses, barns, barracks, canoes, battoes ... to way-lay, attack, and destroying their convoys of provisions by land and water."[13]

The reputation and accomplishments of the rangers soon had an impact on British officers. All wanted rangers to accompany their exped- itions as a foil against the enemy's Canadians and Natives, and because of the rangers' ability to navigate and survive in the merciless wilderness.

Without doubt, Rogers' Rangers, as they became universally known, brought to life the ranger tradition in North America and ensured it would forever endure. Their deeds and prowess have with time become legendary, even if this is not fully deserved.

Indeed, Rogers was repeatedly bested by his Canadian counterparts and normally suffered horrendous casualties. Generals Jeffrey Amherst and Thomas Gage considered the Canadians superior to the American Rangers.[14] In addition, throughout this period, Goreham's Rangers were also active. In 1758, they played an important part in the capture of the strategic Fortress of Louisbourg and a year later assisted in the exped- ition against Quebec. In fact, at the end of the conflict the British high command rated Goreham's Rangers, although rarely mentioned, as the most highly rated ranger organization employed during the war.[15]

Nonetheless, Rogers' Rangers, led by the very adventurous, coura- geous, and exceptionally tough Robert Rogers, created a very romantic image that seemed to both symbolize, as well as define, the strength of the American ranger.

And the American rangers, together with the Canadian rangers, established a tradition of adventurous, if not daring, action that was very aggressive and always offensively minded. The ranger tradition that was created also valorized the concept of individuals who were seen as mav- ericks, outside of conventional military institutions and mentality — men who were adaptable, robust, and unconventional in their thinking and war fighting; men who could persevere against the greatest hardships and despite an inhospitable environment and merciless enemy, achieve mission success.[16]

* * *

The tenacious spirit engendered by the rangers in the eighteenth century would remain with Canada's warriors and be resurrected in future generations. The more contemporary component of Canada's SOF legacy coincided with the explosion of special operations forces at the commencement of World War II (WWII). In essence, modern-day SOF are largely a phenomena of this era.

Paradoxically, they were largely born in crisis from a position of weakness. They were created to fill a specific gap. In the immediate aftermath of the early German victories, the Allies found themselves devoid of major equipment, with questionable military strength, and on the defensive throughout the world.[17]

Despite the still smouldering British equipment on the beaches of Dunkirk, the combative new prime minister, Winston Churchill, declared in the British House of Commons on June 4, 1940, "We shall not be content with a defensive war."[18] He was well aware that to win a war meant ultimately offensive action. Only through offensive action could an army provide the needed confidence and battle experience to its soldiers and leaders. Furthermore, only offensive action could sustain public and military morale. Also, offensive action represented a shift in initiative. Striking at the enemy would force Germany to take defensive measures that would demand a diversion of scarce resources.

That afternoon, Churchill penned a note to General Hastings Ismay of the War Cabinet Secretariat, "We are greatly concerned ... with the dangers of the Germans landing in England," he wrote, "... why should it be thought impossible for us to do anything of the same kind to them?" He then added, "We should immediately set to work to organize self-contained, thoroughly equipped raiding units."[19] After all, exclaimed Churchill, "how wonderful it would be if the Germans could be made to wonder where they were going to be struck next, instead of forcing us to try to wall in the island and roof it over!"[20]

On June 6, Churchill sent yet another missive to Ismay. "Enterprises must be prepared," he wrote, "with specially trained troops of the hunter class who can develop a reign of terror down these coasts, first of all on the butcher and bolt policy." He vividly recounted, "There comes from the sea a hand of steel that plucks the German sentries from their posts."[21] He then curtly directed the "Joint Chiefs of the Staff to propose me measures for a vigorous, enterprising, and ceaseless offensive against the whole German-occupied coastline." He added the requirement for deep inland raids that left "a trail of German corpses behind."[22]

As a result, during the early years of the war a plethora of SOF organizations and units, such as the Special Operations Executive (SOE), the Commandos, the Long Range Desert Group (LRDG), the Special Air Service (SAS), and the American Rangers, to name a few, emerged, creating a means to strike back at the seemingly invincible German military machine.

One of the first unconventional efforts was the creation of the Special Operations Executive, which was a British secret service intended to promote subversive warfare in enemy-occupied territory. It was formed in July 1940 in the aftermath of the disastrous retreat from Dunkirk, as England braced itself for the inevitable invasion. It was designed as a "full[-]scale secret service, the mere existence of which could not be admitted either to Parliament or to the press."[23] The SOE became responsible for "all operations of sabotage, secret subversive propaganda, the encouragement of civil resistance in occupied areas, the stirring up of insurrection, strikes, etc., in Germany or areas occupied by her."[24] Specifically, the SOE was responsible for training agents and organizers, as well as deploying them into the various target countries, with the object of establishing basic subversive organizations that could be expanded as required as the situation allowed. The main functions of the subversive organizations were explained as:

a. Political Subversion and Propaganda: To encourage the population of the occupied countries against the forces of occupation and to undermine the morale of the latter;

b. Sabotage: To build up a sabotage organization wherever the Axis can be effectively attacked, which is mainly in the occupied territories. The object of this activity is to wear down the Axis morally and economically and so hasten the date by which our military forces can take the offensive. Sabotage efforts must be correlated with those of the fighting services especially the bomber forces, and our present short term policy is, therefore, based on the instructions recently given to Bomber Command, whose efforts we intend to supplement by attacking rail, sea, canal, and road transport. The sabotage organization must also be prepared to harass the Axis lines of communication, should Great Britain be invaded, and to intensify its activities in close co-operation with any [A]llied invasion of the [C]ontinent;

c. The Organization of Secret Armies: To build up and equip secret armies in occupied territories. These armies, in co-operation with the sabotage organizations, will be prepared to assist our military forces when they take the offensive, either directly in the theatre of operations or indirectly elsewhere, by attacks on communications, whether telegraphic or transport, by neutralization of seizure of aerodromes, by a general attack on enemy aircraft and personnel, and by producing disorder in the enemy's rearward services.[25]

The Canadian connection was not long in coming. Shortly after its creation, the SOE queried the senior Canadian commander overseas, Major-General A.G.L. McNaughton, for Canadian volunteers. Specifically, they were looking for French Canadians for service in France, Canadians of Eastern European descent for the Balkans, and Chinese Canadians for Far East operations. Clearly, the racial, linguistic, and cultural attributes and knowledge of these volunteers would provide the SOE with, in many aspects, ready-made operatives. Inculcating the specific technical skills would just be a matter of training.

The Canadian volunteers, like the remainder of the men and women trained to serve in the SOE during World War II "were quickly made to forget all thoughts about Queensbury rules and so-called 'gentlemanly' warfare ... [and they] were taught a vast range of sabotage techniques and bizarre methods of killing."[26] Moreover, they were thoroughly trained in advising, arming, and assisting members of the various resistance movements in the enemy-occupied countries.

As much of the art and science of SOF was in its infancy, it is not surprising that SOE selection was inefficient. Initially, it consisted of a three- to four-week selection/training course. However, this was soon deemed too leisurely and ineffective. Many of those on course were failed out at the end of the process, which proved a waste of time and resources. By July 1943 a new selection course (student assessment board (SAB)) had been developed. This applied a variety of psychological and practical tests to candidates over a four day period. In this manner, questionable volunteers were screened out early. The SAB took less time and provided better results.

Successful volunteers went through several phases of training. The first phase focused on ensuring all operatives were in top physical condition. In addition, the course provided all with an in-depth proficiency with Allied and German small arms, as well as expertise in explosives and demolition work. The first phase also provided instruction in the recognition of German uniforms and equipment. The next stage of training was conducted at the commando training centre in Arisaig, in the western Highlands of Scotland near the Isle of Skye. This phase provided rigorous field training and live fire exercises. Following the commando training came parachute qualification in Manchester. At the termination of qualification training, operatives were then separated according to their respective skills and sent to specialized training centres.

The Canadian connection to the SOE went beyond the volunteers who served in the organization. It also extended to the establishment of Special Training School (STS) 103 or Camp X, which was located on secluded farmland outside of Whitby, Ontario. The camp served two functions. The first was to train men recruited in Canada, such as French Canadians and refugees from Eastern Europe, for service with the SOE in Europe. The second function was to give top-secret assistance to the American foreign intelligence service, an activity that could not be done in the United States as long as the United States remained neutral in the war.[27]

Camp X was the first secret-agent training establishment in North America. It opened on December 9, 1941, and trained individuals according to their cultural groups. The officers, less the camp adjutant, were all British; however, the senior non-commissioned officers were all Canadian. Camp X closed on April 20, 1944.

Throughout the war, 227 Canadians served in the SOE in the various theatres of the conflict. In addition, Canadian personnel in the Royal Canadian Air Force and those posted to Royal Air Force units also served in the Special Duties Squadrons used to drop weapons and insert and extract SOE personnel.[28] In the end, the value of the SOE was immense. In a Supreme Headquarters Allied Expeditionary Force (SHAEF) report to the Combined Chiefs of Staff on July 18, 1945, General Dwight "Ike" Eisenhower's staff noted, "without the organization, communications, training, and leadership which SOE supplied ... resistance [movements] would have been of no military value."[29]

The SOE, however, was not the only innovative, unconventional effort. In a remarkable display of military efficiency, by June 8, 1940, two days after Churchill's directive, Field Marshal Sir John Dill, the chief of the Imperial General Staff, received approval for the creation of the Commandos and, that same afternoon, Section MO9 of the War Office was established. Four days later, Churchill appointed Lieutenant-General Sir Alan Bourne, the adjutant-general of the Royal Marines, as "Commander of Raiding Operations on Coasts in Enemy Occupation and Advisor to the Chiefs of Staff on Combined Operations."[30]

The men drawn to the commando idea very quickly brought into being the concept that was expected. Raiding was their primary role. In essence, they were to be trained to be "hard[-]hitting assault troops" who were capable of working in co-operation with the navy and air force. As such, they were expected to execute plans from headquarters and capture strong points, destroy enemy services, neutralize coastal batteries, and wipe out any designated enemy force by surprise.[31] They were also told that they would have to become accustomed to longer hours, more work, and less rest than the other members of the armed forces.

Predictably, the commando units attracted a like-minded group of aggressive, action-oriented individuals. "There was a sense of urgency, a striving to achieve an ideal, an individual determination to drive the physical body to the limit of endurance to support a moral resolve," explained one veteran officer. "The individual determination," he added, "was shared by every member of the force, and such heights of collective idealism are not often reached in the mundane business of soldiering."[32] Together they forged a "commando spirit," one comprised of determination; enthusiasm and cheerfulness, particularly under adverse conditions; individual initiative and self reliance; and, finally, comradeship.[33]

Canada, however, was initially slow to react to the commando concept. Moreover, its commitment to creating an elite commando unit in World War II did not last very long, a reality that betrayed the nation's underlying sentiment toward SOF-type units. In fact, the government's creation of the Canadian "Viking Force" was actually a response to public criticism at home and the opportunity the British raiding program provided. Major-General Harry D.G. Crerar, reacting to public criticism and government pressure to get Canadian troops into the fray, since they had been in England for almost two years and had still not engaged in battle with the enemy, took the initiative as the acting commander of the Canadian Corps and spoke to his immediate superior, Lieutenant-General Bernard Law Montgomery, commander of the South-Eastern Army in England, about utilizing Canadian troops in a commando role.

Montgomery was not a proponent of SOF forces, but he did see raiding as a means to instil offensive spirit and combat experience within his command. As such, Crerar did not have a hard sell. "I believe that occasions will increasingly present themselves for small raids across the Channel opposite the Army front," Crerar argued, "in default of a reputation built up in battle, the [Canadian] Corps undoubtedly would receive great stimulus if, in the near future, it succeeded in making a name for itself for its raiding activities — a reputation which, incidentally, it very definitely earned for itself in the last war."

Montgomery replied, "Your men should be quite first class at raiding" and he gave Crerar the green light to run Canadian raiding activities from the port of Newhaven.[34]

Crerar lost no time and on March 6, 1942, discussed raiding operations with the director combined operations, Lord Louis Mountbatten. Mountbatten was initially reluctant to accept Canadian participation in raiding because he felt that it would dilute the role of the British Commandos, who had a monopoly on the activity. However, Mountbattten was well attuned to political realities and made an exception. He laid out two conditions for the Canadians:

1. ample time should be allowed for proper organization and training — this was stated to be six to eight weeks; and
2. the enterprise should be known only to the Corps commander, BGS (brigadier general (staff)), and a limited number of his own (Mounbatten's) staff.[35]

That afternoon, a second meeting between Crerar, BGS Guy Simonds, and Brigadier J.C. Haydon, commander of the special service force (SSF), transpired.[36] In this forum the senior officers present reached a decision to create a Canadian commando unit of two hundred men, who were to start training by mid-March.

The Canadian commando unit, named Viking Force, was based on 2nd Division. Within a fortnight, 267 volunteers from the division were training at Seaford in the muddy estuary of the Cuckmere River in Sussex. The Viking Force organization was based on the British Commandos but was on a smaller scale. The headquarters section was led by a major and comprised twenty-four all ranks. A further thirty-six officers and men staffed the support squadron (i.e., intelligence, signals, and medical). The remaining 130 personnel were divided into two troops, each consisting of five officers and sixty men. The Viking Force placed heavy emphasis on firepower. In addition to the standard .303 Lee Enfield rifle, each troop carried four Bren light machine guns and eight Thompson submachine guns, as well as two anti-tank rifles and a two-inch mortar.

Within days of the commencement of training, instructors whittled the large group of volunteers down to its official strength of 190 all ranks. From April 4, 1942, personnel from the SSF joined the men of Viking Force to increase the intensity of the training and begin to turn them into hardened commandos. The commanding officer (CO) responsible for whipping the Canadian neophyte commandos into shape was Major Brian McCool of the Royal Regiment of Canada.

During the last half of April 1942, training intensified. It now included speed marches with weapons and sixty-pound rucksacks, river crossings, leaping from crags into sand pits fifteen feet below, cliff climbing, and night manoeuvres. If the men did not get back to the beaches in time to be ferried to the mother ship during these training exercises, they had to swim back with their full equipment .

On April 30, Montgomery visited Major-General Andrew McNaughton, the Canadian Corps commander, and they agreed that the Canadians should form the main striking force for a planned raid on the French port of Dieppe. That same day, McNaughton's headquarters issued a training instruction to enlarge the scale of combined operations training. This new direction was designed to cover the training of 4 and 6 Brigades for the large conventional raid planned on Dieppe. Therefore, before Viking Force was even fully established, BGS Simonds already laid the blueprint for its demise. "Personnel of detachments which have completed [combined operations/commando] training in accordance with Instruction No. 7," he ordered, "will be returned to parent units and employed as a cadre to develop combined operations techniques within the latter."[37]

As a result, Viking Force became swept up in the preparations for Operation Rutter (i.e., the Dieppe raid), and the intensive training that had been reserved for the elite of Viking Force was now extended to the entirety of 4 and 6 Brigades. Quite simply, Major McCool and his cadre became instructors for the others. In this regard, from the end of May to the beginning of July the Viking Force cadre became key to the efforts to help 4 and 6 Brigades master the rigours of amphibious warfare.

However, with the emphasis on conventional forces to take over the raiding role it was not surprising that Crerar wrote on June 4, 1942, "The opportunity to land on enemy shores may not long be denied us." He added,

The training of detachments, units and formations of the Canadian Corps, with this end in view has already proceeded some distance.... It is the intention that it shall be carried through to the stage when every formation of the Corps is thoroughly capable of taking full part in operations involving the landing on beaches in enemy occupation, and the rapid seizure and development of "bridgeheads."

He ended his missive with a revealing, "There must be no need for the Canadian Corps to call upon outside, and special 'Commando' units for assistance in initial beach-landing operation."[38]

The new Canadian approach was a polar opposite to the original intent. Viking Force had been intended as a hard-hitting group of specially trained raiders whose job was to inflict damage on the enemy in limited operations using surprise as a major element and then employing their skills to withdraw before enemy had time to recover. Diluted among the battalions in 4 and 6 Brigades during the ill-fated Dieppe raid on August 19, 1942, the original Viking Force commandos were never given the opportunity to do the job they had been trained for. In the aftermath of the disastrous raid, no effort was made to resurrect Viking Force.[39]

However, the Dieppe raid did lead to the establishment of another SOF-like Canadian organization, namely the Royal Canadian Navy (RCN) Beach Commandos. Their genesis stemmed from the Dieppe raid, where Royal Naval (RN) Beach Parties ("C," "D," and "H") were responsible for disembarking troops and vehicles from assault landing craft, organizing and supervising suitable "beach" areas, and loading serviceable vessels at the time of withdrawal. Of the two hundred navy personnel assigned to the Beach Parties during the Dieppe raid, sixty-three became casualties. As a result, all three RN Beach Parties had to be totally reconstituted. Not surprisingly, soon after Dieppe the Admiralty decided to change the Combined Operations Beach Party Branch name to "Naval Commandos." Accordingly, the Admiralty directed that twenty Beach commandos would be required for the invasion of Occupied Europe (i.e., two each for three assault divisions, one per assault brigade, with 100 percent spare in reserve).[40]

The RCN soon created its own capability and in late 1943 established RCN Beach Commando "W." This unit was modelled upon its Royal Navy counterpart and comprised of eighty-four RCN Volunteer Reserve men (i.e., twelve officers and seventy-two ratings (enlisted personnel). The Naval Beach Commando was described as "a unit especially trained in the control and handling of landing craft on the beaches …[and] is designed to handle landing ships, craft, and barges of an assault brigade group and the further ships, craft and barges landed on the same beaches."[41] Beach Commandos were also responsible for neutralizing beach obstacles, mines, and booby traps.

RCN Beach Commando "W" was assigned to Force "J" on Juno Beach during the Normandy invasion on June 6, 1944, and served with valour and distinction. Canadian newspapers quickly trumpeted the role of the Beach Commandos and described them as the "leather tough Canadians" and "tough, scrappy and self-reliant."[42] Beach Commando "W" was disbanded at the end of August 1944.

Canada's SOF legacy in World War II did not end with the Dieppe raid. One month prior to the disastrous assault, another SOF-like organization that fits into the legacy of Canada's CANSOF community was created, namely the 1st Canadian Parachute Battalion (1 Cdn Para Bn). Although contemporary airborne units are not considered SOF, 1 Cdn Para Bn, like many of the early airborne organizations that sprang up early in World War II, meets many of the SOF criteria. The paratroopers were specially selected, specially trained, and given special missions behind enemy lines. They possessed an indomitable spirit that defied any challenge. In fact, the selection rate for 1 Cdn Para Bn in its infancy was only 30 percent.[43]

At its creation, the army's generals, as well as the media at large, were clear on the type of individual and organization they were creating. Robert Taylor, a reporter for the *Toronto Daily Star*, described the volunteers as "action-hungry and impatient to fill their role as the sharp, hardened tip of the Canadian army's 'dagger pointed at the heart of Berlin.'"[44]

Senior military officers described the new Canadian paratroopers as "super-soldiers" and newspapers, with unanimity, invariably described the parachute volunteers as "hard as nails" representing the toughest and smartest soldiers in the Canadian Army.[45]

One journalist wrote, "They are good, possibly great soldiers, hard, keen, fast-thinking and eager for battle," while another asserted that they were "Canada's most daring and rugged soldiers ... daring because they'll be training as paratroops: rugged because paratroops do the toughest jobs in hornet nests behind enemy lines."[46] Others painted a picture of virtual supermen. One writer invited his readers to "Picture men with muscles of iron dropping in parachutes, hanging precariously from slender ropes, braced for any kind of action ... these toughest men who ever wore khaki."[47] Another simply explained that "your Canadian paratrooper is an utterly fearless, level[-]thinking, calculating killer possessive of all the qualities of a delayed-action time bomb."[48]

But it had not always been that way. Initially, the senior generals had rejected the need for Canadian paratroops, citing a lack of role and purpose for such specialized troops in the Canadian context. However, by the spring of 1942, both the British and Americans fully embraced the concept of airborne forces. And, as the tide of the war began to swing in favour of the Allies, the focus quickly swung from defence to offence. And nothing embodied raw, offensive, aggressive action more than paratroopers. Very quickly, airborne troops became a defining component of a modern army. Not to be left out, senior Canadian military commanders quickly reversed their earlier reservations and recommended the establishment of a parachute battalion to J.L. Ralston, the minister of National Defence (MND). The minister readily agreed and on July 1, 1942, the Canadian War Cabinet Committee approved the formation of a parachute unit, namely 1 Cdn Para Bn.

The unit's training was in many ways innovative for the time and exceeded the challenges faced by other combat troops. Greater demands were placed on the individual soldier for leadership, weapon handling, and navigation. Orders for exercises and later operations were always given to all ranks, so that regardless of the circumstances of a parachute drop everyone had an understanding of the mission and so would be able to execute the necessary tasks whether or not officers or senior non-commissioned officers (NCOs) were present. As such, the unit placed an exorbitant emphasis on courage, physical fitness, tenacity, and particularly on individual initiative.

With no domestic defence role in Canada, the unit was offered up to the commander of Home Forces in England. The British quickly accepted the offer and the government announced in March 1943 that 1 Cdn Para Bn would be attached to the 3rd Parachute Brigade, as part of the 6th Airborne Division. For the remainder of the war the battalion fought as part of a British formation. It established a remarkable record. The battalion never failed to complete an assigned mission, nor did it ever lose or surrender an objective once taken. The Canadian paratroopers were among the first Allied soldiers to land in occupied Europe, the only Canadians who participated in the "Battle of the Bulge" in the Ardennes, and by the end of the war, they had advanced deeper into Germany than any other Canadian unit. Unquestionably, the paratroopers of the 1st Canadian Parachute Battalion, at great cost and personal sacrifice, pioneered a new innovative form of warfare and demonstrated agility of thought and action, as well as an unrivalled warfare spirit in their daring assaults behind enemy lines. They were disbanded on September 30, 1945, at Niagara-on-the-Lake.

Interestingly, in July 1942, at the same time as 1 Cdn Para Bn was established, the Canadian War Cabinet authorized a second "parachute" unit, designated the 2nd Canadian Parachute Battalion (2 Cdn Para Bn). The name of this unit was misleading, however. It was not a parachute battalion at all, but rather a commando unit. The designation was assigned for security reasons to cover the true nature of its operational mandate.[49] On May 25, 1943, the name was changed to reflect this. It was re-designated the 1st Canadian Special Service Battalion and it represented the Canadian element of the joint U.S./Canadian First Special Service Force (FSSF).[50]

Nonetheless, its genesis originated in England with Lord Mountbatten's Combined Operations Headquarters (COHQ) and Prime Minister Churchill's personal support. The original concept, code-named Operation Plough, was of a guerrilla force capable of operations in Norway to attack the hydroelectric and heavy water plants in that country, in order to disrupt the German war industry and the Nazi atomic weapons program.[51] Some thought was also put to using the force to destroy the Ploesti oil fields in Romania and hydroelectric facilities in Italy. In all, the planners reasoned that in destroying any of these targets a hard-hitting raiding force would not only damage Germany's vital war industry, it would also tie up German forces required to protect facilities and chase down the guerrilla force.[52]

The Americans accepted the project and Prime Minister Churchill and Lord Mountbatten very quickly convinced the Canadians to participate as well. As a result, a U.S./Canadian brigade-sized formation was created, with Americans and Canadians serving side by side, wearing the same American uniform, in a military command that was completely integrated. At any given moment, it was impossible to differentiate Canadian from American and vice versa. Each had officers commanding troops of the other nation. At inception, the Canadians contributed 697 all ranks to the formation, representing approximately a quarter of the total number of troops.[53]

As was the case with 1 Cdn Para Bn, the Canadian Army took their commitment seriously and attempted to pick the best soldiers possible for this unique endeavour. Colonel Robert T. Frederick, the American commander of the FSSF, made it clear that he preferred that Canadian volunteers be chosen in the "lower ranks between 18 and 45 [years old], physically rugged and mentally agile, physically able and willing to take parachute training."[54] It became obvious to everyone concerned that superior physical fitness, experience, maturity, and youth were the cornerstones on which the FSSF would be forged.[55] In addition, Frederick also stressed that it was imperative that each man be able to work efficiently independently or in small groups, regardless of the tactical situation or operational theatre. Ross Munro, the renowned Canadian war reporter, noted that the First Special Service Force "will be a continental edition of commandos of the British Army." He added, "In selecting the men to make it up, emphasis will be placed on 'youth, hardness and fitness.'"[56]

As the initial focus of the FSSF was to be sabotage, raiding, and guerrilla-type warfare, the "Forcemen" were trained in a wide spectrum of skills, including parachuting, demolitions, unarmed combat, weapons handling, mountaineering, and arctic warfare. Physical fitness very quickly became the decisive selection tool. Only the hardest of men could successfully complete the training. For instance, members of the FSSF were expected to be "capable of marching [thirty-five] miles a day across rough country or [ninety] miles without rest."[57]

But, after all, the force was to be ready to deploy to Norway on December 15, 1942, for an arduous and very dangerous mission. So, even as the FSSF was in the process of establishing itself, its training regime was in overdrive.

Upon arrival, members undertook their jump training, which in some cases, was all of forty-eight hours as opposed to the more standard three week course. In August 1942, journalist Don Mason captured the contemporary image of the force that was being created in Helena, Montana, where they were based: "The cream of Canada's hard-fighting army youth is training in the United States today for 'aerial commando' raiding which one day soon will make the German and the Jap think cyclones have struck where they thought they were safe and secure."[58]

However, by late 1942 it became clear that Operation Plough was not going to happen. There were three major impediments. First, Frederick's request for the temporary diversion of 750 Lancaster bombers to insert his formation hit an immediate wall. The intractable architect of Britain's strategic bombing campaign, Air Chief Marshal Charles Portal of the Royal Air Force (RAF), responded, "That is our best bomber." He continued, "if you can show us where Plough can accomplish more in its operation than one thousand Lancasters could do on the bombing runs, we shall consider the plane for your uses."[59]

Frederick's next dose of reality occurred when the Combined Operations Command planners briefed him on the Commando raiding program and, more important, the work of Brigadier Colin Gubbins's Special Operations Executive and their Norwegian sabotage campaign. Although the SOE had never even heard of Operation Plough, or the FSSF for that matter, they, too, had plans for sabotaging most of the targets that the FSSF was theoretically earmarked to destroy. Significantly, Gubbins's plan required very few aircraft and only two or three Norwegian soldiers for each target.[60]

The final nail in the coffin resulted from Colonel Frederick's discussion with Major-General Wilhelm von Tangen Hansteen, the commander in chief of the Norwegian Armed Forces. Hansteen bluntly informed Frederick that the king and prime minister of Norway opposed the concept of Operation Plough. They were concerned that the large-scale destruction of power would create a greater hardship for the Norwegian people than it would for the Germans. Moreover, although they welcomed any assistance in ousting the occupying German forces, they did not wish to do so by destroying the vital industrial infrastructure that was key to Norway's economic well-being.[61]

And so, with no aircraft, no host country support, and a competing organization that appeared to have a more efficient, more precise, and less resource-intensive means of achieving the same goal, Colonel Frederick quickly realized that Operation Plough was doomed. Any doubt he may have harboured was quickly dashed when he returned to London to meet with Lord Mountbatten prior to his flight to Washington, D.C. The chief of Combined Operations candidly explained to Frederick that Operation Plough was no longer a pressing issue.

By this time, Combined Operations and the whole raiding concept was under siege by the War Office. The Allied effort, particularly as a result of American might and industrial capacity, was slowly beginning to turn the tide of the war. Raiding and subversive activities, never fully supported by the mainstream military, were further marginalized as large-scale conventional operations such as the invasion of Northern Africa took shape.

Moreover, Mountbatten had no means of influencing the release of aircraft and he conceded that SOE provided a more economical means of achieving the desired result, not to mention at a more politically acceptable price for the Norwegian government in exile in London. As such, both men agreed to let Plough die. Frederick quickly sent a message to his formation in Helena, Montana. True to Frederick's character — it was short and to the point:

> Suspend effort on present line.... New plan may be radically different and not concerned with hydroelectric or other industrial installations.... Cease training on hydroelectric installations and ... stress general tactical training, to include attack of fortifications, pill boxes, barracks, and troop concentrations. Change in weapons may be necessary to provide greater firepower, so suspend further small arms training pending a decision.[62]

On his return to North America, Colonel Frederick briefed General Marshall, the American army chief of staff. He then left for Montana, unsure whether the FSSF would be continued or scrapped. That decision was now left with the General Staff to get a political decision. By October 8, 1942, the Canadian chief of the General Staff forwarded a telegram to Lieutenant-General McNaughton, Canada's overseas commander, informing him of the latest turn of events. The Canadians were now waiting for the Americans to make known their intentions prior to articulating their continuing support.

However, Major-General Murchie's missive provided some telling clues. The alternatives considered were:

a. continue with special service force if Americans so desire;
b. amalgamate with 1st Parachute Battalion;
c. disband and disperse personnel; and
d. retain as an ordinary parachute battalion for service and abroad.[63]

Murchie highlighted the negative effects of options B, C, and D. He stated each has the "disadvantage of unwelcome publicity over cancellation of highly publicized special service forces as have B and C over apparent curtailment of our plans for Cdn [Canadian] Parachute Troops."[64]

In due course, the Americans decided to proceed with the FSSF. On October 17, General Marshall informed Major-General Maurice Pope, the chairman of the Canadian Joint Staff in Washington, D.C., that a decision was reached to retain the FSSF as a special unit.[65] It was now up to the Canadians to confirm their continued participation.

Although a will to continue seemed to be present within the military, the ultimate decision was the purview of the politicians.[66] As such, the War Cabinet Committee discussed the issue on October 28, 1942. From a Canadian perspective the existence of the "elite" First Special Service Force was considered by the government to be of marginal operational value after its original mission was cancelled. The *Minutes of the War Cabinet Committee* noted, "Though the future employment of the unit was doubtful, beyond its existence as a 'stand-by' force, acceptance of the U.S. proposal [continue unit's existence for special operations] was recommended as a token of intimate co-operation between the two countries."[67]

With its existence guaranteed — at least for the time being — the question became: what was its role? FSSF became, in many ways, a highly specialized infantry, capable of a wide range of operations in virtually any terrain. In August 1943, the FSSF participated in the assault on Kiska Island. As the Japanese had already withdrawn from the Aleutians, the FSSF was quickly returned to the mainland and prepared for operations in Italy. Here the force made a name for itself because of its successful assault on Monte La Difensa, a seemingly impregnable German defensive position on the top of a 945 metre (3,100 feet) high mountain. Up until that time, the Germans had repelled numerous Allied attacks and, thus, delayed the advance toward the Gustav Line, the main German defensive line, and Rome, which lay beyond. On December 3, 1943, by a daring night assault that entailed climbing up the rear cliffs of the mountain, which the Germans considered impassable, the FSSF successfully captured the summit. However, the assault and subsequent struggle to maintain their hold over the saucer-shaped mountain top and extend their grip to the adjacent Monte La Remetanea inflicted a terrible toll on the formation. In the aftermath of the battle, the FSSF would never reach its former level of specialized capability or personnel. Reinforcements were simply pulled directly from normal reinforcement pools and given basic training on weapons and tactics.

Nonetheless, the FSSF reinforced its reputation at Anzio in February 1944, where, despite their light armament and only approximately 1,200 all ranks, they held an extended portion (thirteen kilometres) of the vital Mussolini Canal sector. Through aggressive night raiding, they struck fear into the enemy, who believed they were facing up to a small division. The German soldiers were so terrified by the FSSF raids that they nick-named them the "Black Devils." In the subsequent breakout phase, the FSSF advanced on Rome. Upon its capture, and after a brief period of rest and recuperation, the Force seized two of the Hyères Islands in the Mediterranean Sea, to protect the left flank of the landings on the French Riviera in August 1944. The FSSF then joined the Sixth Army Group in the advance through southern France.

The Canadian component of the FSSF, however, proved to be problematic for the Canadian government. Facing a manning shortage resulting from a conscription crisis, the continuing demands to provide reinforcements for the FSSF, which was difficult to administer and in the context of the dying days of the war was also arguably redundant, prompted the Canadian government to make a simple decision. The time had come to pull the Canadians from the force. As such, the FSSF was disbanded at Menton on December 5, 1944.

The disbandment of the FSSF was not surprising. As the tide of the war shifted in favour of the Allies, who by late 1942 had begun to field large modern armies, SOF evolved to provide specific capabilities not resident with the larger conventional military and perform distinct tasks such as raiding, sabotage, and economy-of-effort missions to tie down enemy forces. These activities were soon eclipsed by tasks such as strategic reconnaissance and unconventional warfare. But even at that, the Allied strategy had become a very attritional conventional approach, much akin to a large steamroller simply flattening the opposition before it. As such, the precision and special capabilities provided by SOF were neither required nor appreciated by most senior military commanders.

In the end, despite the overall success and value of special operations, SOF never received full acceptance from the larger military community.[68] The irregular nature of their tactics, the unconventional, if not rakish nature of the operators, who were often seen as lacking discipline and military decorum, as well as the almost independent status of the SOF organizations, were alien and distasteful to the more traditional and conservative-minded military leadership. Not surprisingly, at the end of the war, as already noted, most SOF organizations were disbanded.

Canada was no different. In fact, Lieutenant-General McNaughton provided a clear picture of his perception of SOF. "I have watched with interest the organization here [in England] of such special units as Commandos, Ski Battalions and Paratroops," he noted. He concluded, "The cycle is always the same — initial enthusiasm which is very high, drawing good officers and men from regular units, distracting and unsettling others, and upsetting the units' organization." As a result, he clearly stated his opposition to the formation of such units.[69]

Not surprisingly then, as noted, all Canadian SOF units were disbanded by September 1945. However, a brief breath of air seemed to rekindle the flames of a national SOF capability in 1947. Former members of the SOE, FSSF and 1st Cdn Para Bn developed a plan to resurrect a distinct Canadian SOF entity. Their methodology was as shadowy as the unit they intended to build.

The long, costly global struggle had taken its toll and a debt-ridden and war-weary government was intent on creating a post-war army that was anything but extravagant. Notwithstanding the military's achievements during the war, the Canadian government articulated two clear requirements for its peacetime army. First, it was to consist of a representative group of all arms of the service. Second, its primary purpose was to provide a small but highly trained and skilled professional force that in time of conflict could expand and train the citizen soldiers who would fight that war. Within this framework, SOF had no relevance.

As the army worked feverishly at demobilizing and at the same time creating the structure for the post-war Canadian Armed Forces (CAF), the commanding officer of the small Canadian Parachute Training Centre in Shilo, Manitoba, became instrumental in the next phase of Canadian SOF.[70] He selectively culled the ranks of the disbanded 1 Cdn Para Bn, which also included those from the FSSF. Quite simply, he chose the best from the pool of personnel who had decided to remain in the active force to act as instructors and staff for his training establishment.

Devoid of any direction from army headquarters, the CO and his staff focused on making contacts and keeping up to date with the latest airborne developments. These prescient efforts were soon to be rewarded. It was the perpetuation of links with Canada's closest allies, as well as the importance of staying abreast of the latest tactical developments in modern warfare, specifically air-transportability, that provided the breath of life that airborne and SOF advocates were searching for.

Not surprisingly, Canadian commanders were looking abroad for the way ahead in the post-war environment. In 1947, a National Defence Headquarters (NDHQ) study revealed that British peacetime policy was based on training and equipping all infantry formations to be air-transportable. Discussions with allies quickly ascertained that both the British and Americans would welcome an airborne establishment in Canada that would be capable of filling in the "gaps in their knowledge"

— specifically in areas such as the problem of standardization of equipment between Britain and the United States, and the need for experimental research into cold weather conditions. To its allies, Canada was the ideal intermediary.

Canadian military leaders quickly realized that co-operation with their closest defence partners would allow the country to benefit from an exchange of information on the latest defence developments and doctrine. For the airborne and SOF advocates, a test facility would allow the Canadian military to stay in the game. In the end, for the sake of efficiency of manpower and resources, NDHQ directed that the parachute training and research functions reside in a single Canadian joint army/air training centre. As a result, on August 15, 1947, the Joint Air School (JAS), in Rivers, Manitoba, was established.

The JAS became the "foot in the door." It was responsible for the retention of skills required for airborne and, with some ingenuity, special operations, for both the army and the Royal Canadian Air Force (RCAF). More important, the JAS, which was renamed the Canadian Joint Air Training Centre (CJATC) on April 1, 1949, provided the seed from which a SOF organization would eventually grow.[71]

The hidden agenda of the airborne advocates quickly took root. Once the permanent structure of the army was established in 1947, they quickly pushed to expand the airborne capability within the JAS by submitting a proposal in the spring for a Canadian special air service (SAS) company.[72] This new organization was to be an integral sub-unit of the army component of the JAS with a mandate of filling army, inter-service, and public duties such as army/air tactical research and development; demonstrations to assist with army/air training; airborne firefighting; search and rescue; and aid to the civil power.[73] Its development, however, proved to be quite different, as its name implies.

The initial proposal for the special sub-unit prescribed a clearly defined role. The army, which sponsored the establishment of the fledgling organization, portrayed the SAS Company's inherent mobility as a definite asset to the public at large for domestic operations. A military appreciation written by its proponents argued the need for the unit in terms of its potential benefit to the public. It explained that the specially trained company would provide an "efficient life and property[-]saving organization capable of moving from its base to any point in Canada in ten to fifteen hours."[74] Furthermore, the Canadian SAS Company was framed as critical in working in support of the RCAF air search/rescue duties required by the International Civil Aviation Organization agreement.

The proposed training plan further supported this image. The training cycle consisted of four phases broken down as follows: 1) tactical research and development (parachute related work and field[-]craft skills); 2) airborne firefighting; 3) air search and rescue; and 4) mobile aid to the civil power (crowd control, first aid, military law).[75] Conspicuously absent was any mention of commando or specialist training, which the organization's name suggested. After all, the Canadian SAS Company was actually titled after the British wartime Special Air Service, which earned a reputation for daring commando operations behind enemy lines.

In September 1947, the request for approval for the sub-unit was forwarded to the deputy chief of the General Staff. Significantly, it now had two additional roles added to it — public service in the event of a national catastrophe; and provision of a nucleus for expansion into parachute battalions. However, the proposal also noted that the SAS Company was required to provide the manpower for the large programme of test and development that was underway by the Tactical Research and Development Wing, as well as demonstration teams for all demonstrations within and outside the CJATC.[76]

As support for the sub-unit grew, so too did its real identity. An assessment of potential benefits to the army included its ability to "keep the techniques employed by [British] SAS persons during the war alive in the peacetime army."[77] Although this item was last in the order of priority in the list, it soon moved to the forefront.

NDHQ authorized the sub-unit with an effective date of January 9, 1948. Once this was announced, a dramatic change in focus became evident. Not only did its function as a base for the development of airborne units take precedence, but the previously subtle reference to combat fighting and war, specifically its special forces role, leapt to the foreground. The new terms of reference for the employment of the SAS Company, which were confirmed in April, outlined the following duties in a revised priority:

a. provide a tactical parachute company for airborne training. This company is to form the nucleus for expansion for
   the training of the three infantry battalions as parachute
   battalions;

b. provide a formed body of troops to participate in tactical
   exercises and demonstrations for courses at the CJATC and
   service units throughout the country;

c. preserve and advance the techniques of SAS [commando]
   operations developed during WW II (1939–1945);

d. provide when required parachutists to back-up the RCAF
   organizations as detailed in the interim plan for air search
   and rescue; and

e. aid civil authorities in fighting forest fires and assisting in national catastrophes when authorized by Defence
   headquarters.[78]

The shift was anything but subtle. The original emphasis on aid to the
civil authority and public service–type functions, duties that were attractive
to a war-weary and fiscally conscious government, were now re-prioritized
if not totally marginalized. It did, however, also represent the army's initial
reaction to the government's announcement in 1946, that airborne training for the Active Force Brigade Group (regular army) was contemplated
and that an establishment to this end was being created.

The new organization was established at company strength — 125
personnel all ranks. It was comprised of one platoon from each of the
three regular infantry regiments: the Royal Canadian Regiment (RCR),
the Royal 22nd Regiment (R22R) and Princess Patricia's Canadian Light
Infantry (PPCLI). All of the carefully selected members were volunteers, most with wartime airborne experience. They were all bachelors,
in superb physical condition, and possessed of initiative, self-reliance,
self-discipline, mental agility, and an original approach.

If there was any doubt of the intention of the unit, it was quickly dis-
pelled when Captain Guy D'Artois, a wartime member of the FSSF, and
later the SOE, was posted to the sub-unit as its second-in-command.
However, due to a difficulty in finding a qualified major, he became the

acting officer commanding.[79] After all, his credentials were impeccable. D'Artois had dropped by parachute into Mont Cortevaix in France, then under German occupation, in April 1944. Prior to the sector being liberated, he had trained six hundred partisans, established the Sylla underground, developed an eight-hundred-kilometre secure telephone line; he had also attacked the occupying German troops on numerous occasions within his area of operation. Moreover, he instilled in his French allies a taste for victory. For his feats, D'Artois was awarded the Distinguished Service Order and the French Croix de Guerre avec palme from General Charles de Gaulle. His service with the underground earned him the praise: "Major D'Artois is the embodiment of nobility in figure, strength, and stature, but more importantly, nobility in simplicity and kindness."[80]

D'Artois trained his sub-unit of carefully selected paratroopers as a specialized commando force. His intractable approach and trademark persistence quickly made him the "absolute despair of the Senior Officers at Rivers [CJATC]." Veterans of the SAS Company explained that "Captain D'Artois didn't understand 'no.' He carried on with his training regardless of what others said." Another veteran recalled that "Guy answered to no one; he was his own man, who ran his own show."[81]

But the issue was soon moot. At that point, the continued survival of the JAS and its limited airborne and SOF capability, as represented by the Canadian SAS Company, was largely due to a British and American preoccupation with airborne and air-transportable forces in the post-war period. This was based on a concept of security established on smaller standing forces with greater tactical and strategic mobility. In essence, possession of paratroopers represented the nation's ready sword. This was critical in light of the looming 1946 Canada/U.S. Basic Security Plan (BSP), which imposed on Canada the requirement to provide one airborne/air-transportable brigade, and its necessary airlift, as its share of the overall continental defence agreement. By the summer of 1948, the SAS Company represented the total sum of Canada's operational airborne and SOF capability. Clearly, some form of action was required.

As a result, the Chief of the General Staff directed that training for one battalion of infantry for airborne/air-transported operations be completed by April 1, 1949. After all, the BSP dictated that by May 1, 1949, the Canadian government be capable of deploying a battalion combat team prepared to respond immediately to any actual Soviet lodgement in the Arctic, with a second battalion available within two months, and an entire brigade group within four months.[82] This was the death knell for the Canadian SAS Company.

The Canadian Army was now finally moving toward its airborne/air-transportable active brigade group, which was titled the Mobile Striking Force (MSF). Its effect on the Canadian SAS Company was devastating. The respective highly trained SAS platoons provided the training staff for each of the regular force infantry regiments (i.e., RCR, R22R, PPCLI) that rotated through the JAS for parachute qualification, and upon completion returned to their parent regiments to provide an experienced airborne cadre for each of these regular force infantry regiments. The slow dissolution of the Canadian SAS Company was formalized by the CGS when he announced that the sub-unit would not be reconstituted upon the completion of airborne conversion training by the R22R, which represented the last unit of the three active force infantry regiments to undertake it.

The actual disbandment was so low-key that no official date exists. Its personnel just melted away. Nonetheless, the SAS Company served a critical function in Canadian airborne and SOF history. It was the "bridge" that linked 1 Cdn Para Bn and the three infantry battalions that conceptually formed an airborne brigade (i.e., the MSF). In so doing, it perpetuated the airborne spirit and kept the requisite parachute skills alive. In also perpetuated, albeit briefly, the concept of a selected, highly trained commando force capable of special operations in keeping with the SOE and SAS traditions of WWII.

The nation's SOF lineage went into a hiatus at this point. Neither the existence of the MSF or its successor the Defence of Canada Force represented a SOF capability. Arguably, neither even provided a real airborne capability for that matter.

As always, external factors influenced internal organizational shifts. By the early sixties, the notion of an army rapid reaction and special forces capability gathered momentum, largely fuelled by the American involvement in Vietnam. In 1966, Lieutenant-General Jean Victor Allard, the new commander of Force Mobile Command (FMC — i.e., Canadian Army), decided that the Canadian Army would develop a similar capability. Specifically, he aimed to have a completely air-portable unit, with all its equipment deployed and in the designated operational theatre in as quickly as forty-eight hours. Therefore, on May 12, 1966, the MND announced, "FMC [will] include the establishment of an airborne regiment whose personnel and equipment [can] be rapidly sent to danger zones."

For the army commander, the new airborne regiment represented flexibility and a higher order of professionalism and soldiering. The army commander clearly believed that "this light unit is going to be very attractive to a fellow who likes to live dangerously, so all volunteers can go into it." His creation was to be open to all three services and manned exclusively by volunteers. "We intend," he asserted, "to look at the individual a little more rather than considering the unit as a large body of troops, some of whom might not be suited for the task."[83]

In the spring of 1966, General Allard, now the Chief of the Defence Staff (CDS), took the next step and discussed the formation of what he fondly labelled the new "airborne commando regiment." Colonel Don H. Rochester was appointed as the commander-designate and he was given a further year to refine the "concept of operations," organization, and structure. The prospects seemed unlimited. The "exciting thing about General Allard's concept," recalled Rochester, "was that this unit was to be radically different. Except for aircraft, it was to be self-contained, with infantry, armour, artillery, engineers, signals, and supporting administration." Furthermore, he explained, "all were to be volunteers and so well trained in their own arm or service that they could devote their time to specialist training."[84]

The Canadian Airborne Regiment (Cdn AB Regt) was officially established on April 8, 1968.[85] It consisted of an airborne headquarters and signal squadron (eighty personnel), two infantry airborne commandos (278 personnel each), an airborne field battery (eighty personnel capable of providing two three-gun troops of pack howitzers, or two groups of six medium (82 mm) mortars), an airborne field squadron (eighty-one personnel), and an airborne service commando (i.e., combat service support and administration — eighty-nine personnel).

The regiment's mandate was impressive if not over-optimistic. The Cdn AB Regt was required to be capable of performing a variety of tasks, which included: the defence of Canada; the U.N. "stand-by" role; peacekeeping operations; missions in connection with national disasters; "Special Air Service"–type missions; *coup de main* tasks in a general war setting; and responsibility for parachute training in the CAF. The respective Canadian Forces organizational order (CFOO) stated, "the role of the Canadian Airborne Regiment is to provide a force capable of moving quickly to meet any unexpected enemy threat or other commitment of the Canadian Armed Forces."[86] In addition, the army commander, Lieutenant-General W.A.B. Anderson, ordered the Cdn AB Regt planning team to visit both the U.S. Special Forces Center, as well as the British SAS Regiment to gather the "necessary stimulus and factual data upon which to develop your concept."[87] Moreover, he directed that an element of the regiment must be proficient at: HALO [High Altitude Low Opening] team parachute descents; deep penetration patrols; underwater diving; obstacle clearance and laying of underwater demolitions; mountain climbing; and special service forces–type team missions.[88]

Although outwardly a conventional airborne regiment, it was clear that the Cdn AB Regt, both officially, in accordance with its CFOO, and through direction given by the CAF chain of command, was intended to be capable of special operations. The emphasis on SOF-like capability was also enshrined in the operational concept, as well as in the later doctrinal manual, *CFP 310 (1) Airborne — The Canadian Airborne Regiment.* Under the heading "Special Operations," a long list of tasks was included that were clearly special forces–like in nature. Specifically, the document stated that the

> Canadian Airborne Regiment is to be prepared to carry out the following operations for which it is specially trained: disruption of lines of communications; destruction of critical installations; psychological warfare operations; special intelligence tasks; recovery tasks; deception operations; internal security operations; counter-guerilla operations; and support of indigenous paramilitary forces.[89]

The emphasis on special operations was not lost on the Cdn AB Regt's leadership, which focused at times almost exclusively on daring, direct-action, commando-like raids. Moreover, as a number of former commanding officers noted, if something happened (e.g., a terrorist incident), they knew they would get the call, so they attempted to train individuals in the necessary skills required for special operations.

The quality of the original individuals was incontestable. Official recruiting themes stressed the superior attributes of the new genre of warrior. They emphasised the fact that the new paratrooper had to be an excellent athlete, an expert at small arms, and a survival specialist. Furthermore, they underscored the necessity of their soldiers being robust, courageous, and capable of a high level of endurance.

Not surprisingly, the Cdn AB Regt received a high percentage of the more ambitious, determined, and energized individuals in the CAF. They skimmed the cream of the army. Only experienced officers, non-commissioned officers, and soldiers were accepted. All riflemen within the commandos were required to be qualified to the rank of corporal. This meant that they had previously served within a regular rifle battalion. As a result, they were already competent and experienced in the basic drills of soldiering. Equally important, they were, on the whole, older and, normally, more mature. This allowed the regiment to direct its training efforts toward specialized training such as mountain and pathfinder operations, patrolling courses, skiing, and unarmed combat.

The Cdn AB Regt quickly forged a reputation for undertaking tough, demanding, and dynamic activities. It set new standards for physical fitness and training realism. In consonance with its status as a strategic force capable of global deployment, the regiment travelled throughout Canada and the United States, as well as to exotic locations such as Jamaica, to practise its lethal craft. It conducted training and exchanges with the British SAS, American Rangers and Special Forces, and the French Foreign Legion. By the early seventies, the airborne regiment was at its zenith of power. It had the status of a mini-formation, direct access to the commander of the army, and an increased peacetime establishment of 1,044 all ranks.

The Cdn AB Regt deployed to Montreal, Quebec, during the FLQ Crisis in October 1970, and four years later was dispatched to Cyprus during the Turkish invasion of that island. However, in all cases the regiment functioned solely as conventional infantry. On November 26, 1976, the Cdn AB Regt was moved from Edmonton to Petawawa and its formation status was stripped.[90] It became a simple unit within the newly re-roled special service force (SSF), which provided the army with a relatively light, airborne/air-portable quick reaction force in the demographic centre of the country, one that could be moved quickly to augment either of the flanking brigades (i.e., 1 Canadian Mechanized Brigade in the West and 5 Mechanized Brigade in Quebec) for internal security tasks, to the Arctic, or to U.N.-type operations.[91]

The restructuring inflicted additional wounds. The regiment was dramatically pared and it lost both its preferred standing within the army manning and exemptions from the mundane taskings that other units endured. Out of necessity, it began to accept more junior members across the board (i.e., officers, senior NCOs, and men); this resulted in a corollary degradation of capability. Moreover, it became increasingly under attack by senior CAF leaders, who were not favourable to "special soldiers," particularly during a period of constantly shrinking defence budgets.

Adding to the frustrations of the members of the Cdn AB Regt was the fact that despite the regiment's CFOO and international stand-by status, it was never deployed. Senior CAF leadership argued that to deploy the regiment would strip Canada of its strategic reserve. More realistically, the problem centred around the make-up of the airborne unit itself. It lacked the necessary mobility (i.e., armoured and wheeled vehicles) as well support capability to deploy for extended periods of time. As a result, the army command deemed that it was easier to send conventional units to do the operations, which were all conventional in nature anyway.

Downsizing of the regiment continued, further degrading both the status and capability of the Cdn AB Regt, with the result that it was reduced to battalion status in 1992. Nonetheless, in December of that year, the Cdn AB Regt deployed to Somalia on a U.N. Chapter VII operation, or, in simpler terms, a peace-making operation, under Security Council Resolution 794. Unfortunately, the Cdn AB Regt experienced disciplinary problems in theatre that detracted from their actual performance.[92] The regiment pacified its sector in less than three months, earning the praise of Hugh Tremblay, the director of Humanitarian Relief and Rehabilitation in Somalia, who stated to all who would listen, "If you want to know and to see what you should do while you are here in Somalia, go to Belet Huen, talk to the Canadians, and do what they have done, emulate the Canadians and you will have success in your humanitarian relief sector."[93]

Nonetheless, the mission was ultimately redefined in the media and the public consciousness as a failure, due to the poor leadership and the criminal acts of a few. The inexplicable and lamentable torture killing of Shidane Arone, a Somali national caught stealing within the regiment lines, became the defining image of the Cdn AB Regt's operation in Africa. The public outcry and criticism of the Department of National Defence (DND) as a result of the attempted cover-up at NDHQ, and later revelations of hazing videos within the Cdn AB Regt, created a crisis of epic proportions, and senior political and military decision-makers desperately sought a quick and easy solution to their troubles. They swiftly found one. During an official press release on the afternoon of January 23, 1995, David Collenette, the MND, announced, "although our senior military officers believe the regiment as constituted should continue, the government believes it cannot. Therefore, today under the authority of the National Defence Act, I have ordered the disbandment of the Canadian Airborne Regiment."[94]

The Cdn AB Regt represented Canada's only capability to conduct special operations from 1968 to 1993. A widespread feeling, by former members of the Cdn AB Regt was captured by Brigadier General Jim Cox. "In our hearts," he revealed, "we equated ourselves with the SAS and the SF [Special Forces] in the United States."[95] In the end, although the regiment did not possess all the characteristics of a pure SOF organization, especially toward the latter years of its existence, it did have both the official mandate and the implicit understanding of the senior CAF leadership that it would be the entity that conducted special operations if required. Moreover, the Cdn AB Regt did practise direct action (DA)– and strategic reconnaissance (SR)–type tasks. In addition, it regularly exercised and conducted small-unit exchanges with SOF organizations in the United States and Britain. In the end, it filled an important position in Canada's SOF history.

* * *

Even before the Cdn AB Regt was disbanded, the genesis of Canada's true contemporary SOF capability began to germinate. A fundamental shift in the perception of the nature of the threats to Western industrialized nations erupted in the late 1960s. Political violence, or, more accurately, terrorism, became recognized as a significant "new" menace. Bombings, kidnapping, murders, and the hijacking of commercial aircraft became frequent occurrences, exploding onto the world scene seeming out of nowhere. Not only in the Middle East, but also in Europe, countries descended into a state of violence, as both home-grown and international terrorists waged violent campaigns that recognized no borders or limits. The murder of Israeli athletes at the 1972 Olympics in Munich, West Germany, became one of the defining images of the crisis, as did the 1975 terrorist assault on the headquarters of OPEC in Vienna, Austria.[96]

But the problem went beyond a spillover of Mid-East conflict and politics. In Germany, groups such as the Baader-Meinhof Gang (or Red Army Faction), waged violent terrorist campaigns that resulted in death and destruction. Holland was besieged by Moluccan terrorists, and Britain struggled with the Irish Republican Army (IRA) and the Northern Ireland question. Even in North America, terrorism raised its ugly head. The Americans saw the growth of radical groups such as the Weathermen, the New World Liberation Front, and the Black Panther Party, to name but a few.

In Canada, the Front de libération du Québec (FLQ) began a reign of terror that culminated in the October Crisis of 1970. In addition, foreign terrorists imported their political struggles and launched attacks against targets in Canada. A few examples include the storming of the Turkish embassy in Ottawa by three Armenian men (Armenian Revolutionary Army) on March 12, 1985; the paralyzing of the Toronto public transit system on April 1, 1985, as a result of a communiqué sent by a group identifying itself as the Armenian Secret Army for the Liberation of our Homeland, in which they threatened death to passengers of the transit system; and the downing of an Air India flight off the coast of Ireland on June 23, 1985. This act, which killed 329 people, was the result of a bomb that was planted prior to its departure from Toronto's Pearson International Airport.

Not surprisingly, like other countries around the world, Canada decided it needed a counterterrorist (CT) capability of its own.[97] Its first attempt was to create the Hostage and Rescue Patrol (HARP) under the auspices of the RCMP in 1982. The small, twenty-five-man team was well-trained by foreign SOF personnel, but, unfortunately, a bureaucratic failure to reach a suitable administrative arrangement for the force scuttled the project. The RCMP wanted the operators to do tours of three months in Ottawa and then one and a half months back in their home precincts. The members wanted a permanent posting to Ottawa so they could move their families. In the end, no agreement could be reached and the program was shut down.

Three years later, in 1985, following a number of high-profile terrorist acts committed on Canadian soil, specifically the attack on the Turkish Embassy, the Government of Canada could delay no longer. It was time to establish a CT force of its own. The initial discussion of whether the new CT force should be based in the military or the police became a struggle between the CDS and the RCMP commissioner. Neither wanted the responsibility of creating or owning the force. The commissioner of the RCMP felt the proposed entity was more a military commando unit than a police organization. The CDS was of the mind that the type of individual created in such an organization could be problematic. He feared that once they were done their tour of service they would invariably become mercenaries of one sort or another, and he did not want that type of fallout. As a result, he did not want that type of unit within his Canadian Armed Forces.[98]

In the end, the CDS had his way because the Solicitor General believed the CT task was a policing function. As a result, the following year, in 1986, the RCMP created the seventy-five-member strong Special Emergency Response Team (SERT) as Canada's first hostage rescue (HR)/CT organization. The unit quickly established itself, drawing its personnel from existing trained police emergency response teams (ERT) from across the country. They received comprehensive training, much of it initially from a number of international CT experts. Although SERT was constantly busy, it was never deployed for an actual mission.

By the early 1990s, the continuing efforts of the federal government to combat its enormous deficit led to continuing deep budget cuts to all government departments. The RCMP was not immune. Faced with financial constraints, the requirement to pay overtime to members of the SERT, a force that had been in existence for years but had not yet deployed, as well as the requirement to continually rely on military airlift and other support provided the impetus for change. Moreover, the military in the post–Cold War era was also amenable to taking on new roles.[99] The deputy minister at the time, Bob Fowler, was instrumental in pushing for the DND to take on the role. And so, in February 1992, senior governmental, RCMP, and DND decision-makers decided to transfer the HR/CT responsibilities from the RCMP SERT to a military organization. As such, JTF 2 was born.

The challenge for the unit was immense. It had to select and train its personnel, and establish a new unit and be operational by April 1, 1993. The tight timelines meant that the first CO, Lieutenant-Colonel Ray Romses, had little choice but to utilize the RCMP SERT model for pre-selection, selection, and qualification standards. The RCMP SERT was composed of two distinct entities. Its Dwyer Hill Training Centre was run by an RCMP inspector who was responsible for the infrastructure and training. However, the command and control of the actual SERT was vested in another RCMP officer. Romses, however, would be responsible for both the operational and training functions.

The RCMP trained the first group of JTF 2 personnel. The newly trained military members now became the training cadre, and from the second serial onward, took control of instructing the remainder of the military personnel. Increasingly, the RCMP SERT members maintained less and less responsibility.

Timelines were tight, but JTF 2 was ready for the April 1 stand-up date. A formal handover parade and mess dinner were held at Dwyer Hill on March 31, 1993, to mark the handover of the HR/CT role from the RCMP SERT to the CAF JTF 2. The following day, the unit was already undertaking operational tasks.

From the beginning, the CO realized that the unit would have to evolve. The RCMP SERT had been content to remain strictly a police HR type organization. Initial time constraints meant that JTF 2 had to take on that paradigm and the police culture that accompanied it. However, with the "black" (i.e., CT) role came the issue of utility. How often would it be used? Romses realized this could also create retention issues. Moreover, for JTF 2 to provide utility to the greater CAF a "green" role (i.e., a traditional military SOF role, such as direct action and strategic reconnaissance) would need to be developed.

As a result, the unit began to evolve in the mid to late-1990s, developing a more typical military SOF orientation and capability; however, HR/CT remained JTF 2's primary focus. In 1994, the CDS approved growth for JTF 2, as well as a transition from a pure "black" CT role to other special operations tasks. As a result, the unit undertook tasks around the globe that gave its members both experience in foreign locations, and exposure to senior military and civilian decision makers.

Although the unit was expanding to include a green component, as already mentioned, its focus was still almost exclusively on black skills. A green phase during initial training was largely an introduction to field-craft for the non-combat arms volunteers. Within the unit, there was also tension between those who favoured retaining the exclusive black role and police culture, and those who wanted to push JTF 2 to be more akin to a military organization such as the British SAS and U.S. Delta Force. External events provided the catalyst for change.

On the morning of September 11, 2001, millions watched their television screens mesmerized as events unfolded in New York City. In the early morning hours, a passenger jet had ploughed into the top stories of the World Trade Center (WTC) in the financial core of the city. As most were trying to absorb what happened, a second large commercial airliner came into view and slammed into the twin tower of the WTC. It would only be a short time later that both towers collapsed onto themselves and crumpled to the ground, killing all those inside. A third aircraft slammed into the Pentagon, killing and injuring hundreds more, and a fourth hijacked jetliner, heading for Washington, D.C., slammed into the ground in Pennsylvania, short of its objective, failing on its mission due to the bravery of its passengers. In total, almost three thousand people were killed in the attacks.

Within days, it became clear that the Americans would take military action to strike at the terrorists who planned and conducted the attack and those that supported and abetted them. Osama bin Laden and his al-Qaeda terrorist organization, sheltered in Afghanistan by Mullah Omar and his Taliban government, quickly became the centre of attention. Not surprisingly, the Americans, through the Central Intelligence Agency (CIA), paramilitary forces, and US SOF, in conjunction with the Northern Alliance, an anti-Taliban resistance movement, quickly launched an offensive to oust the Taliban and capture bin Laden and his associates.

The Canadians quickly moved to support their American allies. The CAF mobilized to send ships, aircraft, and ground forces in support of the U.S. mission, titled Operation Enduring Freedom (OEF). Part of the CAF force package was a special operations task force (SOTF) that deployed as part of OEF and was under operational control of the American commander of the Combined Joint Forces Special Operations Component Command. Their tasks included direct action, special reconnaissance, and sensitive site exploitation.[100]

The JTF 2 based SOTF was deployed in theatre from December 2001 to November 2002.[101] At the time, JTF 2 was largely an unknown quantity and its role in theatre was initially marginalized. "They were curious because they [Americans] didn't really know us," conceded one member of the Task Force. He explained, "At the beginning, people said, 'Who the f--- is JTF2?'"[102]

However, it took only one mission to demonstrate their skill sets, and very quickly they became a force of choice. According to U.S. military officials, the JTF 2 SOTF had conducted "[forty-two] reconnaissance and surveillance missions as well as [twenty-three] direct action missions."[103] Tasks included "snatching senior Taliban officials," manning high-altitude observation posts, and combing mountain cave complexes.[104] Their performance earned them the trust and respect of the U.S. commanders in theatre. As stated earlier, the American SOF commanders at first were, quite frankly, reluctant to use them. By the end of the tour, the JTF 2 SOTF had become the designated coalition theatre direct-action reserve force, with American sub-units allocated to it under tactical control (normally Rangers or 82nd Airborne and aviation assets). In the end, the JTF 2 SOTF executed more missions than any other coalition SOF force assigned to the Combined Joint Special Operations Task Force — South (CJSOTF-S).

In fact, U.S. Navy commander Kerry Metz, director of operations for CJSOTF-S, told Congress, "We were fortunate to have the finest special operations ... and we challenged our operators to conduct missions in some of the most hostile environments ever operated in." He explained, "We had special reconnaissance teams operating in the mountains of Afghanistan above 10,000 feet for extended periods without resupply."[105] The CJSOTF-S commander, Rear Admiral Bob Harward, simply acknowledged, "his JTF 2 team was his first choice for any 'direct action' mission."[106]

Unquestionably, JTF 2's participation in OEF was a critical turning point in its evolution and CANSOF history. JTF 2's participation, or, more important, impact in theatre bolstered Canadian credibility. "We had to shoulder our way into the international SOF community," explained Colonel Clyde Russell, the CO of JTF 2 at the time, "but once we got our seat at the table, now we can hold our own."[107]

Participation in OEF also finalized the debate back at Dwyer Hill in Ottawa. JTF 2 was now a Tier 1 SOF organization. One JTF 2 detachment commander explained, "9/11 put us full throttle into the warfighting game and allowed us to pass a number of hurdles that would have taken years in a peacetime environment."

Lieutenant-General Michael Day, one of the Canadian OEF SOTF commanders and a former commander of Canadian Special Operations Command (CANSOFCOM) assessed, "We progressed the unit in maturity decades that first year [in Afghanistan]."

Quite simply, the operation planted the seeds of CANSOF growth and maturation. "It allowed us to move into a kinetic mode," asserted Day, "it showed the connection of the counterterrorism/hostage rescue piece to the expeditionary capability." It not only revitalized the unit, but it also revealed a very potent international capability.[108]

"Stepping out onto the world stage was our first big show," commented Colonel Russell. "From a strategic perspective," he added, "it opened the eyes of the grownups [to] how SOF can be used as a bit of a strategic place marker in a crisis." Russell explained, "we had a small footprint but a large impact. The country got a lot of credit."

Consistently, CANSOF leadership attest to the fact that JTF 2's participation in OEF in 2001–2002 was a seminal event for the unit and CANSOF. "9/11 and Afghanistan allowed CANSOFCOM to grow into a mature combat capable force," explained Lieutenant-General Day, "It was instrumental in shaping our ability to field kinetic forces, which we now use to leverage our ability to shape a theatre."[109] He concluded, "our first deployment will remain the defining moment of who we are."

The CANSOF commanders were not the only ones who recognized the importance of JTF 2's first combat deployment. On December 7, 2004, George Bush, the president of the United States, awarded the JTF 2 component of the CJSOTF-S (later called Task Force K-Bar) a Secretary of the Navy, Presidential Unit Citation. American officials sent the request for Canadian approval prior to its actual presentation to the CAF members. DND issued a press release the following day to announce the presentation. The Canadian governor general congratulated JTF 2 on the award on December 10, 2004, through a media advisory.

The narrative of the citation read:

> For extraordinary heroism and outstanding performance of duty in action against the enemy in Afghanistan from 17 October 2001 to 30 March 2002. Throughout this period, Combined Joint Special Operations Task Force — SOUTH/ Task Force K-BAR, operating first from Oman and then from forward locations throughout the southern and eastern regions of Afghanistan successfully executed its primary mission to conduct special operations in support of the U.S. efforts as delegated to Commander US CENTCOM through the JFSO Component Command JFSOCC to destroy, degrade, and neutralize the TB and AQ leadership and military. During its six month existence, TF K-Bar was the driving force behind myriad combat missions conducted in Combined Joint Operation Area Afghanistan. These precedent[-]setting and extremely high-risk missions included search and rescue, recovery die ops, non-compliant boarding of high interest vessels, special reconnaissance, hydrographic reconnaissance, SSE [Sensitive

Site Exploitation], DA missions apprehension of military and political detainees, destruction of multiple cave and tunnel complexes, identification and destruction of several known AQ training camps, explosion of thousands of pounds of enemy ordnance and successful coordination of UW operations for Afghanistan. The sailors, soldiers, [a]irmen, Marines, and coalition partners of CJSOTF (S)/TF K-Bar set an unprecedented 100 percent mission success rate across a broad spectrum of special operations missions while operating under extremely difficult and constantly dangerous conditions. They established benchmark standards of professionalism, tenacity, courage, tactical brilliance, and operational excellence while demonstrating superb esprit de corps and maintaining the highest measures of combat readiness.[110]

In the aftermath of the award, the Canadian leadership took the opportunity to heap praise on the shadow warriors. "This citation from the U.S.," announced Bill Graham, the MND, "signifies the outstanding counterterrorism and special operations capability that has been developed by the Canadian Armed Forces." He added, "JTF 2 has played a critical role in Canada's contribution to the war against terrorism and will continue to be an important part of our domestic security."[111]

Similarly, General Ray Henault, the CDS at the time, asserted, "The presentation of the U.S. Presidential Unit Citation to members of JTF 2 brings important recognition to a group of incredible CAF members whose accomplishments normally cannot be publicly recognized in the interest of national security."[112] He concluded, "Canadians should be very proud of this specialized Canadian military unit."[113]

The importance of the mission and the recognition of the CANSOF contribution was also evident in the governmental decision to increase the size and capability of JTF 2. The MND quickly realized the strategic impact, at a relatively low cost, that even a small SOF task force could achieve. As such, he pushed for expansion.[114]

Despite the great effort and incredible results, the JTF 2 initial deployment to Afghanistan ended rather quickly. By late 2002, with

THE CANADIAN SOF LEGACY

the Taliban largely routed and the country entering what appeared to be a period of relative calm, Canada withdrew all of its forces from Afghanistan. However, it returned the following year as a contributor to the International Security Assistance Force (ISAF) in Kabul. As part of the redeployment, Canadian SOF also maintained a footprint in the form of a Joint Liaison Team-Afghanistan (JLT-A) in theatre.

But the winds of change were blowing. On December 24, 2004, the Americans requested Canada to deploy another Canadian SOTF as early as possible. The request affirmed that Canada's previous SOF contribution to OEF in Afghanistan in 2001 and 2002 "was highly valued by the United States." Moreover, it confirmed "that relatively small numbers of special operations forces exert a disproportionately large operational impact."

This was no surprise, since JTF 2's performance had elicited praise from the American ambassador, Paul Cellucci. He publicly stated, "Canada's elite Tier 1 JTF 2 is as capable as any Tier 1 [s]pecial [f]orces in the world [and it] makes a significant contribution whenever deployed."[115]

The request was strongly supported by both the CDS, General Rick Hillier, and the deputy minister, W.P.D. Elcock. They explained, "The deployment of Canadian special operations forces to Afghanistan would make evident our ongoing commitment to an active engagement in the Campaign Against Terrorism and it would also demonstrate our direct burden sharing with our closest allies."

The deployment was also in consonance with ongoing strategic object-ive for the CAF in the global war on terrorism. The deployment would assist the Government of Afghanistan in providing security and stability in the country and in supporting reconstruction activities; it would assist with the elimination of al-Qaeda, the Taliban, and other anti-coalition militants, as continuing terrorist threats to international peace and security; and it would support efforts to address the humanitarian needs of Afghans.

The high-level support was not surprising. After all, the leadership were now well-versed in the strength of the unit. "One of my first visits," acknowledged General Hillier, "was to Joint Task Force 2 (JTF 2), our special forces unit based near Ottawa, no strangers to me after the many operations." He explained, "JTF 2 troopers are the Olympic athletes of soldiering, our version of gold medalists, taking on the most difficult missions and tasks with a level of skill and professionalism that has earned the respect of special forces units around the world. Like the U.S. Delta Force or the British Special Air Service (SAS), they get the most dangerous and demanding of missions, from hostage rescues to acting as bodyguards for VIPs (like me!) to operating for long periods of time on their own in enemy territory."[116]

With such endorsement, the Government of Canada authorized the deployment of a JTF 2 SOTF to Afghanistan in support of OEF on June 1, 2005. Its mission was "to conduct combat operations in the Afghanistan theatre of operations (ATO) in support of U.S.-led operation Enduring Freedom for a period of one year." CANSOF was back at war.

Later that year, a JTF 2 SOTF was back in country supporting OEF. Although originally committed for only a year, the mandate was continually extended, lasting in the end until the end of Canadian operations in Afghanistan in 2011. Their mission, however, remained largely unchanged. General Hillier affirmed that Canadian SOF had established a presence on Afghanistan battlefields and that they were effective disrupting the Taliban leadership.[117] He declared, "What we want to do is take out the [Taliban] commanders who are engaged in orchestrating, facilitating, paying, leading, planning, and driving folks to attack us or attack the Afghans or attack the innocent." He added, "And our special forces are focused very much on that.... I said, during a recent speech, that we had removed from the battlefield six commanders who were responsible for the deaths of [twenty-one] Canadian soldiers." Hillier explained, "Well that's changed. We've removed seven commanders who have been responsible for the deaths of [twenty-seven] soldiers."[118]

Canadian scholars have reinforced Hillier's declarations. A team studying operations in Kandahar Province noted that "insurgent operations in 2007 were increasingly characterized by lack of co-ordination and poor planning, which could be attributed to the growing effectiveness of ISAF's special operations forces." They explained:

> SOF units from all ISAF contributor nations in the south were pooled for the task of arresting known bomb[-]making cell leaders [and] drug lords, and a legal case [was] prepared

for their arrest[.] Canadian (and other ISAF) SOF troops would [then] be deployed to apprehend the suspect. As often as not, if the target was a Tier 1 Taliban leader, he would try to shoot his way out, with predictable results. Consequently, Taliban command-and-control capacity in the south in 2007 was less effective than the previous fall.[119]

In addition, conventional commanders also spoke to the influence CANSOF was exerting in theatre. A Canadian battle group commander noted the impressive effect SOF had on his area of operations in Kandahar.

> The SOF strikes had a chilling effect on the Taliban. In one strike they killed an important leader and [sixteen] of his fighters. The Taliban leadership in Kandahar City felt a lot of pressure from SOF. They were moving every day so we saw a reduction in activity. They [Taliban] were being disrupted — they were on the move, on the run.[120]

And this was exactly the effect the CDS expected from his CANSOF SOTF. "Without the proactive operations necessary to precisely track [Taliban leaders], locate them, and attack them," insisted General Hillier, "they with their forces would still be trying to kill us."[121] And so, as the campaign in the Canadian theatre of operations evolved from 2005 to 2011, the specific CANSOF tasks changed also. Their tactics, techniques, and procedures evolved, too, to ensure that the standing CANSOF SOTF in Afghanistan provided the necessary effects to support the ongoing counter-insurgency efforts.

The Afghanistan experience, as already noted, proved to be a watershed for CANSOF. Very quickly the tempo of operations, as well as the demands caused by the execution of myriad missions, clearly highlighted force structure concerns, concerns that prevented JTF 2 from reaching its full potential. A 2003 study paper written by CANSOF staff examined the lessons learned from the 2001–2002 mission in Afghanistan. It identified the need for a Tier 2 SOF capability within Canada to support JTF 2 operations. This call for additional resources did not fall on deaf ears.

In February 2005, General Hillier told his general officers at a special general/flag officer seminar in Cornwall, Ontario, "We need an integrated Canadian Armed Forces that consists of maritime, air, land, and special forces, woven together to make a more effective military."[122] This was the first time that a CDS spoke of Canada's SOF capability within the context as a fourth environment within the CAF. Later that year, on April 19, 2005, General Hillier declared that he intended "on bringing JTF 2, along with all the enablers that it would need, to conduct operations successfully into one organization with one commander."[123] This would prove to be a major step for CANSOF. As a result, on February 1, 2006, as part of the CAF's transformation program, CANSOFCOM was created.[124]

The purpose of CANSOFCOM was clearly articulated: "to force, develop, generate, and, where required, employ and sustain Special Operations Task Forces (SOTF) capable of achieving tactical, operational, and strategic effects required by the Government of Canada (GoC)."[125] The command consisted of a small headquarters; JTF 2; a new, "Tier 2" combatant unit called the Canadian Special Operations Regiment (CSOR); 427 Special Operations Aviation Squadron (SOAS); and the Joint Nuclear, Biological, Chemical Defence Company (JNBCD Company), whose name was officially changed in September 2007 to the Canadian Joint Incident Response Unit (CJIRU).[126] The respective unit responsibilities were given as:

a. JTF 2 — Its mission is to provide a force capable of rendering armed assistance and surgical precise effects in the resolution of an issue that is, or has the potential of, affecting the national interest. The primary focus is counterterrorism; however, the unit is employed on other high-value tasks such as special reconnaissance, DA, and defence, diplomacy and military assistance (DDMA);

b. CSOR — Its mission is to provide high-readiness special operations forces for integrated SOTFs operating on behalf of the GoC. It is also responsible for conducting DA and DDMA;

c. 427 Special Operations Aviation Squadron — Its mission is to generate and employ the integrated aviation element of CANSOFCOM high-readiness SOTFs for the conduct of domestic and international operations. Its range of tasks include CT, DA, and DDMA; and

d. CJIRU — Its mission is to provide timely and agile broad-based chemical, biological, radiological, nuclear (CBRN) support to the GoC in order to prevent, control, and mitigate CBRN threats to Canada, Canadians, and Canadian interests. The unit is a core member of the national CBRN response team, and is also responsible for conducting CT, SR, and counter proliferation (CP).

The unit has three key mandates:

a. respond to CBRN events in conjunction with other elements of the national CBRNE [explosive] response team;
b. provide an agile integral part of the CANSOFCOM Immediate Reaction Task Force (IRTF); and
c. specialized support to CAF expeditionary operations.[127]

Although initially the core of CANSOFCOM was JTF 2, the command has evolved. "We don't talk about deploying units," explained the CANSOFCOM commander at the time, now Lieutenant-General Mike Day, "We talk about deploying special operation task forces, which are absolutely an amalgam of all the parts of this command."[128] One such example was the publicly announced SOTF called "Arrowhead." This task force (TF) was not created for a long-term mission, but instead was designed to allow the Canadian military to quickly put a "footprint" into a crisis area."[129] "Arrowhead will be the precursor" to a larger special forces task force if needed, Day explained.[130] He stated CSOR would be responsible for creating the necessary command team to coordinate the response to an international crisis or mission. However, the task force would be able to draw from personnel in various CANSOFCOM units as needed, and those assigned to TF Arrowhead would be on 24/7 alert to move out.[131]

The solidification of CANSOFCOM as an independent command was further enhanced when, on February 4, 2008, the CDS granted Honour

Bearing status to JTF 2 and CSOR. This honour is "afforded to combatant units whose functional purpose is to close with and conquer, neutralize, or destroy the enemy as an effective fighting force. Only combatant military units are entitled to be publicly recognized for active participation in battle against a formed and armed enemy through the award of battle honours and honorary distinctions."[132] Moreover, the CDS also approved that the World War II 1st Canadian Special Service Battalion (better known as the Canadian component of the FSSF) be perpetuated by CSOR. This meant that CSOR would carry the battle honours of the FSSF from that conflict.[133]

Ten years into its existence, CANSOFCOM has proven itself an integral part of the nation's military capability. It has conducted operations domestically and around the world, and throughout has demonstrated a high level of professionalism and expertise. It has provided DND and the Government of Canada a unique capability, one that is unmatched elsewhere in the CAF or by any other governmental department. "I think it is fair to say the worth of Canada's special forces has been so completely proven to the chain of command — the Canadian Armed Forces and the Government of Canada — that the question is not, 'Does it survive? [And if so, what] is its structure?'" opined Lieutenant-General Day. Rather, "the question is, 'How much do we want it to grow by?'"[134]

These were not hollow words. Others outside of the command agreed. "There is not a more tactically agile capability in the world," affirmed retired Lieutenant-General Michael Gautier, a former commander of the Canadian Expeditionary Command. "They are," he insisted, "as good as any in the world, and what they do is function effectively in chaotic and complex environments."[135]

A former CDS, Vice–Admiral Larry Murray, insisted, "I don't know where we would be today if we didn't develop that [SOF] capability back in the 1990s."[136]

Another former CDS apparently agreed. General Walter Natynczyk "praised the work of the country's SOF," and stated, "they've proven their worth during the past [seventeen] years in war zones from Bosnia to Afghanistan."[137] Natynczyk insisted:

The units [SOF] will remain essential in the future [since] we see that irregular warfare, the counterinsurgency we are seeing in Afghanistan, is occurring and could occur in other parts of the world." He noted, "The one strong aspect of special forces is that it is very surgical in nature. They need a high level of ... competence.[138]

And the national SOF legacy has shown that Canada's SOF organizations throughout their history have demonstrated exactly that. From the earliest days of the rangers, through World War II and the Cold War, to the current campaign against terrorism, Canada's SOF capability has proven to be amongst the best in the world. CANSOFCOM continues this tradition at home and in other trouble spots around the world. Moreover, it continues to evolve and adapt to meet the future threats to the nation.

As such, this volume focuses on six operations from 2005 to 2011 that highlight the contribution that SOF, particularly Canadian special operations forces, provided in the savage insurgency raging in Afghanistan. But more important, it accentuates SOF's greatest strength — the quality of its people. As the six operations revealed in this book demonstrate — they are no ordinary men.

Adept at surviving in the harsh wilderness and proficient at the savage practice of
la petite guerre, Canadian raiding parties composed of French Canadians and their
Native allies proved to be the scourge of the New England frontier. This graphic
depicts a Canadian volunteer and a soldier of Les Compagnies Franches de la
Marine conducting a winter raid against the English fort at Hudson Bay.

Above: Yugoslav Canadians at Camp X training for missions in their former homeland.

Left: Canadian volunteers undergoing gruelling commando training — scaling near-vertical cliffs.

A Royal Canadian Navy (RCN) Beach Commando demonstrates how to silently incapacitate a sentry.

Members of RCN Beach Commando "W" take a cigarette break after a two-day training march, February 1944.

Members of 1 Cdn Para Bn (1st Canadian Parachute Battalion) take a smoke break in the Belgian Ardennes, January 1945.

Members of the FSSF (First Special Service Force) loading a Douglas C-47 aircraft to qualify as parachutists, August 1942. The FSSF ran an abbreviated jump course. In most cases, volunteers were required to qualify prior to undertaking training. This was designed to ensure no effort was wasted on individuals who would fail to complete the parachutist course successfully.

Their original mission in Norway required the members of the FSSF to be proficient at skiing, mountaineering, and survival in arctic conditions, on top of the other, more martial skills they had to master.

Members of the FSSF undergo mountaineering training, December 1942.

Cdn SAS Coy paratroopers emplaning for a practice jump.

Cdn SAS Coy (Canadian Special Air Service Company) officers and senior NCOs (non-commissioned officers) at Rivers, Manitoba. Due to equipment shortages, everyone was forced to make do with various types of American and British jump-training equipment and uniforms.

Paratroopers from the Cdn AB Regt (Canadian Airborne Regiment) conduct counter-insurgency operations in Jamaica, April 1972.

A member of Pathfinder platoon, the Cdn AB Regt, practises a freefall insertion into a denied area.

JTF 2 (Joint Task Force 2) members in their black role practising a hostage rescue.

Members of JTF 2 practise a "stronghold break-in."

Members of JTF 2 practise a vehicle take-down.

Divers of JTF 2 practising MCT drills.

Divers of JTF 2 practising MCT drills.

By the late 1990s, JTF 2 had started to evolve its "green" persona, and its SOAC (special operations assaulter course) included instruction on fieldcraft and patrolling.

JTF 2 members providing close personal protection for former prime minister Jean Chrétien.

Members of the CJIRU (Combined Joint Incident Response Unit) on a CBRN (chemical, biological, radiological, and nuclear) exercise.

DND.

Above: CSOR (Canadian Special Operations Regiment) ski training.

Right: Official CANSOFCOM (Canadian Special Operations Forces Command) crest.

VIAM INVENIEMUS

DND.

CHAPTER 2

LOOKING FOR TROUBLE:
PENETRATING THE DE LAM GHAR TALIBAN SANCTUARY, SEPTEMBER 2005

The soldiers picked their way carefully along the rocky mountain ridge. Loose rocks clattered like so many tiles if a misstep was made. Along the ground, sharp, dagger-like protrusions stuck up as if the ground was trying to protect itself. The mountain walls looked smooth, but were marked by sharp indentations that would rip the skin. Like so much of the land, what seemed benign on the surface promised danger and pain for the unwary.

The terrain was difficult to navigate at the best of times. But, the SOF soldiers from the JTF-2 based task force in Afghanistan were doing it in the dark, in hostile territory. They were venturing back into an area that intelligence analysts had confirmed was an enemy sanctuary harbouring key Taliban leaders and fanatical insurgents. It was their job to ferret them out and capture or kill them.

As the SOF operators moved along the treacherous mountain terrain, straining with the weight they carried, and struggling with the heavy night-vision goggles attached to their helmets, they could hear the bark of gunfire and the tell-tale "swoosh" of rockets as the Apache attack helicopters engaged enemy insurgents. Finally, the game of cat and mouse had ended. The enemy was seemingly found and the fight was on.

The SOF operators dubbed the mission "Algonquin II." This was an unofficial handle, based on the fact that the task was actually a sequel to Operation Algonquin, which was conducted about three weeks earlier. Coalition analysts had categorized the De Lam Ghar mountain as a Taliban sanctuary, and coalition commanders were keen to crack the enemy grip on the area. It had been a long-standing issue.

The analysts believed the De Lam Ghar area housed an important anti-coalition militia (ACM) command and control (C2) hub. In addition, they also noted that Afghan and foreign fighters were trained in this apparent sanctuary. They assessed that at least thirty to forty-five insurgents, armed with small arms, rocket-propelled grenade launchers, and IEDs, were in the area and using caves for concealment and protection. Radios and motorcycles allowed the enemy to communicate with each other and move between camps. In addition, analysts had determined that the Taliban in this sector had access to man-portable air defense systems (MANPADs).

Striking at the ACM in the area, however, was problematic. First, the terrain was inaccessible and incredibly difficult to negotiate. Second, the Taliban had developed an effective early-warning system (EWS), which made it difficult to surprise the enemy. Consisting of a series of two-man observation posts (OPs) located on high features in the mountains, they offered a commanding view of most avenues of approach.

On August 14, 2005, the ACM in the area engaged an American SF patrol and prevented them from penetrating the region. Although the enemy OPs were withdrawn after the initial contact, the Taliban continued to fight and never abandoned the area.

Coalition intelligence pointed to the fact that at least one medium-value target (MVT), Rangin Dadfar,[1] was present during the engagement, and the analysts believed that the enemy had fought hard to cover his withdrawal. As De Lam Ghar was assessed to be an important ACM C2 node in northern Ghorak District, the intelligence analysts felt that the caves in the area might contain material and ACM personnel of intelligence value that could shed light on future enemy operations.

After additional appraisal and consideration, coalition commanders believed that a successful operation in the region would net valuable intelligence on the ACM command and control network in northern Kandahar Province, as well as disrupt enemy training and command and control of ongoing and future operations. Specifically, they decided to target Dadfar, who they now were convinced operated in the area and was vulnerable to capture.

Mullah Dadfar was the Taliban commander in Kandahar Province who was responsible for conducting numerous attacks on coalition forces and Afghan government officials. He was a former Taliban provincial governor, and while in that position, arranged training camps for Arab jihadis. Intelligence analysts believed that Dadfar retained his links to Arab jihadis in Iraq and they considered him to be the most likely of the Taliban leaders to be involved with al-Qaeda (AQ) suicide bombers in southern Afghanistan.

Dadfar's pedigree as a "bad guy" was solid. He was connected to fifty AQ and Taliban fighters hiding in Atalay and Lam villages. He had supported four suicide bombers in July 2005 and was linked to rocket attacks on Kandahar City, as well as Kandahar Airfield (KAF). He was also involved in the abduction and murder of a Swiss female NGO in Iraq in 2004, and had links to other radical mullahs. Ostensibly, Dadfar reported directly to Mullah Omar, the top Taliban commander.[2]

Capturing or killing Dadfar, however, would not be easy. His early-warning system stretched as far west as the Daylanoor Pass, and his sentinels used radio, cell phones, and motorcycles to communicate. Described as a "cave dweller" because he used two caves and a small shepherd's hut near Ateli Karez, where his home was located, to live to avoid detection and capture, he was a survivor who was inured to hardship and a Spartan lifestyle. Adding to the difficulty of interdicting Dadfar was the fact that he was surrounded by a large group that included two sub-commanders and a personal security detail of upwards of twelve fighters, who could be quickly reinforced by another forty to fifty insurgents from surrounding villages, many of whom were believed to be Arab, Pakistani, and/or Chechen — all notoriously ferocious fighters.

However, commander of Combined Joint Special Operations Task Force — Afghanistan (CJSOTF-A) had already set the scene. He approved the concept of a SOF combined task force (CTF),[3] based on formed units with similar skill sets (i.e., SOF Tier 1 organizations), to be organized to conduct a sensitive-site exploitation mission in the vicinity of De Lam Ghar from September 3–4 to confirm or deny ACM activity.[4] The scheme of manoeuvre was simple. The SOF CTF was to isolate the De Lam Ghar objective through a series of insertions on to designated helicopter landing zones (HLZ). This would allow the CTF to establish a cordon around the target, thus sealing escape routes. The blocks also provided a firm foothold and launching point for the subsequent sweep of the objective areas. Once the objectives were cleared, the entire CTF would be extracted by rotary wing aircraft.

The JTF-2–based CANSOF task force was designated the lead nation for the mission. As such, the task force commander, Colonel George Sadler,[5] directed his ground force commander, Jack Rutledge, to conduct the subject-sensitive site exploitation (SSE) in the vicinity of De Lam Ghar, on September 4, 2005. The mission would include substantial coalition support. In order to conduct the SSE of individuals, infrastructure, and equipment in the target sector, Rutledge had the assistance of allied SOF and an Afghan National Army (ANA) element. The planned eight-hour operation fell in line with the scheme of manoeuvre envisioned by the CJSOTF-A commander. The CTF would use the cycle of darkness to insert into four helicopter landing zones (HLZs) in the vicinity of the respective objectives and then secure, saturate, and dominate the terrain.

There, SOF CTF had one major advantage. The closest village to the objective area in De Lam Ghar was approximately six to seven kilometres away. Moreover, intelligence analysts assessed that the target area in question was being used purely in support of ACM activity and, therefore, it was designated as a military target. The probability of non-combatants being present in the objective area was deemed little to nil. Therefore, there was minimal risk of collateral damage and/or negative impact on civilian activity as a result of the mission.

The actual operation held no surprises. It proceeded as expected. The enemy provided initial resistance to buy the necessary amount of time to allow its leaders to escape and then the insurgents tried to melt away, sensing that the tactical advantage was not on their side.

Just as dawn was breaking, the initial wave of troops was brought over the objective. The squadron commander and a small aerial reaction force (ARF) deployed in a Blackhawk helicopter with the aviation commander, and moved over the dominating ridgeline that separated the various allied objective areas. The enemy obviously realized the importance of this terrain and it was quickly established that they had placed a number of defensive positions with RPG launcher gunners along its axis.

"As soon as we hit the objective, we could see all along the ridgeline a series of strong points that could fire down on the landing zones," said Rutledge.

With coalition forces moving into the area along ground routes in the past, the insurgents obviously believed that they would have plenty of warning of an attack and were still sleeping or getting tea ready for the morning prayers as the helicopters came overhead.

After identifying three main positions, Rutledge ordered the ARF to be dropped on the largest position at the far west site on the ridgeline. Norman Jackson, the detachment commander, and a group of his men were dropped off onto the sharp rocks of the north slope, but due to the difficulty of flying in the mountains, with their unpredictable wind currents, the pilot was forced to make an adjustment to his power and the last man of the ARF detachment, Derrick Vanier, the medic, did not make it off the aircraft as it pulled away from the drop off point. Nonetheless, Jackson led his men straight at the enemy position as the Blackhawk moved back along the ridge to the east and into the line of fire of a now awakened enemy position.

"We took fire immediately," remembered the squadron commander, "as we spun around, an RPG just missed the nose of our aircraft." He added, "We all fired at the enemy from the door but as we came around we could see they were still grabbing RPGs so we hit them again."

For a moment it became almost a personal battle between the Blackhawk helicopter and the insurgents in that position. The aviation commander brought his aircraft around and at the same time spoke into the intercom, "you in the back, we're dropping you down to go pick up those weapons." Rutledge recalled vividly:

After his statement, I looked around and remembered that I was now the last man in the back of the aircraft (Al being dropped off with his detachment a minute earlier). The door gunner just looked at me and shrugged. The helicopter could only get to within a couple hundred metres of the defensive position and as I jumped off the helicopter I realized how much weight I had on as I crunched into the mountaintop.

The world all of a sudden becomes very big when you are alone in such a situation. The closest friendly guy was about one kilometre away. I realized, *This is really stupid.*

I began clearing around the position and I'm feeling awfully small. One body is still burning. I just wanted to clear the area, collect the weapons, and get out of there. So I grab the RPG, about four RPG rounds, rifle, bandoliers of ammunition, and binoculars, while the Blackhawk is circling around. Movement back up the slope on the ridge was slow and when the helicopter came down I threw the stuff up on the UH-60 and then I had to climb up the wheel because they couldn't get low enough. I thought I was in shape — but it was exhausting hauling myself up into the helicopter with that much kit and armour at that elevation.

Although it seemed like an eternity, it was but a brief interlude of mere minutes. Meanwhile, Jackson had moved his detachment over the edge of the ridge and had begun to engage the insurgents at close range. After being surprised by the arrival of the force and the quick engagement with the CANSOF detachment, a number of the insurgents made their way down into the re-entrant on the north side of Objective Alpha, while six others remained behind to fight Jackson's men as they made their way into their position.

As more insurgents were identified, two of the Canadian SOF troops used 40mm rounds from their M-203 launchers and hand grenades to dislodge the insurgents as the remainder engaged them with rifle fire. Still, a few tenacious enemy combatants were effectively still using the large boulders on the cliff as protective cover. A strafing run by an AH-64

Apache attack helicopter with its 30mm cannon fire, however, quickly neutralized the stubborn defenders. A sweep of the area by Jackson's detachment prior to being extracted off the top of the ridgeline counted up six enemy dead and a mix of rifles and an RPG launcher. For his leadership in this close engagement, as well as the detachment's overall effective fighting skills, Jackson was awarded the Medal of Valour, and his men received Mention in Dispatches.

Their fight to gain the dominating high ground was crucial. After all, the primary focus of the mission was on Objective Alpha, which was assigned to CANSOF. The Canadian operators landed at approximately 0530 hours, on September 4, 2005, and received enemy fire shortly after disembarking the aircraft. AH-64 Apache attack helicopters and CANSOF snipers responded immediately. The second CANSOF lift, consisting of additional assault troops, was inserted at 0700 hours.

Andre Boisvert, the assault force troop commander, immediately began clearing east along the south ridge of the objective. He had decided to avoid a series of deep valleys and ravines in the area, maintaining, instead, the advantageous, dominating high ground. As they advanced, they came into contact with a number of insurgents, who were apparently on their way to a fighting position or OP. As the enemy tried to work their way to higher dominating ground, they were engaged by the element's 7.62mm general purpose machine gun (GPMG). An Apache gunship also responded to the TIC (troops in contact) and conducted a number of strafing runs. The CANSOF operators quickly swept through the enemy position and captured one wounded insurgent who had a serious gunshot wound to the thigh. He was immediately medically evacuated (MEDEVAC) to KAF by rotary wing aircraft.[6]

The ground assault force continued to move towards their objective and discovered a fortified position on the high ground. The CANSOF soldiers then moved north into Objective Alpha and began their clearance. The extremely rough terrain slowed down movement. In addition, the SOF troops discovered multiple prepared-fighting positions. As they struck deep into the objective, the CANSOF operators once again faced sporadic resistance. Once they reached the extent of their sweep boundary, they took enemy fire from numerous man-made fighting positions and observed a well-camouflaged command and control bunker. The SOF soldiers called in a close air support (CAS) mission that resulted in the dropping of a five-hundred-pound bomb by an A-10 Thunderbolt on the bunker. Due to time limitations, the CANSOF troops moved back to their pick-up LZ for extraction.

Close by, allied SOF inserted into their HLZ on Objective Bravo at approximately 0535 hours. They too quickly found that the rough terrain impeded rapid movement. Nonetheless, the allied SOF elements moved to dominate the high ground and then proceeded southwest out of their HLZ and cleared a number of suspect caves in the immediate area. However, nothing of significance was found. As they moved from the area, they were engaged by two insurgents who were quickly killed. As the allied SOF elements proceeded down the main re-entrant to their objective, they identified numerous mutually supporting fighting positions. A number of engagements with insurgents were experienced as they continued to clear their objective and Apache gunships were called in to conduct gun runs on the east/west corridor of the valley. Other than the numerous fighting positions, which were destroyed by UK GR-7 close air support aircraft and 84mm rocket fire, nothing of significance was found. This was because the allied SOF elements did not make it completely to the bottom of the objective, as they ran out of time due to the terrain and insurgent activity. They were extracted shortly before 1500 hours with two personnel wounded while in close combat with the enemy.

Other allied SOF elements met with similar results. Their two chalks (i.e. aircraft loads) inserted at 0530 hours and 0700 hours respectively onto Objective Charlie.[7] With the snipers on the high ground in over-watch, the allied SOF ground force began to clear west onto their objective. They very quickly found, however, that they were unable to complete the sweep of their entire area, due to time and terrain constraints. AH-64 attack helicopters were brought in to conduct speculative fire on suspected caves but with little result. The allied SOF operators did uncover two grave sites that upon examination revealed two bodies, both of which had their hands tied behind their backs and both of which had been shot in the back of the head.

Concurrently, once the allied SOF detachment and their ANA component arrived at their HLZ, they quickly cleared their target area, Objective Delta, and then pushed northwest along the ridgelines and the main road leading out of the mountains. As the ANA moved along the road, they encountered a large group of local men. The A-10 aircraft providing air cover was requested to drop low for a show of force over the assemblage. This seemed to sedate the group who stated that they had come up to the area to see what the fighting was about. They were then escorted by a few ANA soldiers to the east, but as the remaining ANA and allied SOF soldiers continued to move west, a couple of vehicles came speeding toward them. The vehicles stopped a few hundred metres away and a number of men jumped out firing their weapons in the direction of the coalition troops. The ANA fired back and took cover, but as they were out of effective supporting-fire range, the joint terminal attack controller (JTAC) directed the A-10 aircraft to converge on the site and engage the vehicles with cannon fire. After two strafing runs, there was no further reaction from either the vehicles or the men, who ran into the hills to the north.

The ground force commander ordered the CANSOF assault detachment assigned to the air reaction force to respond to the stricken vehicles on the main road. On inspection, two wounded insurgents were treated and detained. One of the detainees claimed to be a driver for the district governor, while the other detainee claimed to be a driver for a Taliban commander who had fled the area with the group to the north. Once the wounded insurgents were dropped off with the assault force headquarters in Objective Alpha, the ARF was again dispatched to an area in Objective Charlie to search a Toyota Hilux pickup truck that had been spotted, as well as a nearby cave. Nothing of significance was discovered and the vehicle was destroyed by AH-64 fire after the ARF was recovered.

With regard to the other forty-five individuals, the allied SOF team and the ANA detained them and subsequently evacuated them to an American forward operating base for further processing and questioning. However, the next day they were all released, since they did not meet the criteria established for detention.

Overall, the mission appeared to be underwhelming. Objective Alpha, particularly because it was declared the primary focus, proved to be a disappointment. Overall, enemy resistance throughout the objective area was relatively low and no items of intelligence value were collected by CANSOF or its allied elements. At 1900 hours, the CANSOF operators, as the last component of the CTF SSE, were extracted and returned to base.

However, the CANSOF and CTF commander, Colonel Sadler, took a positive perspective. "Operation Algonquin," he asserted, "was a successful proof-of-concept mission for the SOF CTF." Sadler added, "In the larger context of the overall coalition operations underway, this coordinated task force succeeded in causing disruption to a known ACM C2 node that had operated with impunity in the region of De Lam Ghar."[8]

He had a point. At the end of the day, the CTF had disrupted the enemy leadership, destroyed equipment and fighting positions, and, it was later learned, had killed a confirmed thirteen insurgents, with the count being as high as a possible thirty — all at the cost of no casualties and no equipment losses.

Although multiple-source reporting indicated that the operation had a serious impact on the enemy, the aftermath resembled what follows after a pit is dug on the edge of the ocean: as the coalition forces stopped "digging" and pulled away, the insurgents promptly rolled back in, like the tide, and filled in the hole. Intelligence sources noted that key Taliban leadership returned as early as September 6, and the sources began to discuss the impact of the SOF operation. Not surprisingly, task force planners decided that there was an opportunity to exploit. As a result, commander CJSOTF-A quickly appointed the CANSOF task force as the lead for the fourth Canadian-led SOF CTF mission — unofficially dubbed Algonquin II, for obvious reasons. CANSOF and their allies were going back to De Lam Ghar.

With regard to the enemy and their main target, the command and control node at De Lam Ghar and Taliban chieftain Mullah Dadfar, nothing much had changed. Analysts still placed Dadfar at the location. However, extensive ACM C2 activity in the nearby village of Atalay the day after Operation Algonquin gave them a new target to focus on. Also, in De Lam Ghar the enemy presence seemed to shift north from where it had been previously.

Colonel Sadler assigned his ground commander the mission of denying the use of the De Lam Ghar sanctuary area from September 23 to 24, 2005, in order to disrupt ACM command and control. The focus of this operation was Objective Echo, which was several kilometres to the northeast of the Operation Algonquin focal point, Objective Alpha.

The scheme of manoeuvre was expected to take approximately eight hours. The CANSOF assault force, reinforced by allied SOF with their integral ANA platoon, was to be deployed in a two-lift rotary-wing insertion into HLZs close to the objective area. Blocks were then to be established to the south, east, and west. Withdrawal to the north was to be prevented by an ARF. Once all the blocks were in place, thereby sealing off escape routes and establishing a firm foothold, allied SOF and the ANA would clear through Objective Echo. Once the mission was complete, the combined task force would link up with elements of a conventional task force, who would take control of the objective area while the SOF ground force extracted by helicopter.[9]

Once again, the target area was outside of civilian inhabited areas. The closest village was identified as being seven to eight kilometres away. The De Lam Ghar objective area was once again assessed as being purely under ACM control. Therefore, the entire objective area was classified a military target. Despite indications that the villages of Lam and Atalay, which were approximately eight kilometres to the south of the target area, supported the ACM, they were still scheduled for civil military operations (CMO), specifically a CMO aid package, at the conclusion of the operation. The conventional TF was responsible for this task after conducting the battle handover with the SOF CTF.

The command element of the SOF CTF attended the aviation task force air mission brief at Kandahar Airfield at 2300 hours on September 23, 2005, to cover the ground tactical plan for the pilots. Once the details of the insertion were finalized, they moved to a nearby American FOB for pickup. The first lift, which consisted of elements of CANSOF, allied SOF, and ANA, departed for the objective at 0203 hours on September 24. AH-64 Apache gunships reported the designated HLZs clear of enemy activity as the aviation commander's aircraft approached the objective with the first chalk of the ground assault force. Approximately thirty minutes after takeoff, the initial elements of the CTF SOF ground force were inserted into the objective area without incident.

Boisvert, the troop commander, and two of his assault detachments (C/S 11 and 13)[10] were inserted into an alternate HLZ but moved immediately to the southeast to seize the high ground. The other CANSOF elements were also dropped away from their designated HLZs, but all were able to quickly move to high ground to dominate Objective Echo.

As the first wave of soldiers consolidated their positions around the objective, Rutledge, the squadron commander, was made aware of a large number of unknown individuals in the middle of the objective area. The surveillance operator stressed that he could not make out who they were (i.e., no positive identification as enemy was obvious). As a result, the force commander was in a bit of a predicament.

"I'm wondering where all these people are coming from," explained Rutledge, "we went in looking for Dadfar and his bodyguards — we didn't expect a large AQ camp." The squadron commander had to consider that at least some of the group, failing positive identification as enemy, could be Bedouins, women or children.

CANSOF snipers occupying a good position of fire and observation quickly reported approximately twenty to twenty-five personnel moving south to north in the objective area. "We couldn't PID [positively identify] them with weapons so we didn't engage," explained Wilson, one of the snipers. Elements of allied SOF were dropped to the east of their intended HLZ and moved promptly to secure high ground to their west. Following the insertion, the CH-47 Chinook medium lift helicopters faded into the darkness as they returned to the staging forward operating base to pick up the second lift.

In the interim, at 0242 hours, a Predator unmanned aerial vehicle (UAV) reported Objective Echo clear after sweeping the area from north to south. However, approximately forty minutes later it observed six individuals moving along a ridgeline with no identification friend or foe (IFF) markings. Nine minutes later, at 0333 hours, the number of possible insurgents had grown to approximately twenty. The UAV noted they were moving very quickly north-northwest. It now appeared that there were two large groupings of potential enemy in the area.

The number of possible enemy grew even further. About twenty-nine ACM were moving between HLZ "P" and "N." Nonetheless, the aviation TF was able to land the second lift of the assault force without incident at 0400 hours.

Shortly after the second insertion, the ground force commander authorized the on-station AC-130 Spectre gunship to fire a warning shot in front of the large group of personnel now moving west through the valley. The AC-130 fired a second warning shot at 0415 hours, which seemed to divert the group from travelling west.

And so, as of 0430 hours, September 24, 2005, the AC-130 was tracking approximately fifty individuals moving about the area while CANSOF snipers were observing another large mass of twenty possible insurgents in Objective Echo. Unfortunately, the AC-130 could not engage at that time as it did not have positive identification on any of the groups to identify whether or not they were insurgents. At 0449 hours, the AH-64 Apache attack helicopters had returned from refueling at Tarin Kowt and the AC-130 then left station.

Meanwhile, Rutledge, the squadron commander, used his ARF to reinforce positions in his cordon in reaction to the potentially large enemy presence. He also moved his allied SOF and ANA elements to interdict and verify the identity of the large group of people moving about the areas. However, by 0619 hours, visual observation of the groups had been lost and the SOF CTF leadership assessed that they "went to ground." At this point, the Predator began flying west along the valley to see if "squirters" (i.e., enemy personnel attempting to escape) had made it out.[11]

At 0626 hours, the tension was finally broken and the tedious game of cat and mouse reached its apex. The aviation commander was frustrated by this point that the "enemy" was seemingly moving about with impunity, and sent a message across the net declaring "we need to do something about this." He then piloted his Blackhawk with coordinated support from an AH-64 Apache and flew very low east to west through the valley. Suddenly, a thunderous echo reverberated through the length of the valley as the enemy opened up with a barrage of RPGs and small arms fire. The AH-64 returned fire and conducted three strafing runs to punish its antagonists. Rutledge then pushed components of his CANSOF assault force north along the west side of the objective to try to get observation on the TIC site.

Shortly after the initial engagement, at 0715 hours, allied SOF and the ANA platoon began sweeping through Objective Echo from the south to the north. They quickly discovered a campsite in the vicinity of a group of suspected caves. During exploitation of the campsite, a number of push-to-talk radios, blasting caps, wires, and other potential IED components were found. At the same time, assault detachment call sign (C/S) 12 moving south from HLZ "L" discovered and cleared a fighting position on the high ground.

Concurrent to the clearance of Objective Echo, CANSOF elements continued to observe the area where the AH-64 engaged the enemy. An A-10 Thunderbolt CAS sortie conducted an additional strike on the target, immediately after which CANSOF snipers engaged a number of insurgents. The enemy activity prompted additional strafing runs in the same area. On conclusion of the A-10 runs, the ground force commander ordered his troop commander to sweep the area in order to finish dealing with the ACM in the areas and to conduct an SSE. However, the treacherous terrain made it impossible for the CANSOF operators to move off the mountaintop into the low ground. As a result, Boisvert coordinated with allied SOF elements to move into the area while CANSOF provided over-watch from the high ground.

As the ANA and allied SOF elements began the sweep of the TIC area, CANSOF snipers observed six individuals attempting to move into positions to engage the unsuspecting coalition troops. The CANSOF elements acted quickly to disrupt the enemy plan. The six individuals then suddenly popped up from cover. They were quickly engaged by the CANSOF snipers. A C-6 GPMG was also put into action and several 84mm rockets were launched at the ACM, resulting in numerous kills.

Following the engagement by the CANSOF troop and snipers, the A-10 Thunderbolts flew a number of sweeps over the area of the most recent contact. Once this was completed, allied SOF and the ANA continued to conduct their sweep of the objective area. Rutledge also requested additional aviation assets to move troops around the battlefield. As a result, an additional UH-60 Blackhawk helicopter and another AH-64 gunship arrived in the area at around 1115 hours. Rutledge then proceeded to use his ARF and move troops around to interdict squirters.

At noon, the allied SOF elements engaged another group of insurgents, resulting in the wounding of an ANA soldier. "The ANA were brave," insisted Tim Wilson, "they assaulted with guts and glory — assaulted a small cave head-on." A C-6 GPMG quickly marked the larger enemy position by firing tracers at the target. An Apache attack helicopter then conducted a strafing run on the out-gunned insurgents. Shortly thereafter A-10 aircraft were called in on a suspected enemy bunker in the same location.

Just as events seemed to be winding down, the area around the first main TIC appeared to have grown into a hornet's nest. At 1540 hours, about twenty heavily armed ACM were discovered in caves and bunkers approximately one hundred metres south of the previously mentioned main contact. The enemy had cleverly camouflaged their fighting positions. They used burlap and hessian "curtains" hung recessed in the cave openings to make them appear shallow and empty. In addition, they had thatched coverings over openings from which to fire, described one of the CANSOF snipers, "and they had tents within the caves themselves."

Sean, another sniper commented, "these guys are crafty."

As time wore on and it was clear that the time for redeployment was not going to be adequate due to the nature of the current engagement, the ground force commander requested additional time on the objective and asked that the extraction be on call if the helicopters were available. This request was relayed back up the chain of command and approved minutes later. Rutledge quickly requested helicopters once again to move troops around the battlefield. At the same time, the allied SOF elements and ANA troops on the ground pulled back so that CAS could pound the area.

Quick coordination between the joint terminal air controller (JTAC), the aviation commander, and the ground force commander put a plan in place to redeploy forces and continue hammering the enemy positions with close air support. As the additional helicopters arrived at 1710 hours, Rutledge used the CH-47s to pick up elements of a sub-unit from a conventional TF and lift them to the top of a ridgeline a kilometre to the north of Objective Echo into HLZ "P" in order to cover that flank. The Chinooks were also used to redeploy the CANSOF headquarters, as well as elements of ANA and allied SOF into the north portion of the objective as well.

Time began to run out. The adjusted extraction of the SOF CTF was quickly approaching but still none too soon. The ANA was dangerously low on ammunition and the entire ground force was running low on radio batteries. And then the unavoidable friction of war came into play. The extraction was delayed — indefinitely.

By 2030 hours, September 24, hours after the initial extraction was to have commenced, Rutledge called for a resupply. He forwarded the exact locations of all friendly forces and a summary of the day's activities. Rutledge also reported that although the SOF CTF maintained a loose cordon in place, he was certain once the moon rose and provided adequate illumination the insurgents would be able to stealthily escape the area.

The reply to the squadron commander's message was a mix of good news and bad. His resupply request was approved and a Blackhawk and an Apache helicopter were assigned to the mission. They arrived at 0145 hours the next morning. However, extraction was not to occur, at the earliest, before 0630 hours, September 25.

The majority of the area surrounding the enemy defensive location was covered by coalition troops and they were able to observe that the objective area still indicated enemy activity. As a result, the ground force called in close air support at 2230 hours, prior to moon illumination. Two A-10 aircraft slowly lumbered into the valley and dropped four GBU-12 bombs and conducted six 30mm gun-strafing runs over the enemy-dominated ground. "During this action," reported Rutledge, "one impact had numerous secondary detonations at the bunker location." However, one of the bombs fell without detonating, and had to be called in by the JTAC as a dud.

The night proved to be extremely uncomfortable. "During the day it was forty some degrees [Celsius]," explained Wilson, "at a night it was cold at twenty." He added, "guys were wrapping up in personal camouflage nets, panel markers, whatever they had."

The CANSOF linguist was blunter. "We froze our asses off," he stated.

Richard Desjardins, the assault force squadron sergeant-major, made best use of a body bag to keep off the chill. Between the drop in temperature and the winds in the mountains, the SOF troops spent a very unpleasant night.

The next morning, prior to first light, Rutledge established communications with headquarters to confirm the extraction plan. At first, it looked good for a pickup later that morning but a CH-47 Chinook crash in Zabol Province quickly changed coalition priorities. Since there were no indications at all when extraction would occur, Rutledge decided to conduct a detailed SSE of the valley. By mid-morning higher headquarters warned off the CTF that pickup would not be before 2245 hours that night.

The squadron commander requested that the allied SOF with their ANA counterparts conduct a sweep of the enemy defensive position, but with the potential of a five-hundred-pound dud sitting in the middle of the position, the allied SOF commander refused to move his men into a potentially dangerous area. Considering the potential importance of an SSE of the objective, and taking into account the fact that his two explosive ordnance disposal personnel were actual bomb technicians, Rutledge made the call to take his own tactical headquarters down into the position with some ANA. Although not the most desirable plan of action to take as a commander, he figured that the allied SOF commander was well-qualified to continue on with the mission should anything happen.

The small HQ element made its way into the enemy position and slowly advanced along the old stream bed, which was littered with ordnance and boulders. They carefully cleared each small area, locating a number of additional insurgents killed by the A-10 strikes the night before. A couple of hundred metres into the sweep, the group came across a wounded insurgent pinned under a tree. Although his situation was initially confusing, it became clear what had transpired to the man the night before. Rutledge described him, relatively speaking, as "the luckiest guy on earth." He had a sucking chest wound that was partially bandaged up from the firefight the day prior, and he had been making his way, possibly with help, down the stream bed to the west when the dud round had come in. The bomb had apparently struck the side of the ridge, sheared off its fuse and split open, depositing the explosive compound inside all over the area in an orange shower of small chunks. The large casing had continued to the bottom of the chasm and knocked the tree over pinning down the wounded insurgent. This pushed him down beneath the large rocks of the streambed subsequently shielding him from the next bomb, an airburst, which shredded everything in the area.

A MEDEVAC was subsequently called for him. To conduct the evacuation the MEDEVAC bird was hovering for thirty minutes as they tried to hoist the casualty up three hundred feet on a cable to the helicopter. This rescue created some criticism later on due to the fact some felt that the helicopter and aircrew were put at risk to airlift a confirmed insurgent from an area that still contained an unknown amount of enemy. Rutledge brushed the criticism aside. "I was not about to kill a wounded prisoner," he stated matter of factly. "The moral (and legal) requirement to ensure the safety of the enemy wounded once they were in our custody," commented the squadron commander, "was part of my responsibility as a professional and, as well, as a human being."

Luckily, nothing happened. The enemy held their fire. Rutledge hypothesized that they held their fire because they feared it was a trap designed for them to give away their position so that the coalition forces could call in more close air support. This was not surprising considering the hammering they had taken the previous day. Another plausible theory to explain the lack of gunfire was the fact that the enemy were most likely aware of who was being brought out of the chasm.

The ground force commander estimated that the close fighting had resulted in at least twenty enemy killed. But there was still a minimum of twenty or more ACM still in possible caves around the area. Moreover, the SSE had confirmed the enemy possessed a number of weapon caches and specialist equipment such as night-vision scopes. In addition, they had numerous covered routes throughout the area. Adding to these realities was the fact that throughout the day, the coalition troops observed individuals in and around the objective, a number of which were engaged with 105mm rounds from a battery of artillery assigned to the conventional TF that had been moved within range of the force.

Static so long in enemy territory, Rutledge began to be concerned about a possible counter-attack during the next period of darkness. After all, it would be very easy for the ACM, with their detailed knowledge of the terrain, to re-infiltrate the area and strike at the coalition forces. The anticipated counter-attack never materialized, however. The pounding the enemy had taken over the previous forty-eight hours had made them melt away until the coalition forces decided to pull out. The extraction commenced at 1430 hours, on September 26, and the last of the CANSOF troops were back at their FOB by 1730 hours that evening. The eight-hour task had dragged on for almost sixty hours.

The actual impact of the mission was hard to determine. SOF CTF killed a probable forty enemy, with at least twenty confirmed kills. But a body count is always deceptive in such a conflict. The Taliban had absolutely no problem regenerating low-level hired guns. The SSE also netted one detainee and a score of captured equipment, including two RPGs, a PKM machine gun, five AK-47s, two sets of binoculars, a commercial thermal (night-vision) sight, a satellite phone solar panel, an FM radio, a GPS, and assorted IED assembly components, such as wires, cables, batteries, clamps, and an unidentified white powder, as well as captured documents, including a book with phone numbers and documents in Urdu detailing how to use a GPS for targeting purposes.

Although the SOF CTF did not capture Dadfar or any other key leaders, or for that matter uncover an intelligence bonanza, they did confirm that the De Lam Ghar area was a main ACM defensive belt, with fortified positions, an ACM C2 node, as well as a sanctuary for an IED cell. More important, the CANSOF-led SOF assault force penetrated the enemy stronghold and created, for the second time in a month, massive disruption to the Taliban in the area. "Algonquin II succeeded," claimed Colonel Sadler, "in disrupting a major C2 node in the De Lam Ghar region of Ghorak." This alone bought time for the conventional forces and the Government of Afghanistan to continue the program of reconstruction and recovery.

CHAPTER 3

NEVER SAY DIE:
INTO THE JAWS OF DEATH AT CHENARTU

The special operations forces soldiers sat uncomfortably in the cargo-net seating against the fuselage of the chubby CH-47 Chinook medium-lift helicopter. They were loaded down with weapons, ammunition, and other equipment that made sitting intolerable, no matter how they tried to position their bodies. The noise just added to the discomfort. The loud, deep "wup, wup, wup," of the large dual rotors of the aircraft, in combination with the whine of the overworked engines in the heat and altitude of southern Afghanistan, made it impossible to talk or sleep.

It was almost midday and they had just finished scrambling for the mission. With half the assault troop just returning from a mobility patrol in the Khod Valley less than forty-eight hours prior, they had spent most of their time planning for another mission, one that was cast aside to execute this time-sensitive task instead. It had been a whirlwind of on-again/off-again activity. But they were in the air, so each SOF operator lost himself in his own world. Some tried to peer out the small portholes to catch a glimpse of the passing terrain; some tried to sleep, and others just watched the activities around them. However, none were too excited about a rotary-wing insertion in broad daylight.

The flight passed quickly and the CH-47 began to flare for its approach. The flight engineer was talking into his headset although no one could make out what was being said. The SOF troops were less than pleased with the fact that they had no connection with what was transpiring — no headsets were available and their radios were incompatible. They had to trust the aircrew to get them to the target and on the ground at the right place and the right time, and hope there were no surprises when they stepped off the rear ramp.

The helicopter seemed to lurch forward and pick up speed once again. Clearly it was an aborted landing, but "why?" was the general concern. And then, the chaos began. The SOF soldiers could see the crew chief, door gunners, and flight engineer become increasingly animated and excited. The noise made hearing difficult, so the troops did not take notice of the bullets slapping and tearing into the metal skin of the helicopter. But there was no mistaking the smoke and flame that erupted from the right rear of the airframe. They had clearly taken a hit. This became even more apparent once the helicopter began to shudder and rock, seemingly entering its death throes.

The aircrew fought the fire and actually put it out, but only for a few seconds. The Taliban were not to be cheated today. The flames erupted once again and this time with a renewed energy. The aircrew strapped themselves in and told everyone to brace themselves. The next seconds passed without allowing those on board to fully comprehend what was about to happen. The helicopter was quickly losing altitude, seemingly not slowing down in concert with its descent. All realized they were about to enter the fight by way of a crash landing.

The opening minutes of the operation in Chenartu, Shah Wali Kot District, in Kandahar Province, on December 4, 2005, were proving to be disastrous. Commanders and planners had hoped that this mission would net them an elusive key Taliban leader. Now, most were hoping they could simply avoid serious losses.

In many ways, the mission had begun already in mid-November 2005. The target was Mullah Abdul Ghafour, a former security coordinator for Mullah Mohammed Omar and the current principal Taliban commander in northern Kandahar Province. Ghafour commanded an anti-coalition militia (ACM) cell that was responsible for IED activity in northern Shah Wali Kot, as well as attacks along the Kandahar–Tarin Kowt road. He was also responsible for two IED zones in the Mianeshin Valley. His known associates included a number of Taliban commanders who were identified as MVTs.

Although Ghafour had numerous areas that he frequented, he rarely stayed in an area for longer than a few hours. This made it extremely difficult for the coalition to target him. Furthermore, the location of his movements offered a double-edged sword for the coalition forces. The areas in which Ghafour was most vulnerable were those where he spent the least amount of time, making targeting difficult. The areas where he spent more time were regions where Taliban support (and, thus, support for Ghafour) was high. This support meant that he was less likely to be caught in such places; it also meant that it would be more dangerous for coalition forces to operate there.

Analyst believed that Ghafour and his three- to five-man personal security detail (PSD) would most likely flee any area he was in if the ACM early-warning system identified coalition forces en route to wherever he was. So, surprise was critical. And, if successful, the pay-off would be great. Analysts believed that capturing or killing Ghafour would reduce operational capability within the Shah Wali Kot and Mianeshin Districts of Kandahar Province and hinder future Taliban operations.

In mid-November 2005, Mullah Ghafour was believed to be in the village of Chenartu. In addition, the coalition also suspected other Taliban leaders were nearby. During this period, a combat element from a conventional task force received small-arms fire from approximately twenty ACM in the vicinity of Gaskol. The task force ground elements attempted to surround the Taliban and they believed that they had cornered Mullah Ghafour and a number of other MVTs. Subsequently, an assessment was made that the Taliban leaders and a large group of heavily armed fighters were located in Zamto and Chenartu.

Chenartu was comprised of scattered hamlets along the Rahka River in a mountain valley that is impassable to vehicles past De Chenartu Tangay in the north.[1] However, the valley widens out into a fertile farming area around the village of Chenartu in the south. The main access route is from the southwest and runs through the village to the northeast with the primary north–south road splitting off and running through Takht Kalay to the Baghtu Valley.

Chenartu itself is located where several valleys converge, and it has always been an excellent venue for the Taliban to meet since they have always considered it to be a safe haven. Moreover, coalition intelligence staff believed it to be a staging area and probable command and control node for several IED cells targeting the Kandahar–Tarin Kowt road. The coalition certainly considered the village to be a likely refuge for ACM elements. Planners believed that a coalition operation in Chenartu would potentially disrupt IED operations and cause further ACM dispersal. Furthermore, they insisted that an SSE in this town would probably uncover weapons, explosives, and intelligence related to current and future plans to attack coalition force convoys.

The commander of Combined Joint Special Operations Forces Task Force — Afghanistan (CJSOTF-A), the senior headquarter for the JTF 2–based Afghanistan task force, was adamant that the coalition strike at the ACM leadership. He wanted to maintain unrelenting pressure on the ACM, even as the campaign season was coming to an end. As such, he directed that his forces pre-empt ACM attacks, as well as conduct specific operations to defeat ACM forces as they moved to their winter sanctuaries. In this manner, he believed he could prevent ACM from consolidating, reorganizing, or planning for their spring attacks. He planned to do this by conducting offensive combat operations, foreign internal defence (FID), information operations (IO), and civil military operations (CMO) to support the Combined Joint Task Force 76 (CJTF 76) winter offensive against the ACM.[2] The desired end-state was the disruption of the ACM's ability to reconstitute forces through the winter months and the impacting of their ability to conduct spring attacks and potentially increase the likelihood of reconciliation.

As part of this campaign, the commander CJSOTF-A created SOF Combined Task Force (CTF) operations throughout the Afghanistan theatre of operations (ATO). Within this framework, CJSOTF-A authorized specific operations that were based on the combined forces of the CANSOF task force and elements of allied SOF. This CTF was responsible for conducting high-tempo disruption operations in the period leading up to, during, and after, the national elections.[3]

Sensing that Ghafour was potentially vulnerable, the Canadian led CTF began to plan for the conduct of an SSE mission. Within CJSOTF-A, all operations and targets were bottom-up generated by the task force special operations intelligence centre (SOIC) or handed to the CANSOF task force by other forces who required assistance. Nonetheless, both the in-theatre national Canadian chain of command, as well as the commander CJSOTF-A, approved the concept of operations (CONOP) for the Canadian led CTF to conduct an SSE in the vicinity of the Village of Chenartu on November 22, 2005, in order to confirm or deny ACM activity. Quite simply, the commander's intent was to obtain intelligence to ascertain whether or not Chenartu was an enemy command and control node.

Therefore, using the SOF CTF as a cordon and SSE force, the plan was to insert in the vicinity of the Chenartu, isolate it, and conduct a detailed SSE on personnel, infrastructure, and equipment. In addition, the mission also entailed delivering a CMO humanitarian assistance package to the village. When the SSE/CMO was complete, the CTF was to extract itself from the area.

The scheme of manoeuvre was to be equally simple. The plan called for a rotary-wing insertion on a landing zone that dominated the objective. A cordon would then be clamped into place through the use of blocks, domination of key terrain, and the use of air reaction forces. The block positions ensured a secure foothold to launch the village sweeps; they also sealed off possible escape routes that could be used by any ACM elements attempting to slip out. The CMO humanitarian package was to be passed to the village prior to withdrawal to reinforce the legitimacy of the Government of Afghanistan (GoA).

The mission, however, was never executed because the intelligence picture did not reveal enough to act.

However, it resurfaced weeks later. At 1200 hours, on December 3, 2005, a conventional task force forwarded a target intelligence package (TIP) through Peter Alaby, the CANSOF liaison officer, at Kandahar Airfield to Colonel George Sadler, the commander of the CANSOF task force. The conventional task force requested CANSOF to prosecute a

Level II capture/kill time-sensitive target related to Mullah Ghafour on their behalf. During the previous week, Ghafour had been tracked to a compound in the vicinity of De Chenartu Tangay and the Americans believed that he was potentially vulnerable. As a result, CANSOF began battle procedure to conduct a direct-action mission on the specified objective to capture or kill Ghafour.[4]

The task force intelligence officer (J2) briefed the target information package to Colonel Sadler and his operations staff at 1515 hours. He ordered his staff to confirm that CJSOTF would sponsor the concept of operations and provide the necessary resources to conduct the mission. Subsequently, at 1630 hours, the CANSOF commander accepted the mission; thirty minutes later, Alain Picard, his squadron commander, began the mission planning.

Although the task force headquarters had already been working on the new target since noon, when the operation spooled up, the squadron was in the process of planning for another mission that was to be conducted that night. They had already done the planning, issued orders, and conducted their review of concept (ROC) drill.[5] Clearly, the new target was a priority, but the CANSOF ground force now had to reorient its focus and begin planning anew.

Norman Jackson, the troop commander, had a huge challenge before him. A portion of the troop had literally just returned from conducting a thirty-day mobility operation and they had just started planning for another mission. They now dropped tools, refocused, and started planning for a completely new mission to be executed in less than twelve hours.

At 1815 hours, the squadron commander back-briefed the task force commander.

His mission was clear — CANSOF was to capture or kill Mullah Ghafour in the vicinity of De Chenartu Tangay in order to disrupt ACM activity in Kandahar Province. The concept of operations had not changed much from the plan several weeks back. In essence, Picard planned to dominate the high ground, establish key block positions, maintain an ARF, and then sweep through the target. There were two major changes. One was the absence of an allied SOF element. In its place, the CANSOF ground force would be reinforced by a twenty-two-man ANA company.

Another change in the overall concept revolved around a battle handover with a sub-unit of a conventional task force, who were assigned the task of taking over the objective area once the DA and SSE were complete.

The allocated H-Hr (i.e., start time) for the operation was 0615 hours, December 4, 2005, approximately twelve hours later. And then, the inevitable friction of war set in. There were some complications. At 1900 hours, intelligence confirmed that Ghafour was leaving De Chenartu Tangay and was moving to Chenartu. Due to his frequent movements, it was unclear at which objective he would actually be. As a result, at 2100 hours the squadron commander revisited his mission planning based on a possibility that the target area would be centred on Chenartu. Needless to say, the fact that it was difficult to define the location of the target meant that the intelligence picture was not optimal.

An hour later, his CONOP was briefed to commander CJSOTF-A for approval, which was received at 2300 hours. The mission, with a possible modified objective location, was a go. The actual execution of the task now hung on an actual trigger — the confirmation of Ghafour's location.

However, before any action the squadron commander issued a final warning order and final planning guidance to his squadron HQ and troop commander at 2345 hours. Approximately two hours later, they briefed him on a refined concept of the actual plan of attack. Picard then gave formal orders to the ground assault force.

The mission remained the same; however, the objective was now Chenartu. CANSOF and ANA elements would conduct a one turn rotary-wing insertion to isolate the target compound. CANSOF operators were tasked with establishing a cordon around the objective, by placing blocks to the south, east, and west. The remaining Canadian SOF troops, in conjunction with the ANA, would establish a block to the north, thus, sealing off any possible escape routes. The blocking positions also created a firm foothold from which to conduct follow-on tasks. Once all blocks were firmly established, the CANSOF and ANA forces in the north would then systematically sweep through the objective moving north to south. Once the target area was secure, elements from the conventional task force would then be called forward to conduct a handover of the site. In addition, they would support the CMO assessment that was scheduled once the objective was cleared. Once the CMO assessment was complete and the target area had been handed over to the conventional task force, the CANSOF and ANA elements would withdraw by helicopter.

The abort criteria for the mission were also clearly laid out. The loss of one CH-47 helicopter on the first chalk; a downed aircraft en route; or the lack of AH-64 Apache helicopters for infiltration would scuttle the mission. H-Hr was moved thirty minutes to sunrise, or 0645 hours, December 4, 2005.

In theory, it was a relatively simple plan. The mission was scheduled to take only eight hours. At 0330 hours, the ground force conducted their ROC drill, which consisted of the different ground elements explaining on a large map of the objective area exactly what they would be doing throughout each phase of the operation.

At 0430 hours, the CANSOF task force commander, Colonel Sadler, issued a "Frag O" (fragmentary orders) to update the situation. Very little had changed, except for the objective. The mission now revolved around capturing or killing Mullah Ghafour in vicinity of Chenartu village in order to disrupt ACM activity in Kandahar. One other change, this one minor, was the caveat that CANSOF had to be prepared to stay on the objective for an additional period of time if required to conduct a detailed SSE.

With orders and preparations largely completed in the CANSOF forward operating base, the ground force moved to "thirty minutes notice to move," awaiting the trigger to launch the operation. They eventually located at the landing zone at the adjacent American FOB installation. Meanwhile, at 0445 hours, the squadron commander moved to KAF to brief the aviation unit responsible for the rotary-wing insertion.

Picard remained at KAF and attended the aircrew mission brief (AMB) at 0530 hours. Initially there was some confusion of the actual objective. In addition, the intelligence brief provided did not accurately reflect the information that was available. The commanding officer of the aviation unit caught the problem and clarified the mission. Picard also repeated the brief on the ground operation.

This was not the only harbinger of existing problems. From the receipt of the TIP from the conventional task force right through

CONOP development and mission planning, the CANSOF task force had consistent difficulties in communicating with non-CANSOF units. Due to a lack of secure communications between the CANSOF FOB and American units, all communication had to go through Alaby, the KAF liaison officer. As such, at the tactical level, all intelligence or planning products, flowing either way, were pushed through the CANSOF KAF liaison officer who physically walked the products to the various units. This proved to be extremely time-consuming, particularly when time was so short. As a result, passage of information was slow, which affected the ability of various units to plan effectively.

In addition, the CANSOF operations centre did not have direct access to all of the feeds that provided information on the battlespace. This led to a complicated process of passing information through the chain of command to the CANSOF KAF liaison officer, who was now located in the tactical operations centre of the conventional task force, in order to relay information. The result was a delay in the passage of information and a loss of situational awareness and perspective with regard to what was actually happening on the ground. Picard explained, "Neither the aircrew nor the ground force were getting a good idea of what to expect on the ground."

Then the push died down. It appeared the trigger was not met and the mission would be delayed at least twenty-four hours. Picard, who had now been on the go for thirty-six hours planning for one mission or another, decided to stay at the CANSOF "B" Echelon at KAF and put his head down for a few hours. Around mid-morning he was awoken and told the mission was on. He called the task force commander to confirm the order. A broad daylight insertion was always tactically risky. Once he confirmed the order, he prepared his troops to launch.

What became disturbing, however, was the fact that a number of ANA members, as well as some interpreters, were caught making phone calls on the landing zone prior to take-off.[6] It was no secret that many Afghan, including those in the ANSF, were sympathetic to the insurgent cause and would share information for reasons of ideology, family, or profit. Nonetheless, whether there had been a potential security breach or not, at 1048 hours, intelligence put Ghafour on the objective. Nine minutes later Colonel Sadler launched the mission. The aviation task force arrived at the American FOB with the aviation package at 1127 hours to pick up the assault force.

When the helicopters arrived, the pilots were once again briefed that the southern objective, Chenartu, was the primary target. At 1140 hours, the reconnaissance (recce) element consisting of an AH-64 Apache attack helicopter, a UH-60 Blackhawk helicopter, and the aviation commander in another Blackhawk helicopter departed the American FOB. The remaining aircraft, consisting of another AH-64 Apache helicopter and two CH-47 Chinook medium-lift helicopters carrying the main body of the ground assault force, lifted off three minutes later. For better or worse, the mission was underway.

The recce element arrived on the objective area at approximately 1210 hours and began conducting sweeps of the area. They reported normal village life but no enemy activity. Subsequently, they reported some "squirters" running from compounds in all directions. Nonetheless, the lead aircraft called "green" on all four helicopter landing zones (HLZs), indicating they were safe for insertion.[7]

At 1213 hours, the first Chinook helicopter arrived on its primary landing zone, HLZ Juliet, and with the Apache helicopter in an over-watch position commenced its approach. However, the CH-47 Chinook could not land because of high trees in the area. It then flew four hundred metres north of the HLZ looking for a better spot. At that point, the left side crew chief saw two insurgents exit a compound and point a weapon at the aircraft. The crew chief asked for permission to shoot, and after receiving authority engaged and killed the enemy.

The first Chinook now found that the secondary HLZ was also unsuitable for a landing due to the high walls of a nearby compound, which were too close for the rotor blades. It then proceeded to retrace its route back down the river valley to an open field south of HLZ Juliet. While on approach to the field, the aircraft started receiving small-arms fire from the ridgeline, hillsides, and valley area.

On the arrival of the first Chinook, its protector, an Apache helicopter, had broken east, all the while continually checking on the HLZ areas. As the Chinook came back to its primary landing zone (i.e., HLZ Juliet), the accompanying Apache helicopter saw enemy begin to engage the vulnerable Chinook helicopter. The AH-64 gunship desperately tried to provide covering fire, but it discovered its 30mm gun would not work. It then circled to the right to put itself in position to fire rockets. Simultaneously, the aviation commander called an RPG launch. Subsequently, the Apache helicopter reported that the Chinook helicopter was on fire.

Jackson, the assault element commander, recalled, "In the CH-47, the pilots gave me 'one minute out' [i.e., one minute from touch down at the LZ to allow the chalk to prepare for disembarkation]."

"As we approached the LZ, I saw that the LZ was not good and the pilots started looking for an alternate LZ. They over flew the LZ, turned around and exposed themselves to a ton of fire," continued Jackson in disbelief. "We then received a burst of bullets from the rear to the front and the C-6 [machine-] gunners opened up."[8]

Chaos was not far behind.

"We then 'heard fire in the back,'" Jackson said. "I turned around and confirmed fire in the rear port side of the bird."

The squadron medic recalled events similarly. "I was seated first man port side near the C-6 gunner," he explained, "As the chopper was flaring and we were inserting into our initial LZ, word was passed that it was not suitable to land." He continued:

> Once I heard that, the C-6 gunners on both sides opened fire. I also heard what sounded like small-arms fire coming through the chopper. Seconds later, I attempted to look out the ramp, but could not see due to large flames coming out the port side of the aircraft. The message was passed up that there was a fire, and that's when the aircraft started its quick descent. I prepared for a crash landing by bracing myself.

Key to the operation was the reliance on a Blackhawk helicopter to insert a team onto the high ground before the arrival of the CH-47s into the target area. This would allow the CH-47s to come in supported by observation and some covering fire from the ground. However, this did not transpire as planned.

"Right from the beginning things were fucked up," asserted the JTF 2 linguist.

There was hesitation to land the small team because of the enemy contact. But finally they were put down, albeit too late to help the first Chinook coming in to land. The American pilots struggled to maintain orientation, although they were under fire as they waited for the troops to unload. Things didn't improve. Once the CANSOF operators got out of the helicopter, they were pinned down by enemy fire almost immediately.

"We were taking fire from everywhere," explained the CANSOF linguist, "the villagers were on their roofs firing everywhere."

The linguist and the snipers he was with did not know what was going on. The communications were pretty much blocked as everyone was trying to communicate their individual dramas happening across the small valley battlefield. The enemy was equally communicating but in a different context.

"Brothers," encouraged a Taliban leader, "you will be rewarded for your work this day."

At that point the small isolated team realized something big was going on. Then they saw huge black smoke and the AH-64 Apache helicopters firing everywhere. It was not until Jason Ashburn, the sniper detachment commander, and the rest of the snipers crawled forward to the edge of the cliff that they were able to get "eyes-on" the objective and the calamity that was transpiring below them.

At the same time, the second Chinook was in the process of dropping off a number of CANSOF operators (call sign (C/S) 11) at HLZ Hotel, to form the south block. However, they too ran into problems. The loading of the all-terrain vehicles (ATVs) had not been optimized, and as a result, the pilot reported, "with the ATV in the way, a few passengers took as long to offload as it does a full manifest of passengers — way too long." The CH-47 then proceeded to "bunny-hop" to the vicinity to the west of HLZ Golf to insert the remaining CANSOF and ANA elements on board. It then loitered, waiting for word that the landing zone was clear for insertion. The aviation commander reported over the radio that he observed RPG fires and instructed the second Chinook helicopter to drop off the passengers into the objective area without delay.

Blair Sturgeon, the detachment commander of C/S 11, and his men, who were responsible for the southern block, had made their way off the helicopter with difficulty because of the obstruction. They adopted a defensive position and waited until the Chinook departed. Immediately after the helicopter was out of ear shot, "we were able to hear noise other than the helo [helicopter] itself," reported Sturgeon, "we heard MG [machine gun] fire." He added, "All of the fire was coming from the north of our location. As we were not under contact, we carried on with our primary task." The detachment commander explained:

At this point it was clear that the AH-64s were engaging something to the North. After observing to the north we saw large amounts of black smoke approximately five hundred to seven hundred metres away. About five minutes later, I received on comms [radio] what I thought was "a chopper is down." At this point I decided to push my C/S north and forego the blocking position. After establishing comms with the assault force commander, it was clear that a helo had been downed, and this was the cause of the black smoke. As briefed in orders, this was now the primary mission.

The Apache gunship that had escorted the second CH-47 helicopter to HLZ Hotel for its first insertion observed, as they were in the process of moving to their second drop location (i.e., HLZ Juliet), the first Chinook helicopter turn around after over-flying HLZ Juliet and head back south toward their originally intended landing zone. They then noticed four enemy in the river firing and running towards the second CH-47, while another six enemy were running towards the first Chinook helicopter, which was now on fire.

"I engaged the enemy with 30mm killing ten as they were firing on both Chinook helicopters," recalled the aircraft captain. "We continued to observe and cover the burning CH-47 as it landed on fire near LZ Juliet." He added, "All personnel exited the stricken helicopter before the aircraft was completely engulfed in flames."

The first Chinook helicopter itself did not notice any RPG fire while it was being engaged. The helicopter's left fuel pressure light illuminated and the ramp aircrew member reported a fire in the cabin. Crew members extinguished the flames but they flared up again. At the same time, the aircraft started to vibrate heavily, as the controls were getting stiff due to loss of hydraulics.

Jackson remembered, "The CH-47 clearly lost power and dropped a little bit before going back up for few seconds and then lost all power and crashed."

Luckily, the mortally wounded CH-47 was able to make a controlled crash landing in a field near its original HLZ.

The tragedy unfolded, taking mere minutes, while the command and control helicopter was orbiting the battlefield, trying to bring order to the spiralling chaos. Both the aviation commander and Picard were on board the C2 bird. As the first Chinook helicopter was turning south towards HLZ Juliet, the aviation commander and his right crew chief witnessed enemy running into the treeline. Subsequently they saw an insurgent emerge with a tube on his shoulder. The Taliban fighter then adopted a crouching position and raised the tube to his shoulder, aiming it at the first Chinook helicopter as it flew by. As the right crew chief began to inform the aviation commander of the impending engagement, the enemy fired the RPG. The crew chief saw a puff of smoke come from the tube on the Taliban's shoulder and, subsequently, flames coming from the bottom of the first Chinook helicopter at its five o'clock position. The flames were at the rear of the aircraft and began to travel up the left side of the fuselage. The aviation commander quickly looked out of his UH-60 Blackhawk and saw that the first CH-47 helicopter was indeed on fire.

"From my vantage point in the UH-60," said Picard, "it seemed as if it [the first Chinook] was travelling in slow motion as the flames engulfed the rear of the CH-47."

Unfortunately, the pilots flying the C2 bird did not have the same vantage point, so they brought the helicopter around to the right. As the Blackhawk made its sharp turn, more ACM emerged from the treeline and another tube-launched weapon was aimed skyward, but this time at the C2 Blackhawk carrying the two key on-site commanders. The crew chief could not verify the exact type of weapon that was being aimed at them since they were at approximately one thousand feet above ground level (AGL), but he immediately yelled, "RPG at five o'clock" into the intercom. At the same time, the CMWS system aboard the aircraft expelled flares from the dispenser on the right side of the helicopter. Both the aviation commander and the right crew chief saw a plume of smoke emit from the weapon and a smoke trail coming menacingly towards them. The crew chief saw the missile narrowly miss the aircraft and fly towards the flare location. The aviation commander and his crew chief later acknowledged that the missile passed underneath the right side of the aircraft at a distance of approximately five to ten feet.

Simultaneously, the pilot banked sharply to the left and away from the missile. The right crew chief also heard what appeared to be a loud "boom" or "thunder clap" as the missile went by. The crew chief had been unable to return fire due to the aircraft's height and the presence of friendly forces in the vicinity.

As the command helicopter came around, they could see that the burning Chinook helicopter had made a controlled emergency landing and everyone was exiting the aircraft. The scene was surreal, more akin to a scene from the film *Apocalypse Now* than what one would expect from a mission based on a tempered risk assessment.

The aviation commander swept up the unfolding events and quickly informed the accompanying Apache helicopters that they were being engaged by small arms and RPGs while flying over an orchard and compound north of the crash site. His bird then swooped down and he threw a smoke grenade into the orchard so that the Apache helicopters could blanket the area with rockets and 30mm fire. At least one enemy was killed.

As the CANSOF linguist looked down from his mountain perch on the western side of Chenartu, he could see the entire battlefield. "The chopper [first Chinook] looked like an elephant jumped on it, and it was burning. I thought everyone inside was dead."

But they were not.

As the battle quickly sucked everything within reach into its vortex, C/Ss 12 and 14, who were to land at HLZ Juliet and establish the northern block and then sweep south, were now fighting for survival. Their CH-47 had crashed hard into the unforgiving Afghan soil. Flames licked at the survivors in the badly scorched and bullet-riddled aircraft. Outside the burning hulk, Taliban bullets zipped through the air before ploughing into the earth, or — sometimes — a coalition target.

On impact, the squadron medic was thrown forward and he hit his head on the cockpit separation panel. He stood up only to discover that the aft of the aircraft and most of the port side was on fire, so he escaped through the C-6 gunner hatch on the starboard side. The rotor blades were still turning but they were starting to get very low.

"I yelled out, watch your heads," he recalled.

The warning came too late. On evacuation, one of the crew chiefs was seriously injured when he was struck by a rotor blade. He slipped in and out of consciousness and was later evacuated.

According to the squadron signals NCO, "The aircrew left the CH-47 through the starboard side door in the front where the C-6 is installed, and one of them got stuck at the door because of his backpack. I removed the backpack from the crew member and left the CH-47 by the same door. Outside, we were under serious enemy fire."

"The crew left the CH-47 through the starboard side door in the front," affirmed Jackson. "I confirmed that the evacuation was underway and evacuated myself through the front C-6 gunner hole." He elaborated, "Outside, we were under heavy enemy fire from the west mountain ridgeline and the north and east compounds. We initially returned fire to these positions."

Harold Rossier, the detachment commander for C/S 12, recalled, "On landing, the fighting force exited the burning aircraft and began to take up firing positions." There were multiple injuries due to both small-arms fire and the hard landing. "We had three CANSOF and two ANA casualties," he added. Although Rossier was one of the wounded, he continued to fight his with detachment in the break-contact action that ensued.

Meanwhile, still in the aircraft, Martin Pelletier, the most seriously wounded SOF operator, could not exit the aircraft on his own.[9] Help was not far away. Dan Tessler, a detachment second-in-command, re-entered the chopper to extract his wounded comrade as a twenty- to thirty-foot fire raged on the port fuel cell. Braving the heat and incinerating aircraft, he ensured Pelletier was pulled from the flaming wreckage. He later received the Cross of Valour for his heroic actions.

As the evacuation was taking place, the crash LZ was under constant enemy fire. "Once we hit the ground," recounted Paul Hellyer, the detachment commander for C/S 14, "our call sign immediately exited the rear of the aircraft via the ramp [and] we took up fire positions covering the four to eight o'clock [nose of aircraft pointing twelve o'clock] position." He elaborated, "We were taking fire from the high ground east, west, and north of us. After a hasty consolidation, I determined that moving into the high ground to the west was the best location for a rally point." The detachment commander continued, "we moved first to secure a toehold to cover C/S 12, the ANA and wounded off the "X" [crash site].

To add to the problems, the downed aircraft appeared to be operating in isolation.

"No communications systems worked at that point, and I decided to break contact to the east on a piece of high ground, in order to regroup," explained Jackson. "C/S 14 and the aircrew moved to the hilltop while we covered them and then I coordinated our break contact, covered by C/S 14, [which] had exited to the rear of the CH-47 and moved to the high ground."

The assault force commander was then advised that he had some serious casualties. He immediately ordered his JTAC and signal NCO to call for a MEDEVAC. Jackson then ordered his force to consolidate on the high ground and move the casualties close to HLZ India for extraction. By this time, C/S 11, who had continued to move to the northwest to link up with the assault force at the crash site, arrived and assisted in the extraction of the casualties to a safe area.

Meanwhile, C/S 13, acting as the ARF in a UH-60 Blackhawk, was eager to assist their comrades struggling on the ground. But it was still unsafe to land and Jackson told them to remain airborne. "Feeling that we were taking control and not wanting to lose another helo, we inserted them once enemy fire had subsided." And so, on order, the ARF inserted into HLZ India to reinforce the assault force. At the same time, the aircrew from the crashed CH-47 helicopter and the casualties already at the landing zone were evacuated.[10]

The Apache helicopters continued to fire rockets north of HLZ Golf into the river valley where small-arms and RPG fire was observed. Communications were now established with the ground force joint terminal air controller, and fidelity was gained on friendly locations east and west of the valley. But not before a near disaster.

The ground force was taking fire from the western mountain and called the Apache gunships to take out the problem. The Apaches began their approach and quickly noted the activity on the hill, which in fact was the product of the CANSOF snipers. The actual enemy position was approximately fifty metres lower on the mountain and farther to the west. Luckily, both the ground force commander in the C2 bird and the snipers themselves caught the potential disaster in the making and were able to call off the strike and direct the AH-64s to the correct target.

Once the AH-64 gunships finished with that target, they responded to a newly detected RPG team that was identified five hundred metres northeast of the downed aircraft. Both unleashed a torrent of rockets and cannon fire into a compound in the vicinity of HLZ Juliet.

The snipers from C/S 15, who had just averted a friendly fire incident, were still taking heavy fire from the eastern mountain, from enemy located north of HLZ India. The snipers then proceeded to direct the attack helicopters onto the target and both Apaches once again engaged with rockets.

As the drama was unfolding on the ground, a second ordeal began to unfold in the air. The second Chinook, having been ordered by the aviation commander to land the remainder of the ground force as quickly as possible, swung from the northwest to the south and began its run-in.

The pilot reported "heavy smoke everywhere." The intended landing point was a ploughed field approximately five hundred metres from the burning hulk of the first CH-47. However, it soon became the focus of the enemy's fury. Small-arms fire ripped into the thin metal skin of the Chinook.

The pilot immediately initiated a climbing right turn out of the objective area. But it was too late. As the pilot pulled on the controls, he observed his control panel light up, indicating a number of malfunctioning hydraulic controls. In the back, hydraulic fluid began to spew, much like blood flowing from an artery. The effect was the same. The bird was quickly dying. The second Chinook immediately reported that it was making best speed to the abandoned FOB Tiger, which was nearby, for a "hard landing."

The "hard landing" by the second CH-47 at FOB Tiger caused an additional two ANA casualties. And then there was a brief TIC (troops in contact) with insurgents, which was quickly dealt with. However, no time was lost. After confirming with the aviation commander, Picard directed that the element under Roger Deluth, the squadron sergeant major, with most of the ANA, be picked up from FOB Tiger and inserted back into the objective area. As a result, the aviation commander ordered up a third CH-47 from KAF to fly to FOB Tiger to pick up the stranded coalition forces and deliver them to HLZ India to reinforce the assault force commander.

This sat well with the SOF operators now stranded in the abandoned FOB. "There were guys under fire on the ground," explained one operator, "and the biggest thing on the minds of those stuck at FOB Tiger was 'Can you get us in that fight?'." Quite simply, no one wanted to leave their comrades in harm's way.

By this time, Jackson had regrouped in his position four of his assault detachments, as well as the ANA. "I then decided," explained Jackson, "to clear the north ridge, which posed a threat to us, with two of my sub-C/S (11 and 13), in order to secure the area and bring in the MEDEVAC helicopter." He added, "After clearing this ridgeline, enemy fire stopped. We then completed the MEDEVAC and consolidated on the position."

Simultaneously, the command and control helicopter dropped Picard, the ground force commander, and the remainder of snipers into HLZ Golf to reinforce the small element that was located there. This was particularly critical, as it finally allowed Picard to have adequate communications with both the assault force and higher headquarters. It had taken approximately forty-five minutes after the initial insertions and the crash of the first Chinook before the ground force commander was landed.

Picard's initial thoughts at the beginning of the contact had been, "Holy shit! How are we going to get out of this one?" For a moment it seemed as if he was back on training and the directing staff had given him a problem and then just kept piling more crap on top of it. However, he soon overcame his initial reaction and set about assessing the demands of the situation. He now put his mind to making the situation work.

The poor turn of events failed to derail the CANSOF operators for long. Once they had consolidated and evacuated their wounded, they immediately turned to the offensive. Aided by the AH-64 attack helicopters, C/Ss 11 and 13 began to clear the high ground to the north of their position. As that was occurring, the replacement helicopter, the third Chinook, inserted the remainder of the ground force, which had temporarily diverted to FOB Tiger, into HLZ India.

The AH-64 gunships continued to blanket the area with fire as requested. The JTAC specifically had them unleash rockets on a hilltop northeast of HLZ Juliet. The attack birds were now virtually on empty and conducted a handover with the two relieving Apache helicopters who had escorted the third Chinook from KAF in order to pick up and insert the stranded troops from FOB Tiger.

The CANSOF troops were grateful for the courage of the Apache helicopter crews, who had stayed on-station longer than their standard operating procedures allowed. They had burned through their 10 percent safety fuel margin to remain and provide the necessary fire support to allow the assault force to get consolidated. Of exceptional note was the aviation commander. The UH-60 Blackhawk barely cleared the fence at FOB Davis in Tarin Kowt, landing basically on fumes, in an effort to evacuate the remaining serious casualties to safety.

Once the high feature to the north was secured, thus providing the CANSOF and ANA troops the dominating ground and a secure foothold, Picard ordered Jackson to take his assault force and clear a portion of the objective area. The snipers on the opposite hilltop provided over-watch.

As the tide of the battle swung back in favour of the assaulting force, and the actual sweep of the objective, as well as adjacent compounds, was conducted, elements of the conventional task force, were moving north up the Tarin Kowt road to reinforce the CANSOF effort. A sub-unit from the conventional task force now formed a solid southern block. They were told to hold until the clearing of the compounds was complete, however. At this juncture, no one wanted a "blue-on-blue" friendly fire incident.[11] The CANSOF and ANA troops conducted a hasty SSE on the suspect compounds but nothing of significance was found. It was the normal list of a few weapons, ammunition, and drugs, along with Taliban propaganda originating in Pakistan.

By 1815 hours, coalition forces controlled Chenartu. Only women remained in the village. Six ground force casualties had been evacuated during the course of the action: two CANSOF members and four ANA soldiers. Only two enemy bodies were found. They belonged to two insurgents who were shot in the exposed river wadi, which explained why their bodies had not been recovered. One was a local man, while the other was a Pakistani. However, coalition forces tallied fifteen confirmed enemy kills, with an estimated ten additional enemy dead.[12]

While two platoons from the conventional force waited for word to move forward into Chenartu to conduct the handover, one of the elements, red platoon, was attacked by insurgents. Quickly reinforced by its sister platoon, the fight was not prolonged. However, it was clear that much of the ACM had simply moved to the northeast and remained a persistent threat.

It was also clear from radio chatter and other activities that the insurgents were still lurking around Chenartu. As a result, Picard tasked his ANA soldiers with sweeping any additional compounds in the area.

The task that now lay ahead was to check the CH-47 crash site and determine the status of sensitive equipment, as well as confirm possible locations for suitable HLZs. But there was more. CJSOTF-A was not going to allow the Taliban an IO victory. As such, higher headquarters ordered the CANSOF ground force to dismantle, chop up, and/or blow up the burnt-out carcass of the crashed Chinook helicopter, pack it in sea containers, and have it lifted out of the area. The troops were to leave no trace of its destruction that could be leveraged in any way by the Taliban.

Intelligence analysts later assessed that the assault surprised Mullah Ghafour and several other Taliban commanders who were meeting in Dad Mohammad Kalay to conduct a major *shura* (assembly). They believed that Ghafour was likely moving to, or away from, the actual meeting site. Furthermore, they appraised that the first Chinook was likely shot down by RPG and/or small-arms fire from Ghafour's personal security detachment as they engaged the coalition force to cover the withdrawal of the Taliban leaders to the north.

An allied SOF element at a southern American SOF FOB stood by to reinforce; however, it was not required. By 1815 hours, the CANSOFTF assault force and other coalition elements linked up and each consolidated defensive positions for the coming darkness that was beginning to descend on the valley.

However, the hunt for the ACM was not over. Ghafour was still on the move, as were other ACM leaders as a result of the strike on Chenartu. As a result, a long-range surveillance detachment (LRSD) from the conventional task force inserted into the area and moved south, tracking the MVTs that had been flushed from Chenartu. With the assistance of aerial assets, as well as the CANSOF JTAC, they identified both individuals and compounds of interest. A Taliban leader was suspected to be part of the first group they identified. As a result, at 0130 hours, December 5, an AC-130 Spectre engaged targets scoring a number of kills.

Another group was identified at 0322 hours. Ghafour and another MVT were believed to be in this band. The LRSD continued their relentless pursuit of their quarry into the mountains and at 0530 hours they located their prey. The LRSD activated their strobes and the CANSOF JTAC vectored in an A-10 Thunderbolt aircraft to hit the target. Two of the enemy escaped and the LRSD continued to use the A-10 to engage targets until 0700 hours. An SSE of the ACM that were killed indicated that at least one MVT was probably eliminated.

For CANSOF and ANA on the objective, the night had been extremely unpleasant. Tasked for an eight-hour mission and expected to be lifted out shortly thereafter, the soldiers were now stuck in the Afghan mountains with no food, water, or warm clothing. The day had been hot and the troops had sweated profusely with their heavy loads and exertion. Now, as the December sun dropped below the horizon, the mercury plunged and the coalition troops suffered accordingly.

Throughout the morning of December 5, 2005, the CANSOF ground force pushed into the valley in vicinity of its original objective clearing compounds and continuing the dismantling of the burned wreck of the first Chinook helicopter. As more elements of the conventional task force, as well as the LRSD, moved into the area, CJSOTF-A pushed overall ground force command of the vicinity around Chenartu to CANSOF. This made perfect sense as a joint special operations area (JSOA) box had already been designated for the Chenartu valley area under control of the CANSOF ground force commander. This meant that anyone entering or working within the box required authorization from Picard to ensure that coalition movement and strikes were coordinated and deconflicted. Once the command issues were worked out, the next priority was the coordination of an MC-130 resupply airdrop for that night. After that was done, all hunkered down for yet another frigid night in the valley.

At approximately 0800 hours, December 6, the first of the sea containers arrived, slung under a CH-47 Chinook helicopter. An hour later, the second container was inserted in the vicinity and the task of dismembering the remains of the doomed CH-47 commenced. A sub-unit from the conventional task force secured the outer cordon, while the CANSOF and ANA troops manned the inner cordon.

The area, however, was still not tamed. The aviation task force aircraft, assisted by the ground force JTAC, continued to engage ACM. In addition, during the morning, ANP attached to Blue Platoon were involved with a firefight with four ACM. As a result of the activity, a follow-on sweep and clearance of additional compounds in the outlying area was conducted by CANSOF. They soon uncovered an insurgent with a PKM machine gun.

An emergency resupply by rotary wing arrived at 1530 hours on December 6 and the opportunity was used to remove one of the sea containers that was now full of aircraft debris. The chopping up of the helicopter took longer than expected, so explosives were used to blast the remaining pieces of the downed Chinook. By last light, the CH-47 was completely dismantled and largely loaded into the remaining container.

The next morning helicopters arrived to remove the last sea container and to pick up the CANSOF troops. A sub-unit from the conventional task force secured the HLZ and assumed control of the area following the departure of the CANSOF ground force. The JTF 2 operators arrived at their FOB at 0825 hours, December 7, 2005. The eight-hour mission had lasted almost three days. Intelligence later that day confirmed Ghafour was still on the move.

The operation in Chenartu had proven to be costly. The coalition forces suffered three CANSOF, three American aircrew, and three ANA wounded. In addition, one CH-47 was destroyed, another was badly damaged, and several other airframes were riddled with holes caused by small-arms fire.

However, in return, various reporting indicated that coalition forces killed eighteen ACM, with thirteen confirmed bodies. The three Taliban leaders known to have been in the area were not identified among the dead, but analysts believed some were probably killed in the air strikes on the morning of December 5. Information disclosed at a later date from a *shura* in Pakistan indicated the Taliban had lost approximately fifty individuals during the battle and follow-on pursuit.

With regards to the operation, "While not achieving mission success in capturing or killing Mullah Ghafour," concluded Colonel Sadler, "[we] significantly disrupted ACM activity in the Chenartu region of Kandahar Province." He explained that the subsequent SSE indicated "that coalition forces disrupted a potential future operation in the planning stages and severely dislocated several MVTs in their operations." Sadler assessed, "Although a costly operation in terms of coalition WIA [wounded] and loss of equipment, this was partially offset through ACM disruption."

Despite the self-critical examination, not all was bad news. The official after-action review stated that the cost was high, but the gain was proportionate. Jackson agreed. "The target was worth it," although he conceded, "we did not set all the conditions for success." He did emphasize, however, that "actions on the objective were a complete success." Jackson concluded, "This was our worst and our best day ever."[13]

Brigadier-General Jack Sterling Jr., the deputy commanding general of Combined Joint Task Force 76 agreed. He declared, "Afghan and coalition forces are going to continue to bring the fight to the enemies of Afghanistan, no matter where they are, no matter where they are trying to hide." He added, "This is a resounding victory for Afghan forces and for the Afghan people. We located and closed with the enemies of this nation and as we have said we would in the past, brought them to justice."[14]

An American colonel shook his head in disbelief at the end results. "You should have about thirty guys beside you horizontal [dead] on the ground," he informed the task force commander

"We had luck that day," agreed the assault force commander, "but I always say you create your own luck." He explained, "Everyone turned a shit situation into success. It was a function of our immediate action drills, training, and quality of operator."[15]

The JTF 2 soldiers had once again lived their motto — Deeds not Words.

CHAPTER 4

WHERE NO MEN DARE TRAVEL: PENETRATING THE BAGHRAN VALLEY

The slight evening breeze brushed away the oppressive Afghan heat and made movement tolerable. The Canadian special operations forces troops from JTF 2 finished loading their heavily burdened vehicles and prepared to move out. The strategic reconnaissance/direct action SR/DA HMMVWs, commonly referred to as Humvees, looked menacing as they were brimming with weapons and ammunition that betrayed the firepower and capability of death and destruction that they possessed.[1] The gun trucks groaned loudly as they lurched over the speed bumps at the exit of CANSOF FOB Graceland as they rolled out of the camp's gate, which was located near Kandahar City.

The sky was a typical charcoal grey and although the half moon seemed to be covered by a thin, sandy veil, it still threw off an amazing brightness, revealing those who would rather fade into the darkness. The SOF operators appeared relaxed in their vehicles as they slowly pulled out of camp. They were heading out on a mission that all knew would be filled with challenge and no doubt excitement. There was also the realization that the task was exceedingly dangerous. But most had already experienced combat and all had extreme confidence in themselves, as well as in the ability of their comrades. Although they all made a point of never underestimating their very clever and wily opponents, none could realize the ordeal they were about to face.

Operation Audacious Beast, as the SOF operators unofficially titled the operation, was a daring venture into an area of the country that had not seen many coalition troops. The north Helmand region, specifically the Baghran District, had been without a coalition force, or, for that matter, an Afghan National Security Force (ANSF) presence, for more than five months. The vacuum caused by an absence of Government of Afghanistan (GoA) representation was quickly filled by a mix of insurgent and criminal elements whose aim it was to discredit and destroy the remnants of GoA institutions throughout the region.

The anti-coalition militias, ACMs as they were referred to at the time, conducted a sweeping and often brutal campaign of removing government officials from their duly assigned posts. These actions buoyed the enemy forces and provided them with localized victories and momentum to reinforce their successes. Peace in the area was based largely on the accords made between the Taliban and the primary narco-syndicate in the region based on the Akhundzada clan.[2]

The absence of coalition and ANSF was not entirely an oversight. The insurgents within the Baghran Valley possessed the capability and intent to attack and kill any interlopers. The string of successes, such as the seizure of the Baghran District Centre, the attacks on the Musa Qala District headquarters, and the assassinations of regional and GoA/provincial officials, had filled the valley with a high number of known insurgents that were confident in their abilities.[3] Although they normally operated in groups of twenty to thirty fighters, they had the ability to concentrate three hundred men in a short period of time. In addition, they had support weapons such as heavy machine guns and mortars.

As was consistently demonstrated throughout Afghanistan, the insurgents possessed a very effective early warning system. In addition, they also maintained a very developed and robust command and control network that allowed them to conduct coordinated attacks with fighters from different regions. In short, the insurgents, as well as the criminals, in the Baghran Valley were well organized and tenacious. Not surprisingly, the Baghran Valley had become a Taliban transit area, if not a temporary safe haven. They also used the valley as an infiltration point into Uruzgan, and particularly into the Khod Valley.

Coalition intelligence analysts deduced that the most likely enemy course of action in response to the CANSOF special reconnaissance into the Baghran Valley would be to deploy an insurgent early warning system to assess and track the coalition/ANSF movement to and through the valley. Then, as the SR patrol made its way through the restricted terrain, they would be interdicted by improvised explosive devices (IEDs) and/or IED-initiated ambushes. If the insurgents were unable to accomplish this in one area, they would pass the task on to the next group of insurgents in the valley. Not surprisingly, if an attack was successful and the appropriate authority was given, insurgents would reinforce their success with follow-on attacks.

In the end, the enemy's intent was to overrun the force in contact. Taliban fighters were adept at both manoeuvring and sustaining contact as long as they felt they had a chance of retaining the tactical advantage. And in the Baghran Valley, they had a number of advantages. Most of all, they knew the terrain, which would allow them to plan excellent ambush positions in the heavily canalled ground. Additionally, they knew all the escape routes so they could practice hit-and-run attacks. The rugged terrain also provided a vast number of locations that could be used to cache weapons.

The local population in the area was not seen as a significant factor. Most of the estimated eighty-two thousand residents located in the approximately 460 villages there were considered indifferent bystanders. That is, as long as the coalition force was not seen as part of a poppy eradication effort. Any action by coalition forces that was seen as threatening the opium trade would instantly arouse the ire of the locals.

There were several other potentially problematic issues also. There had been very little coalition exposure in the area previously and the level of education in the district was very low (i.e., less than 14 percent literacy rate).[4] As a result, the local nationals had no understanding of the outside world. Normally xenophobic in any case, they were highly suspicious of the "foreigners" venturing into their land. Such skepticism was not surprising; however, the locals could often be downright hostile, instead of friendly.

Further complicating things was the fact that the centre of gravity for the area was the town of Baghran, which was a large population centre and the site of a recent Taliban "takeover" of the local government office.

The mission of the Canadian JTF 2 based task force was actually part of a larger operation, namely Operation Mountain Thrust, led by the Americans under Operation Enduring Freedom. The operation was designed to disrupt enemy operations and set the conditions for NATO's International Security Assistance Force (ISAF) to take responsibility for southern Afghanistan in accordance with its Stage III expansion plan in the summer of 2006.[5]

As far as CANSOF was concerned, the intent of their immediate commander and headquarters, Combined Joint Special Operations Task Force–Afghanistan (CJSOTF–A), was to conduct full spectrum operations in order to destroy Taliban command and control, as well as to deny them safe havens. In addition, they were also to extend enduring GoA control and influence in Uruzgan and northern Helmand provinces, as well as to set the conditions for the transfer of responsibility to ISAF.

The CANSOF task force's specific mission was to conduct a mobility-based special reconnaissance patrol in the Baghran Valley in order to shape the area for follow-on coalition operations. The commander CJSOTF-A ordered the CANSOF task force, reinforced with some Afghan National Army (ANA) elements, to identify enemy command and control (C2) nodes, key terrain, and actionable intelligence, so that they could set the conditions for successful follow on operations by an American task force based on the U.S. 2nd Battalion, 87 Infantry Regiment (2-87 Infantry) as part of the Operation Mountain Thrust scheme of manoeuvre. A number of "named areas of interest" (NAIs) throughout the route were designated for the CANSOF operators to locate, identify, and observe. Based on results, they were also to be prepared to exploit either through direct action (DA) themselves, passing the target to another coalition DA strike force, or kinetic strike.

This operation was to be conducted in three phases. During Phase I (i.e., infiltration) the CANSOF/ANA force was to deploy out of the

Canadian FOB and conduct a two-day infiltration into the Baghran Valley with a final resupply in FOB Price prior to entering the valley. The next phase (i.e., conduct of SR/battle handover (BHO)) was to begin with the move into the Baghran Valley. The CANSOF patrol tasks during this phase included route reconnaissance (recce), helicopter landing zone (HLZ) identification, recce of blocking positions, "squirter" route confirmation, definition of anti-coalition militia organizations, and link-up and BHO with follow-on coalition forces. Phase II was to conclude with the actual BHO with 2-87 Infantry. The main effort for the patrol during phase II, however, was the accurate definition of ACM forces and activities within the identified NAIs in order to set the conditions for successful follow-on operations as part of Operation Mountain Thrust.[6]

The final phase (i.e., exfiltration) was to be the redeployment back to the CANSOF FOB. CJSOTF-A headquarters's intent was for the patrol to glean actionable intelligence, as well as disrupt the ACM.[7] The coalition planners believed that the disruption of the insurgent operations in the valley would damage Taliban effectiveness in Baghran and the surrounding districts. This in turn, they thought, would provide an opportunity for the GoA, with the assistance of coalition forces and the ANSF, to influence the local population in a manner favourable to the locals and the GoA. The presence of a robust ANA force throughout the area was also seen as being highly influential in regaining the respect of the locals.

Jack Rutledge, the squadron commander, worked out his own scheme of manoeuvre. His under-strength squadron would be augmented by an undermanned ANA reconnaissance company. Rutledge decided to conduct the mobility operation based on a force package of two manoeuvre groups. In addition, the SR patrol was to be self-sufficient for a number of days and would then be resupplied by air. The patrol was broken up into two manoeuvre elements. Troop "A" consisted of SR/DA and cargo Humvees, as well as Polaris 6x6 (Gator) all-terrain vehicles (ATV). It also boasted a substantial arsenal that included C-6 7.62mm general purpose machine guns (GPMG), MK19 40mm automatic grenade launchers, .50 calibre heavy machine guns (HMG), and MK 48 60mm mortars. The second manoeuvre element, Troop "B," was comprised of a similar vehicle and weapons package.

Although venturing into the valley alone, the squadron commander knew that he had a DA strike force package available that incorporated an allied SOF team reinforced by an infantry company, as well as the myriad ISR and fires platforms. However, reinforcements by ground were over one hundred kilometres away, and air assets were never fully guaranteed.

But failure was not an option.

The CJSOTF-A commander defined the CANSOF SR of the Baghran Valley as "decisive" to the conditions for the 2-87 Infantry offensive operations that were an important element of Operation Mountain Thrust. As a result, the CJSOTF-A commander designated the CANSOF patrol as the main effort for the "shaping" opening phase of the larger U.S. operation. In addition, he also established a temporary area of operation (AO) box, code-named "Canada," which encompassed the entire Baghran Valley for the duration of the mission. All units entering this AO were required to coordinate with the CANSOF squadron commander.

Rutledge articulated the objective of the SR in greater detail than that of his higher headquarters. He asserted that the SR would "focus on ground analysis, ACM communications, HUMINT [human intelligence] collection, … discussions with local elders/villagers, and questioning [of suspected anti-coalition fighters]." He specified that they would also collect information on movement in and out of the identified named areas of interest. Rutledge explained, "[G]enerally, this relates to element size, time of movement, and activity within the vicinity of the NAI." He expected that his higher headquarters would relay intelligence that confirmed the targets were in the NAI in order to facilitate the patrol's ability to visually define and readily identify the target(s). Rutledge set the specific tasks for the designated observers: to identify any activity related to IED transport or deployment; to report on the transportation of weapons or possible weapons systems to and from the NAI; and to record the schedule(s) of meetings (of a specified designated size) of personnel inside the NAI." The mission commander elaborated that information gained from the surveillance would be combined with current and historical intelligence to exploit and decisively engage the enemy.

Initially, however, the intent of the larger operation was for other coalition forces to engage the enemy based on the information provided by the CANSOF SR patrol. The plan called for them to do a battle handover. Specifically, the 2-87th Infantry was to conduct a BHO with CANSOF at Musa Qala as the Canadian SR patrol exited the Baghran Valley on June 8, 2006.[8] In addition, an allied SOF element was to synchronize their move into the north of the valley with the 2-87th Infantry as well. The entire Baghran Valley was to be split between a north and south AO. The centre of gravity for the 2-87th Infantry was to be Baghran City. They were to establish a static location that would give them access to population centres in the north but not make them a target within the city itself. From this base, they were to try to influence the population centres through leader engagements and patrols.

However, first the CANSOF patrol would have to complete the special reconnaissance. As the mission commander, Rutledge assessed the overall residual risk as "medium." There were a number of hazards: compromise of presence and their route by the enemy; IEDs; ambush; weather; and fratricide. However, Rutledge knew that control mechanisms they would put in place, such as leading with reconnaissance (recce) elements, utilizing two manouevre groups for mutual support, coalition fires (e.g., fixed-wing, aviation, artillery), and ISR (intelligence, surveillance, and reconnaissance) assets, would mitigate the threats.

And so, under a watchful Afghan moon on the night of May 19, 2006, the CANSOF patrol rolled out of their compound on their way to the Baghran Valley. The long column of Humvees was initially slow in its departure as the vehicles snaked their way through the dirty, narrow streets of Kandahar City, trying to shake out into their spaced formation. Everyone was alert. No one actually expected trouble until they hit the objective area, but, nonetheless, all had learned never to underestimate the enemy.

The lead vehicles were approximately two kilometres from the start point, only about fifteen to twenty minutes into the actual mission when there was suddenly a change in the atmosphere. Something just did not seem right. The SOF operators in the lead vehicles noticed shop lights suddenly appear on their right, and then go off. Just a little further ahead, it happened again on the left, and then on further again on the right. Fingers now took up the slack on the triggers of every manned weapon system. It did not take a rocket scientist to figure out what was about to happen.

Events happened rapidly as the vehicles shot through the near-deserted streets. One second, the Canadians noticed the light show, which was obviously marking their progress and being used as a system to initiate an ambush, and the next second the darkness erupted into a festival of colour that would rival a fireworks demonstration on the nation's birthday. The air became filled with lead and shrapnel as the rounds hissed by the narrowly contained convoy.

The lead SR/DA Humvee was at the focal point of the skirmish. Rounds ploughed into the earth around the vehicle and tore into its metal skin. One 7.62mm round struck the engine and caused a "mobility kill." Those vehicles in a position to react lashed out in return, unleashing a deluge of fire at the muzzle flashes of their unseen antagonists. The curtain of fire being thrown up allowed the vehicles at the front of the convoy to pull out of the kill zone.

Bob Reynolds was returning fire from his vehicle, which had just died in the kill zone. Another enemy round sliced into the side of the barrel of his GPMG at a 45-degree angle, approximately half-way up the barrel, causing it to jam. As Reynolds leaned forward to clear the weapon, another enemy round penetrated his helmet, glanced off his skull and exited out the back of his head gear. Fortune was with Reynolds that day. Had he not leaned forward to clear the jam in his machine gun, he would have taken the round square in the face. Equally remarkable, Reynolds was oblivious to the wound he had just received as he continued to return fire while his vehicle was pulled from the kill zone.

Amazingly, the entire convoy was able to disengage from the ambush and return to FOB Graceland. The lead vehicle was towed back to camp. The remainder of the night was used to cross-load the weapons, communications gear, and other equipment from the dead vehicle to a replacement. The delay also allowed Reynolds to get seven stitches and provided time for his headache to recede before heading out mere hours later.

The next morning, May 21, 2006, the SR patrol departed once again, this time selecting a different exit gate and route. They drove without rest

WHERE NO MEN DARE TRAVEL

and pushed toward their next objective, FOB Price, where they would rest for the night before making their way to the Baghran Valley.

It was, however, a busy day. The Taliban conducted numerous attacks across the Sangin District. It did not seem to bode well for the Canadian patrol.

The convoy had driven straight through the day, and night had already enveloped the land when it approached the town of Gereshk. The vehicles had their lights off, realizing that a long convoy of lights at night could signal only one thing: a coalition convoy. As the patrol neared, an Afghan National Police vehicle control point (VCP), the lead two vehicles slowed and cautiously approached.

Jim Fields, one of the allied SOF embedded-training team (ETT) members and a squad of his ANA soldiers, as well as Blair Simpson, a CANSOF operator in call sign (C/S) 11, which had taken the brunt of the ambush in Kandahar City the night prior, moved forward to conduct a link-up with the ANP. As they rolled forward, the lead vehicle, which had put on its headlights, was fired on by the checkpoint. Believing that it was a warning shot, the second vehicle now put on its white lights and they all yelled out in English, "coalition, coalition." They also called some ANA soldiers to make contact with the ANP. The vehicles were fired upon a second time, and as the ANA advanced, a high volume of small-arm fire slapped into the exposed vehicles.

As they were now taking effective fire, the lead vehicles opened up and returned fire. At the same time, the remainder of the gun trucks in the convoy reacted and conducted an "ambush right" drill. The hapless ANP outpost never knew what hit them. The overwhelming barrage was like a rogue wave building up and crashing down on all before it. The wall of fire quickly silenced the ANP aggression.

Once the incoming fire ceased, Rutledge called for a ceasefire. The ANA company commander and three of his squads moved forward to link-up with the local ANP commander. The squadron commander also quickly moved forward to speak with the apparent local ANP chief, who, like his men, was dressed in local garb.[9] The ANP senior apologized for the confusion and stated that his men fired in error. He explained they had just been in a running battle with Taliban insurgents less than an

139

hour ago and that his men were "jumpy." He informed Rutledge that he had three wounded men but that they could take care of them themselves.

Rutledge was concerned about the casualties, but the commander waved it off as nothing and insisted that they just leave. The mission commander was skeptical; his men reported seeing a number of bodies being loaded into the bin of a truck. But, after ensuring there was nothing that he could do, Rutledge declined the offer of an "escort out of the area" and the convoy departed, still somewhat perplexed by what had just happened.

The following day, May 21, 2006, the story was already circulating amongst local nationals that coalition forces had attacked an ANP check point. According to the gossip, the ANP noticed vehicles approaching their VCP without lights and opened fire, thinking they were Taliban. As a result, the Canadians engaged the ANP, killing two and wounding four. The gist of all these tales was that the Canadians had initiated the aggression and killed innocent ANP personnel.

The truth, however, was quite different. When the convoy reached FOB Price the next day, they discovered that the Taliban had attacked across the entire region. More important, 3 Parachute Regiment headquarters at FOB Price had received information that the checkpoint in the area of the firefight had been under heavy assault during the day of the contact and that it was most likely overrun by the Taliban in the evening. An allied SOF team, also at FOB Price, stated that they were informed that the checkpoint, which was never manned by more than five to eight policemen, who were armed only with AK-47 assault rifles and who were usually in uniform. was, in fact, overrun and that the area was in Taliban control at the time of the CANSOF "troops in contact" (TIC).

When the squadron was engaged, there were thirty-plus fighters armed with AK-47s, PKM machine guns, and rocket-propelled grenade launchers. When the Taliban at the checkpoint were hit with the wall of fire from the patrol, they seemingly decided the best course was to end the fight and to allow the patrol to get out of the area. This also explained why the apologetic "ANP commander" seemed unconcerned about his casualties and why he wanted to "escort" the convoy out of the sector.

The CANSOF patrol rested, refuelled, and then departed the British FOB. They then set out and made their way to the Baghran Valley. As they approached the western route toward Musa Qala, the patrol had to move through a built-up area which was not on the maps and was clearly an opium production centre. Very quickly, the patrol suspected that the local EWS had already picked up the convoy and that plans were being made to engage it. However, the Taliban held off attacking the Canadians. The local leaders had not yet fully identified the size of the convoy, or its purpose.

As the day wore on, the enemy EWS continued to monitor the squadron's activity and northern progress into the valley. "We would have to go through crevices and gullies," said the CANSOF linguist, "and we would be shadowed by a guy on foot on the ridge who would pass us off to someone else at his boundary." He added, "[T]hat's how dedicated they were, they would follow you on foot for a whole day."

There was no sign of either ANA or ANP anywhere. More disconcerting was the news that an ANA convoy near Sangin was ambushed and wiped out and a number of their vehicles and uniforms stolen. This raised the issue of the possibility of anti-coalition militias moving into AO Canada disguised as ANA. In light of the previous night, this meant, of course, that interaction with government forces would be done very carefully.

On May 22, Rutledge pushed his patrol out just as the day was showing signs of beginning. He wanted to get the squadron into the complex terrain and moving as quickly as possible. He had four hours of air coverage and wanted to use it to his best advantage. He anticipated that he would be in the valley by late afternoon.

But the inevitable friction of war played its hand. Vehicle breakdowns required the patrol to be broken into two elements. The troop warrant officer with some vehicles would patrol the local area while the patrol commander and the remaining vehicles were in a laying-up position (LUP) to allow the mechanic to work his magic and fix the unserviceable vehicles. While in the LUP, however, they noticed eight to ten individuals with weapons moving on the high ground to their west. It was clear that these belligerents were monitoring and reporting on the squadron activities. The enemy was also considering placing an IED on the route most likely to be taken by the coalition forces.

The enemy eventually acquired an IED and decided to position it. However, their actions too were being watched. The location was easily located, as they placed it in obvious view in the main wadi, expecting that the patrol would use the easy approach.

With half the squadron held up with maintenance, Rutledge moved the troop warrant officer and his vehicles through rough terrain to the southwest of the ambush site and easily pushed the group of twelve to fifteen insurgents from the ambush site. The Taliban in turn moved to the west and the CANSOF operators pursued. The group of enemy that had laid the IED ambush were then observed moving up into high ground to the west. At the same time, ANA soldiers dismounted and cleared a number of compounds where the Taliban fighters had been seen prior to withdrawing. Some Pakistani documents were found and the locals revealed that there were a number of Pakistanis with the ACM forces.

The CANSOF force continued pursuing the group of insurgents, which could be seen moving up a high ridgeline off to the west some two kilometres away. The lead ATVs, squadron commander, and the troop warrant officer began to move through a small wadi to the north of a small village when they were engaged from less than twenty-five metres away. The vehicles broke contact and joined the remainder of the half squadron group four hundred metres back to the east of the village.

The ANA and C/S 14 moved to the south and engaged the enemy on the opposite side of the village. A B-1 bomber then executed three runs and pounded the north portion of the village (which was made up of old ruins) with three two-thousand-pound JDAMs (joint direct attack munitions) prior to the dismounted ANA soldiers conducting a sweep. The bombing easily neutralized the north enemy position and created havoc on the west position.[10]

There were no bodies discovered in the village after the sweep, but there were a number of blood trails and articles of clothing, as well as ammunition (mainly RPG rounds). Discussion with the elders after the clearing of the village confirmed that the ACM normally came from the west. The patrol elements then moved back to the LUP. The ANA proved themselves brave and effective.

"Very pleased with the tactics and skills of the ANA in the TIC today," reported Jack. "They are chomping at the bit when it comes to dismounting and getting into the fight."

Five days later, the patrol would learn that one hundred fighters withdrew through neighbouring villages after the fight. The insurgents, revealed Rutledge, "proved to be well-organized and disciplined." He assessed that they were accustomed to dealing with ANP and others who normally took established roads and tracks. As a result, explained Rutledge, "the cross-country movement to their flank caused [them] some concern and they ordered all their elements to move to the high ground when they realized they did not have the advantage." Astutely, the mission commander realized that the enemy would "most likely be regrouping [later that night] for dealing with [them] tomorrow as [they] push[ed] west."

On the morning of May 23, an AH-64 Apache attack helicopter that had escorted a resupply flight for the CANSOF patrol, flew by a suspected enemy observation post (OP) and identified a number of cave entrances to the west of the LUP. The squadron commander, still held up by the forced maintenance pause, decided to push elements of his squadron up to this area with the ANA company to try to locate the OP and check the suspicious caves.

As the patrol element moved within the heavily canalled terrain near the high ground in question, enemy small-arms fire began to ping off the rocks. In addition, the patrol could see enemy "squirting" out of the area in an attempt to avoid the approaching coalition forces.

The half squadron deployed another six hundred metres to the west and then halted out of RPG range. Coalition assets indicated there were more insurgents on the north side of the high ground. Rutledge assessed that the enemy was trying to lure his force into the canalled terrain, where they could launch an ambush and where the CANSOF heavy weapons could not be optimally employed because they would have a difficult time elevating their weapon systems to the required height. Instead, the squadron commander used his superior range and fired the .50 calibre HMG and MK-19 grenade launchers to great effect.

To not get decisively engaged with the enemy close to their positions, close air support was called in on the west and north ridgelines. The B-1 bombing runs made a significant impact. The aerial attack consisting of ten JDAMs clearly frustrated the insurgents, who often referred to the bombing runs as "low-life tactics."

The ANA then began scaling the west ridge and after a brief skirmish at the crest with insurgents who were withdrawing down the west slope toward the village of Charmestan, secured the location. The ANA cleared the ridge and bunker but found nothing of value.

The patrol observed a squirter move off to the west. Days later, the Canadians discovered that the enemy had lost a number of men. Despite the setback, the insurgents showed that they were not at all intimidated by the presence of the coalition forces. However, they were very frustrated by the coalition's air superiority.

The next morning, on May 24, the patrol elements left the LUP and scattered to the wind, taking completely different routes and travelling in different directions as deception to confuse the ACM with regard to their actual intentions and true direction. This seemed to work, at least initially. By early morning, however, the enemy once again gained observation. "They located us by dust trails as the sun came up," revealed the patrol commander, "but the squadron had been on the route for an hour before the enemy had eyes on us again."

The squadron commander's intent for the day was to move toward NAI 10, well into the northern portion of the valley, which was described as "hilltop, friendly, over-watch for northern battle position." The patrol left before first light and with the ANA leading and an A-10 Thunderbolt aircraft providing overhead cover, the squadron rumbled through the forbidden valley.

Despite the slower than expected progress due to enemy contact and vehicle difficulties, the "overall moral[e]," according to Richard Desjardins, the squadron sergeant major, "[was] extremely high due to our success."

As well as the Taliban, the terrain was also proving to be an enemy, and the vehicles soon began to show the effects of operating in this region. Damaged and worn-out alternators, voltage regulators, batteries, and ball-joints caused endless toil for the overworked mechanic.

It seemed the vehicle electrical systems had difficulty coping with the demands of the heat, terrain, radios, and computers. Nonetheless, the ceaseless effort by Charles Lemar, the vehicle technician, who worked through the nights to keep the vehicles running, made him the unsung hero of the operation.

The deeper and farther north the Canadian SR patrol ventured, the more difficult became the terrain. It was so rough that the majority of the time the elements had to use the local trails. At one point, the terrain was too severe for the ATVs and one flipped, rolling over six times, seriously injuring Marc, one of the CANSOF operators. He was medically evacuated by a UH-60 Black Hawk helicopter. The Polaris 6x6 ATV was beyond local repair and since they were deep in Taliban territory, it was destroyed in place.

"The ground was crazy," explained Norman Jackson, "it [was] either the mountain peak or the bottom of the valley." Continuing, he noted that "the valley [was only] fifty metres wide with walls on each side." Jackson added, "[T]here [were] no arcs of fire [i.e., no ability to adequately cover one's movement by being able to observe out to a distance and engage with one's weapon if a threat emerged]; … [the] other option [was] taking the Humvees up on the mountain and over the peaks."

While Trevor Lapointe, the troop warrant officer, secured the helicopter landing site and awaited the MEDEVAC, the troop commander pushed to NAI 11, which was estimated to be the location of a "high value" Taliban leader. The ANA searched a number of compounds of interest. Although there were some signs of Taliban activity in the area, the villagers insisted that there was absolutely no ACM in the region. Once the MEDEVAC was complete, the squadron linked up and began moving into the canalled ground to the northwest.

The ACM monitored the patrol along the entire route, passing off responsibility from group to group as the convoy progressed along its route. There were a number of areas during the day that proved to be of concern because enemy personnel could be seen with weapons watching the patrol. Precision fire drove them away. Coalition assets observed twelve to fifteen personnel in an area with tents, two large pickup truck–type vehicles and two small compounds. There were no women or children in the area. An additional report noted the discovery of a large cave from which about five to eight individuals exited and then returned to when the aircraft was heard. The area seemed to be swarming with enemy.

"Movement became very difficult today," lamented the ground force commander in his daily situation report (SITREP). "Movement is so slow that the ACM see you coming for three to six kilometres and have plenty of time to slowly walk over the next ridgeline."

The squadron drove through a few kilometres of heavily canalled terrain to the area of the planned resupply drop that was to occur the next day. Two more vehicles had broken down and the mechanic assessed it would take at least four hours to repair them. As a result, Rutledge decided to remain in place and push onto NAI 12 the next day before first light. Since his LUP was only 1,400 metres away from the cave complex the unmanned aerial vehicle (UAV) had discovered earlier in the day, he had the patrol keep a sharp eye on the rock face and then conducted a sweep of the area with ANA and CANSOF troops, confident that this would "deter any movement from this area down to the LUP."

To that point, the CANSOF SR patrol appeared to be highly successful. They had inflicted casualties and kept the ACM off balance and in a reactive mode for several days. They assessed that they were now in the enemy's decision-making cycle — a position that the Taliban were not reacting well to. Furthermore, the CANSOF patrol believed that any pressure exerted by them would likely keep the Taliban off balance; however, the Canadians also realized that the Taliban had an uncanny ability to quickly adapt their tactics, techniques, and procedures (TTPs), and, therefore, they should not be underestimated. The patrol concluded that the targeted personalities were definitely dispersing, which was evidence that some insurgent leadership had been temporarily pried out of their comfort zone.

The patrol departed at first light and made good progress west until C/S 11 slid off the treacherous route into a wadi and destroyed its front steering rod. Recovery and repair would take well over an hour so the troop warrant officer and his elements were pushed forward into the gap that led to NAI 12, which was identified as an enemy observation post or early warning system position. The ground was nothing short of hostile.

"It took the better part of the morning," noted the mission commander, "to negotiate the canalizing [i.e., canalled] ground safely."

At one point, Tim Wilson and Tony MacMillan, two of the patrol snipers, rode well ahead of the forward troop in their Polaris 6x6 ATVs. "We could see the enemy pulling back and we had to recce the wadi so we got a little cocky," explained Wilson. "We were a ways ahead of the forward gun truck and we went into the wadi," he continued. "When I looked up the fifteen-foot-tall wadi wall and I saw three guys standing there with RPGs and small arms — then a PKM machine gun lit up." The RPG struck the bank to the left of Wilson, deafening him and showering him with dirt and debris. The previously tranquil air was suddenly filled with the angry hammering of the light machine gun as rounds whistled through the air.

The lead gun truck now entered the wadi and found itself also caught in the tight kill zone. "We pulled around and tried to get the hell out of Dodge," recalled one SOF operator, "when a target popped up unexpectedly." A burst of fire from virtually every weapon in the vehicle disposed of the threat.

Meanwhile, the remainder of the vehicles in the forward recce element, realizing that some of their troops were in trouble, now rushed forward to the rescue, firing their armament at the enemy position. However, this left Wilson, MacMillan, and the lead Humvee in the unenviable position of trying to extricate themselves from the kill zone without crashing into one another, while at the same time avoiding the deadly crossfire. "There [were] bullets everywhere," described Wilson, "and I [was] trying to find a safe place between the crossfire to get out of that wadi."

Wilson would later shake his head in disbelief and recall, "there were two ATVs and a Humvee caught in that tight bend in a kill zone and there was not a shot in any of them." Once again, the CANSOF troops seemed to live a charmed existence. The question remained — how long would it last?

The rear elements, having finished repairs, caught up soon after lunch at NAI 12, which marked roughly the half-way point through the valley. Jackson, the troop commander, then took the lead and moved south to the town of Emam Robat.

As the patrol picked its way forward, enemy transmissions seemed to be emanating from one location. The patrol suspected that there was an enemy radio rebroadcasting (RRB) site on one of the nearby mountains. The snipers proceeded to comb the mountains inch by inch with their scopes. Eventually, they identified a pair of yellow poles standing up and discovered the RRB. Rutledge requested permission to destroy it by close air support because of the threat of IEDs in the area. Permission was denied, however, as higher headquarters wanted the site exploited and pictures taken to determine its composition.

With permission to destroy the site by air denied, they advanced toward the RRB on ground. As they approached the village of Emam Robat, approximately eighteen to twenty males quickly fled the town. Vehicles were placed in an over-watch position to cover dismounted operations. The ANA company was then sent in to search the town. Unexplainably, the ANA commander became very nervous and refused to continue unless there was a show of force. Rutledge called the B1 fighter bomber that was on station to assist. The B1 flew in at five hundred feet and fired off chaff and flares. The demonstration had the necessary effect. Enemy spotters vanished and did not return for thirty minutes. (The town elders later explained that these squirters were simply men afraid of the ANP.)

The ANA completed their important sweep of the town. Two individuals who appeared very suspicious were questioned. Six full AK-47 magazines and six boxes of AK ammunition were confiscated from their compound, which housed a significant guesthouse with eight beds inside. A third individual was also questioned, but since there was no substantive justification to detain the individuals, they were all released. The search of the town revealed only a few AK-47s and ammunition.

Although repairs had been done on a number of the vehicles prior to the company's arrival in town, vehicle problems once again plagued the patrol. The rough terrain, heavy loads, and reliance on cross-country travel began to cause wiring, steering, and brake problems. After a brief recce of the gap leading into the approach to NAI 10, the entire squadron moved into their LUP, which was adjacent to their drop zone for their resupply, for the night. The patrol was exhausted and also needed to spend time addressing their equipment issues. As a result, the next day was designated a maintenance day.

The enemy had remained relatively subdued throughout the day and contented themselves with simply tracking and assessing the patrol. They had demonstrated commendable command and control as they passed observation tasks from one group to the next as the patrol advanced on its route. The final insurgent group in the Antrak Valley assessed the patrol strength "as light or weak." They kept tight control of their spotters during the patrol movement and implemented a new tactic. They placed children, normally two to three young boys aged eight to ten years old, in the observation posts with the four to six fighters so the CANSOF patrol could not fire on the spotters to move them off the high ground. "They would be standing on the hill with their kids," stated one SOF operator in disgust, "reporting on us." He added, "they knew our ROEs."

By this time, the overall plan began to change as well. The 2-87 Infantry no longer planned on conducting a northern block as they felt this would add no value to the operation. Its original planned operation was compromised. The mission had also been briefed to some of the ANA leadership and word of the operation found its way to the Taliban. In addition, the allied SOF element was not planning on entering the Baghran Valley before June 5-6 at the earliest and then only south of Baghran City. As a result, the CANSOF SR patrol would not need to recce the northern end of the main valley. Ominously, the enemy now decided to focus all its intention on the CANSOF SR patrol. With this new information Rutledge set to recalibrate his planned route.

The parachute resupply did not go as planned. The actual drop was early and farther from their location than desired, but since it was only five hundred metres away, the consequences were not severe. The patrol maintained security on the site overnight and then recovered the material at first light.

The morning of May 26 was busy. A number of spotters were observed along with one observation post. Only 150 metres to the south of the LUP, the post was run down. The fighting-age males escaped toward the town of Emam Robat but two young boys (aged eight to ten) were stopped. The ANA questioned the boys and then sent them on their way back to their village.

Also noted to the south of the LUP was a lone small building away from the main village. While members of CANSOF were observing this area, approximately eighteen males exited the structure and "departed in a bomb burst of directions." Rutledge quickly assessed that this was probably a *shura* (leadership meeting) conducted by the local leaders to discuss the next course of action against the patrol.

Later that morning, the troop commander took a ten-man dismounted patrol of CANSOF personnel and ANA to exploit the suspected RRB site that was located previously. The climb up the steep mountain, particularly because of the heavy equipment the patrol carried, "really sucked," according to those who participated. For their efforts they uncovered an RRB site that consisted of:

- ICOM repeater box;
- large 12 V battery;
- alligator clip/jumper cables;
- solar panel;
- 12 AA batteries;
- large amount of wire (common copper wire and coaxial cable);
- antennae portions/bag;
- large bag of possible explosives; and
- two twenty-foot bamboo poles (used for antennae mast).

The site was not set up for operation when the patrol checked it out, although all items were in working condition. The repeater box was removed from the site for further exploitation. In addition, the patrol also found IED manufacturing components in a small cache nearby. Because the squadron did not have sufficient explosives to blow the entire site, close air support was called in. Four two-thousand-pound JDAMs subsequently destroyed the site and all the remaining components.

In the interim, another element of the SR patrol visited the village of Sar Akhtak so that the ANA could fill their jerry cans with well water, purchase food, and speak to the elders. The villagers described themselves as farmers and when asked if Taliban entered the region, they categorically stated that there were no Taliban in the area, and that they did not transit through the area. Although used to discover real information and to help foster better relations, the discussion with the elders was also part of a deliberate disinformation plan to provide an element of deception with regard to the route that the squadron intended to take the next day. The ANA recounted to the villagers that the patrol was conducting a recce for a new FOB that would be established and that the patrol also planned on visiting Mian Akhtak and Akhtak as it drove straight north. The visit overall was uneventful and all personnel returned to the LUP.

Discussion with young adults in the vicinity of the LUP during the day revealed information on the suspected Taliban commander in the NAI 10 area. It appeared his name was Mullah Zahir Azimi and he lived in the village of Gurz. Supposedly the entire village was controlled by the commander who had thirty to forty fighters that continually lived in his compound, which the locals referred to as the "Castle." Azimi was also reported to own one Land Cruiser, twelve pickup trucks, and ten motorcycles. The locals also indicated that Azimi could muster up to one hundred to two hundred fighters into the area.

That evening, as the daily squadron leadership was wrapping up its commanders' orders group, there was the sound of low-flying aircraft and a number of explosions off to the southwest near the gap toward NAI 10. The coalition JTAC tried multiple times to contact the attacking aircraft and ISR platforms, but to no avail.

It became apparent to the patrol leadership that they had been successful in uncovering Taliban leadership. As the Taliban leaders became unnerved and spooked they would attempt to escape and evade the area. This made them vulnerable. Coalition air assets would appear, uncalled by the squadron, to attack the targets that the patrol had uncovered without fully knowing it. The CANSOF soldiers deduced that their patrol activities were flushing out Taliban commanders who, Rutledge described, were "sparking up in all areas we have been active in." In turn, coalition higher headquarters tracked the enemy leadership and attacked them once they determined probable locations.

There was a negative aspect to all of this, however. The Taliban were quick to spread false information throughout the valley and they soon spread the "news" that the air strikes had killed innocent women and children. This made for hostile receptions when the patrol entered areas where there had been bombings. As the only direct coalition connection to the air strikes, the CANSOF troops were put in a potentially unfavourable situation.

The next day, May 27, began with a search of Siah Sangak, the village with the lone building that spewed out eighteen fighting-age males the day prior. The village and target building were searched by the ANA, but nothing of significance was found. Three squirters were seen heading east on motorcycles as the coalition forces approached, but once again, the village elders insisted that there were no Taliban in the area.

Throughout the morning, breakdowns continued to plague the patrol. Despite the mechanical problems, all of the operators adored the Hummer. They swore that the robust, squat, to some even ugly, beast was the best cross-country vehicle available. Most were amazed at the spots it "would drag you out of" and the "punishment it would take." The breakdowns are more testimony to the extreme expectations of the operators and the sheer difficulty of the terrain, rather than a reflection on the durability of the vehicle itself.

As repairs were undertaken, Rutledge pushed a patrol element forward to conduct a detailed recce to the south at the intended crossing site, which was later, unfortunately, found to be completely impassable to vehicles. With repairs ongoing and last light only an hour away, Rutledge made the call to remain in position for the night.

The situation was a tense one, though. They knew the Taliban were active all around them.

Fortunately, the night passed without incident. However, the next morning activity appeared to erupt. At approximately 0900 hours, May 28, 2006, a local commander directed his personnel to report on the size of the squadron for planning purposes. He also ordered all his people to consolidate. Not surprisingly, the CANSOF troops took this as a precursor to an imminent attack.

At first light, the squadron pushed out and proceeded up the valley to the north, on the route that had been described to the elders in the village of Sar Akhtak. At the last moment, however, the patrol swung east and back to the pass taken three days earlier. There were no difficulties getting through the choke point. The ANA cleared the high ground and the track itself was physically cleared by CANSOF personnel. However, the terrain had become increasingly difficult for mobility operations. Although map and over-flight appreciations proved beneficial, ground truth was a different matter altogether. The terrain was dominated by low- to medium-elevation rolling hills, cut with deep, sharp wadis that could not be detected from overhead imagery.

Once in the adjacent valley to the east and moving north, there was a spike in enemy radio chatter. It now appeared the squadron's earlier deception plan had worked. The enemy had positioned three of their five ambush positions along the route that the elders were told the squadron would be using to get to Akhtak and from there into the Baghran Valley. Coalition ISR assets located approximately three ambush sites along the route within the west valley, a fourth at the northern exit of the valley, and the fifth in the major wadi that allowed access to the main Baghran Valley.

Once the enemy discovered the CANSOF SR patrol was in the east valley, they began to move fighters from both the east and west to the main ambush position at the choke point into the valley. The terrain in the east valley, in which the patrol found itself, was passable to HMMVWs along the bottom of the main wadi. However, this made the convoy vulnerable to ambush, particularly because of the soft sand in which vehicles could become stuck. As a result, the CANSOF patrol picked their way carefully along the high ground on the east side of the valley, which allowed them to dominate by fires from both sides of the wadi.

The squadron stopped short of the village of Nekatu and conducted a recce of the major-obstacle crossing. The command recce group moved on foot up the high ground to the north to look at the large east–west wadi leading to the main Baghran Valley to the east. At that point, three individuals who purported to be the village elders approached the patrol and stated that there were no Taliban in the area. They also offered information indicating that the major wadi that would take the squadron to the main Baghran Valley was passable for the vehicles. In fact, they stressed repeatedly that the wadi to the east that led to the main Baghran Valley was excellent for the patrol vehicles. They went so far as to assure the squadron safe passage through their village and offered to guide the patrol through the immediate area.

The ANA leadership present stated that they had never seen elders come out and offer safe passage through an area before. Rutledge suspected that the Taliban were setting up a very large and coordinated ambush on the main, and only, east–west wadi going from Nekatu to the main Baghran Valley. Rutledge thanked the elders for their help, declining their offer, but questioned them again about the route to the east that they had recommended.[11]

Since one vehicle required approximately three hours of work and since the next bound would have to be completed in one cycle of daylight, Rutledge decided to form a LUP south of the obstacle. He would then conduct a deliberate crossing of the major wadi to the north of Nekatu the next morning. This would position him to break out of the heavily canalled ground by the next evening.

Up to that point, the methodology of continually changing their TTPs, as well as seeding disinformation, had allowed the squadron to keep the initiative over the ACM and prevented them from being decisively engaged. Rutledge was confident that the same tactics would prove successful now. Recording his assessment of the situation at the time, he stated, "With the successful push to the northeast tomorrow, we will be able to break into the main Baghran Valley by the 30th for the next resupply." Continuing, he revealed, "I am optimistic that major vehicle problems are being worked out, but the terrain and heat is taking its toll." He realized that the deliberate crossing the next morning would be a challenge, as it would more than likely be opposed once the Taliban determined the patrol's real route.

The night passed quietly with the exception of a small fire. One of the sentries in the turret of a Humvee stepped on a smoke grenade and inadvertently pulled the pin. The activated smoke grenade then set off the remainder of the smoke-generating munitions in the ammo box, which started a small fire. There was minor damage to the individual's kit and some communications equipment but nothing serious.

Just after first light on May 29, 2006, the squadron crossed the line of departure. Their intent was to push northeast and then east into the main

Baghran Valley, with the aim of making it to their next planned LUP and resupply location. "It took approximately an hour and a half to get into position," revealed the patrol commander, "due to the usual surprises of the terrain." Luckily, there was no resistance to the obstacle crossing.

However, the enemy was perplexed. They had no idea what was taking the squadron so long to get to their ambush position. Once the Taliban determined that the squadron had taken a different route, they collapsed the secondary ambush position to the north and most ACM personnel moved to the south to their main attack position.

The squadron made its way across the major obstacle without contact, although they did experience difficulty due to the terrain. It took the CANSOF SR patrol a considerable amount of time to negotiate the next eight kilometres. The terrain was incredibly complex and there were no local tracks through the area for vehicle use. At one point, the movement was so slow that the ACM, who were busy trying to locate the CANSOF troops, concluded that the Canadians were lost. After thirteen hours of hard slogging with little rest, the patrol reached its next destination and set up an LUP.

It seemed that the squadron had dodged a bullet once again. Rutledge assessed that the main enemy ambush position was actually located to the east of the actual crossing point on the major obstacle. Choosing a more difficult route had allowed them to avoid the ambush. However, the ground had been taxing. "All I can say about the terrain," noted Rutledge in exasperation, "is that God did not intend vehicles to travel this area." He explained, "Only the types of HMMVW with the right tires and trained drivers allowed us to make it through this challenging ground."

The morning of May 30 began routinely. The patrol awoke and made its preparations to continue its trek. The first portion of the day was through very steep hills, which proved very difficult, especially when trying to stay off off the existing tracks. It took six hours to move not even six kilometres. Finally, the patrol had no choice but to use some tracks to move into the main wadi to the east. Luckily, there was enough accessible dominating ground to accomplish this safely. After seven hours of tedious driving, the squadron broke out onto the floor of the main Baghran Valley. The terrain now transitioned to gentle rolling hills that allowed for the necessary mobility formations.

The day finished in a relatively uneventful way in terms of enemy activity. The patrol reported, "The area in which the squadron travelled today demonstrated little ACM activity." They noted, "There was some activity which could be considered suspicious, such as probable spotters, but nothing concrete."

This prompted Jim Brighton, the squadron intelligence analyst, to conclude, perhaps somewhat prematurely, "We've won. The enemy has disappeared." However, he did clarify that "there is a possibility that a few insurgents who haven't heard the word will continue to monitor CANSOF progress with EWS." He also surmised, "Insurgents will attempt to conduct ambushes on targets of opportunity through surprise and canalizing ground using IEDs and close small-arms/RPG fire."

The following day, May 31, was designated another maintenance day following the air resupply drop from the previous night, which due to marginal winds, narrowly missed the sleeping ANA. Some of the vehicles were in really bad shape and the patrol required resupply of some critical parts. During the day, the ANA and some CANSOF elements conducted leadership engagements in the villages within walking (and direct-action support) distances. Throughout the day, there were no ACM spotters and there was little to no radio chatter.

During the night, although the squadron was left unmolested, the enemy was not idle. The Taliban focused its attention on bringing larger weapons into the area. On June 1, the squadron moved northeast and crossed the Baghran Valley for a push to the village of Syahcaw. The patrol commander split his squadron into its two elements approximately five kilometres from the objective and they enveloped the village and surrounding area. Soon a fully loaded Hilux pickup truck was seen quickly leaving the main village and heading north. The A-10 Thunderbolt aircraft on station also observed what he believed to be eleven squirters from the main village move north into what had been identified as a local Taliban leader's safe house in this village. However, when it was later searched, there were only two men and fifteen women and children inside. Once the village itself was examined, nothing of intelligence value was discovered.

The squadron then regrouped and moved back toward Baghran City. Movement was actually easier than anticipated. "This speed," explained Rutledge, "has allowed us also to keep ahead of the enemy EWS and surprise them on occasion." The better than expected progress prompted Rutledge to recce the Baghran Regional Centre prior to moving to a LUP.

As the CANSOF SR patrol neared the actual town of Baghran, it discovered the surrounding villages were surprisingly empty. "There were no people," said the patrol linguist, "just shovels in the fields. The people ran away." There was, however, one old man who seemed to be waiting for the CANSOF troops. He spoke to the ANA commander and told him that the Taliban had mined all the high features leading to Baghran, which proved to be a very picturesque town surrounded by hills.

Rutledge ignored the warning of the old villager who just so happened to be waiting for them. Most agreed he was obviously a plant by the Taliban. By now they had realized that the CANSOF patrol did not use the obvious tracks and roads. As a result, the Taliban tried to lure them down into an ambush along the main routes leading into the town.

The squadron, however, took the dominating high ground and pushed forward. Rutledge once again split his squadron into two elements — one moving to the north and the other moving to the south. Once the squadron commander felt that the area surrounding what he thought was the regional centre was secure, by both observation and fire, the ANA moved in to recce the area.

The ANA soldiers encountered no ACM resistance. In fact, it appeared as if local enemy commanders had told their fighters to keep out of sight in the bazaar. When the ANA made it to what the squadron had thought was the regional centre, they discovered it was a school. This was verified by locals. One of them then pointed out the whereabouts of the real regional centre.[12]

The patrol commander jockeyed his vehicle to get a better view of the regional centre and came within two hundred metres of the bazaar.

This movement sparked a good deal of enemy activity. Significantly, there were numerous pre-positioned old Soviet defensive positions surrounding the district centre. One had an excellent overview of the centre itself and all the positions provided interlocking arcs of fire. As the patrol to the north moved for a better position, they realized that the comment from the old man may have been partially true, as locals later revealed that the insurgents were surprised that "they [the squadron] have not blown up yet!" They were referring to the northern element travelling on the high ground.

Rutledge decided not to push the ANA into town to check out the actual building and he did not collapse his cordon any tighter. All the indcators were there that a large number of insurgents were getting ready to fight if the ANA and CANSOF troops entered the area and Rutledge did not want the squadron decisively engaged within the city. As a result, all elements were regrouped on the south side and the squadron moved into a LUP just south of the city itself.

Although there was no direct contact with the Taliban at first, they quickly decided to strike at the coalition forces. They tracked the patrol for a while and then planted an IED on the route they projected the squadron would travel. The CANSOF vehicles avoided the IED by staying off the track, which sent the insurgents into a scramble to retreive it so they could reset it. The enemy became agitated when the SR patrol moved through the villages to the northeast and the insurgent EWS quickly sent warnings all along the route allowing enemy to withdraw long before the patrol arrived.

The Canadian patrol had avoided contact throughout the day. They now hunkered down in their LUP to await the next play in the drama to unfold. They did not have long to wait. Prior to first light, at 0228 hours, the insurgents unleashed their attack on the coalition forces. The Taliban poured automatic small-arms fire, as well as volleys of RPGs into the LUP. The initial deluge of fire was short, only about five to ten minutes long, but it was extremely intense. It was delivered from only two firing positions, approximately twenty-five metres apart. They were also located in the low ground only seventy-five metres from the lead vehicle in the LUP defensive perimeter.

As luck would have it, one of the SOF operators had decided for the first time on the patrol to remove his pants and boots to air them out while he slept that night. When the Taliban struck, the patrol linguist found himself fighting in his tactical vest, underwear, and flip flops.

More fortunate were two other SOF operators who had fallen asleep beside their vehicle. The alert sentry, caught sight of two heads in the pitch darkness approaching the position from a distance and quickly but quietly woke his two mates so that they could take cover behind the vehicles. No sooner had they repositioned themselves when the first rounds cracked into the position right where one of them had been sleeping.

Although the duration of the initial attack that drenched the position with heavy fire was only five to ten minutes, the extended firefight lasted well into the early morning hours. Once again the squadron came through relatively unscathed. Only one CANSOF operator was struck by shrapnel and had to be evacuated later by helicopter.

After the attack, footprints belonging to an adult, as well as a child, were found leading from the village through the low ground close to the position. The CANSOF and ANA commanders suspected that these tracks belonged to a close reconnaissance party that conducted a recce of the position conducted earlier in the evening. The presence of a child was not surprising. The insurgents knew that children act as shields. Coalition troops will not fire if children are present and there is less likelihood that someone accompanied by a child will be detained or questioned.

The patrol discovered that there was a large group of enemy in the vicinity of the Baghran Bazaar. They also learned that a Taliban leader was wounded during the night attack. Some insurgents had attempted to manoeuvre into a more advantageous position in a Hilux pickup truck. A Hellfire missile fired from the supporting aerial assets destroyed the vehicle and killed five to six enemy personnel, one of which was a local insurgent leader. The strike, however, was quickly exploited by the enemy, who spread false stories that a large degree of collateral damage had resulted from the air strikes.[13]

So, as the morning of June 2 developed, indicators pointed to the fact that the Taliban were gathering for a big fight. They were in the process of redeploying as many insurgents as possible from the ambush they had developed in the northern reaches of the valley to strike at the anticipated arrival of the 2-87th Infantry and instead utilize them to hit the CANSOF SR patrol.

"The radio chatter indicated the enemy was pissed off at us about something," explained Aaron, one of the CANSOF operators. He added, "We knew they were hunting us down." Accordingly, as the CANSOF elements departed the LUP area, all expected an eventful day.

Talk of coalition bombing in the valley, specifically the false accusations of collateral damage of the previous night, raised local anger. One old villager, who stated he had lost two of his daughters in the strike, advised the patrol that the nearby villages were armed and ready for them and that they would kill the foreigners if they came near. "I promise you that you will not leave the valley," he ominously warned.

The prospect of an angry mob was quite concerning to the patrol. Jackson explained, "If rumours of collateral damage spread, the chance of being confronted by locals with picks and shovels would be high and it would become a no win situation. Therefore, the ANA commander and ourselves agreed it would be best to move out quickly to avoid a possible confrontation."

Realizing that the Taliban information operations were effective and that a known insurgent force of two hundred to three hundred enemy were en route from the north, Rutledge decided to make a break for the one viable choke point in the valley and try to get through it before the enemy could set up an effective ambush. This would allow him to gain access to the more open and defendable southern reaches. He decided to catch the enemy by surprise and go down to the valley's main wadi and "floor it."

The patrol was aware that the insurgent EWS monitored their progress and continued the process of passing off the convoy to other groups as it proceeded down the valley. However, once the CANSOF SR patrol entered the Baghran River wadi, they learned that the enemy had ordered locals to remove the women and children from the village areas in the vicinity of Ghargharab. This was never a good sign.[14]

An eerie silence seemed to hang over the wadi as the vehicles groaned over the inhospitable terrain. Then, almost as a relief, breaking the tension that had existed since all knew an attack was imminent, it began. "I remember going through the wadi and there [was] this cold chill going through the back of my neck," recalled Rutledge, "and I flicked off the safety of the C-6 GPMG." Then the world erupted in a kaleidoscope of sound and colour.

The insurgents initiated the ambush with RPGs. The swish of the rockets and their subsequent explosions made everyone instinctively duck. The Taliban tried to isolate the rearmost part of the patrol and destroy it piecemeal. Once the ambush was started, AK-47s and PKM machine guns poured fire into the coalition vehicles from both the west and east ridges. "The bulk of the vehicles made it through the first portion of the pass," said Rutledge, "then the insurgents struck the last four vehicles with RPGs and machine gun fire." Lapointe's Humvee was targeted by three RPGs, but they were fired from too close a distance and did not detonate. Bullets slapped into vehicles everywhere.

The Taliban had chosen their ground well. The ambush site was situated in an "S–turn" in the heavily canalled terrain that the Taliban knew the patrol would have to traverse after committing to the wadi. It provided them with observation, excellent fire positions and escape routes through the high ground if required. They further exploited the terrain by positioning their RPGs on the high ground and their small arms lower on the ridge to effectively support one another.

Approximately fifty to eighty enemy fighters were concentrated at the focal point of the attack. Estimates of the total number of enemy involved in the ambush range from 150 to five hundred fighters. Whatever the actual number, it actually does not matter.

Still, there was no panic or confusion. The CANSOF patrol lashed back calmly, with unrestrained fury. Heavy machine guns barked in reply with their distinctive "boom, boom, boom, boom, boom," while the Mk-19 40mm grenade launchers quickly chugged their bulbous rounds and spat them out, spreading death and destruction along the enemy lines. Every other available machine gun and carbine also responded, adding to the exchange of lead and molten metal that seemed to fill the air.

The initiation of the ambush elicited a simple, "So here it begins," from Lapointe as he began to return fire. "There were so many enemy," he said, "that it was like shooting plates at the range."

Rutledge remembered, "It was so surreal, I almost had to laugh. The guys were so wound up and everyone was firing in a 360 degree arc — there was enemy everywhere."

Another SOF operator quipped he could have just loosened the turret and gun and have someone just spin him around.

"Everyone was so calm," remarked the CANSOF linguist, "despite the overwhelming odds."

The calm of the operators belied the actual situation. The patrol were on their own. They called for close air support, but literally a minute prior, an allied SOF patrol on top of a mountain in a different sector was compromised and was forced to retreat. They were running for their lives. The limited air assets available had been sent to that location, leaving the Canadian SR patrol to fight themselves out of their predicament alone.

Jackson reacted instantly. He guided his vehicles to some high ground and created a firebase. His troops poured a devastating fire into the enemy and Jackson then sent the ANA company to sweep through the Taliban positions, reversing the role of hunter and hunted. This allowed the vehicles in the kill zone to push through and link up with the remainder of the squadron. The squadron then continued to make their way through the canalled ground, leap-frogging from ridgeline to ridgeline under the covering fire of the stationary CANSOF element. But with the tables reversed, the insurgents lost resolve and withdrew before the ANA soldiers could reach the Taliban positions.

It seemed simple science that no one could escape the density and intensity of the fire that was being exchanged. "Five or six rockets exploded right around our vehicle," exclaimed Leo Cormier, one of the detachment commanders. "How no one was hit," he exclaimed, "I'll never understand." The patrol did not lose a single man. Even the vehicles pulled through with only bullet holes.

During the enemy ambush, two ANA soldiers found themselves left in the kill zone — left behind. Many of the ANA were uncomfortable fighting from the vehicles and had dismounted. These two hapless men found

WHERE NO MEN DARE TRAVEL

themselves abandoned when the vehicles, having unloaded a volley of fire at the insurgents, pushed through the ambush site. Nonetheless, the patrol commander and C/S 14 braved effective fire to stop and pick them up prior to moving to safer ground.

On another spot on the battlefield, one of the gun trucks broke down at the most inopportune time. Nonplussed, the mechanic moved to the immobile vehicle and while under fire crawled beneath the broken Hummer to fix it. He was awarded a Mention in Dispatches for his courage that day.

Enemy activity revealed that they were bringing forward vehicles during the desperate fight to retrieve their dead and wounded. The enemy had suffered heavily.

Having escaped miraculously without casualties, less the heavily punctured vehicles, from what should have been certain death, the CANSOF SR patrol continued on its way. The patrol now moved through the mountain pass instead of through the wadi trail and pushed through the night, making it into the southern reaches of the Baghran Valley by first light.

The lack of air support caused some frustration with higher CANSOF task force headquarters back in FOB Graceland. "Last night was a nightmare for allocation of CAS in support of your TIC," complained the task force operations officer, "We were constantly being bumped for assets by elements not in contact."

The overall task force commander reinforced the displeasure. He lamented, "We missed a golden opportunity to do some real damage to a sizeable Taliban force."

The following day was uneventful as the CANSOF squadron took stock of their narrow escape. As the Canadian patrol settled in for the night of June 3, there were ominous signs that indicated the ACM were planning another attack. As such, the CANSOF and ANA troops hunkered down for another fight. Apparently, the enemy intended to attack in the early hours of the morning; however, there were problems within the Taliban ranks determining who would initiate the assault. Although remaining vigilant, neither the sniper OPs, nor the AC-130 Spectre gunship, which burned a five kilometre ring around the LUP, spotted any movement.

Rutledge suspected the enemy were trying their hand at deception. "They know we have sources," he acknowledged. Rutledge deduced that they were either moving more fighters into the area, monitoring the CANSOF troops to gauge how they would react, or a combination of the two. Whatever the case, the follow-up attack never occurred.

June 4 dawned with all still alive and well. "After a sleepless night of anticipating an ACM attack, it ended up to be uneventful," reported the mission commander. The enemy activity was either a ruse to keep the coalition soldiers awake all night, or they were unable to mass enough troops to fight in such a short period of time.

Having regrouped, rested somewhat, and having made the necessary repairs to battle damaged equipment, the SR patrol struck out for yet another day in what was clearly enemy territory. Insurgent spotters continued to monitor the squadron, but this had become a familiar sight for the patrol.

During the day's travel, it became evident that two motorcycles were shadowing the patrol. After warning shots were fired, the individuals stopped and appeared to begin working in the nearby fields. When a CANSOF element with its ANA component conducted an envelopment of the location where the individuals were, the two were captured. They explained that they were harvesting in the wheat field.

Of approximately five males in the area, most were questioned and released; however, the two on the motorcycles were detained. The first, Salaam Jawed, whose name was provided by an intelligence source, was believed to be the owner of a house that was locked during a search and believed to belong to an insurgent. The individual was noted to have prayers written on pieces of paper throughout his clothing. The individual stated he was Afghan-born but Pakistani-raised.

The second individual was named Hamid Gul. He was in possession of camouflage-pattern pants with worn out knees. The commander of the ANA company commented that the worn knees were indications of spotter activity. More significantly, his motorcycle had two homemade electronic detonators rigged for transport hidden in the frame. Also in his possession was a piece of paper with numbers and names, which the intelligence analyst deduced might represent frequencies associated with remote controlled IEDs. In the end, the motorcycle was blown up in place and the two individuals were detained by the ANA.

It quickly became apparent that the enemy was looking for their two lost compatriots. The aggressive approach to dealing with the ACM spotters paid dividends. The local Taliban commander became unhinged at losing his men and not knowing where the squadron was located.

Aside from the small distraction of the two captured insurgents and indications that the ACM were in the process of trying to plant an IED, the day passed uneventfully.

The squadron moved into a LUP at last light and completed a rotary-wing resupply with two Black Hawk UH-60 helicopters after last light. A fixed-wing resupply air drop was also scheduled for that night but was less than desirable. The aircraft refused to drop on the strobe (even after authentication) and instead dropped the load on a grid, which ended up placing the supplies almost three kilometres to the north. It took CANSOF elements a large amount of time to find the dropped supplies. Significantly, as a result of the distance, the squadron had to collapse half of its defensive position so it could send a force out to secure the drop zone with the supplies.

The mission commander was very unhappy. "To make matters worse tonight," he reported, "it seems that the bundles did not have IR glow sticks on them."[15] Rutledge added, "The point about dropping on a fixed grid and not on the strobe, after having contact with the JTAC confirming the exact drop grid, is not acceptable." He stated, "It wasted time [and] energy, and increased risk to the TF." Rutledge concluded, "With the ACM in a hunting mood, we are now keeping all of our personnel up tonight to secure the site, once located, till first light."

The inflexibility of the aircrew to drop the resupply near the patrol created undue danger and hardship on an already overtaxed group of men. The squadron now had to send elements out into difficult terrain, in enemy territory, to find the supplies at night. Moreover, the patrol was now split in half, providing less force protection and less rest, as both positions now had to maintain the same level of vigilance with fewer personnel. It was a needless drain of resources.

At first light on June 5, the mobility patrol set out once again to recce out the last of the potential enemy withdrawal routes in the valley, and then struck out to the south to begin making its way to Musa Qala for the battle handover with 2-87th Infantry and the allied SOF element. The terrain, however, proved decieving. Although it looked like gently rolling hills, the ground was cut by deep wadis every five hundred to seven hundred metres. Moreover, the flat terrain east of the mountians was covered by large boulders that were not passable by the SR/DA HMMVWs.

As one of the Humvees was limited in its performance due outstanding repairs that could not be completed due to lack of parts, the squadron was forced to take one main wadi, following the road for six kiometres. "This was a bit unnerving after the other day of seeing the burned-out hulks on the side of the wadi from Soviet War era ambushes," conceded Rutledge. As they made progress, the patrol also noted that they were being tailed by a dark SUV, which they recognized as the one belonging to some elders they had spoken to the day prior with regard to the men the ANA had detained.

The patrol commander stopped them and he discussed the situation, explaining that the two men had to be taken to Musa Qala for "further questioning and if they were found to be 'good men' then they would be allowed to go home." Rutledge reiterated that the detainees were being treated very well, and he told the elders to stop following the squadron so as to avoid any danger should they come in contact with insurgents. The elders then left and proceeded due south. "I assume to Musa Qala," commented a jaded squadron commander, "to bribe the local regional commander for the release of their men."

The squadron then made its way to its final LUP for the night. The next day would be a run for Musa Qala and the BHO with the Americans. From all reports to date, it was clear that the CANSOF shaping operation had caused great disruption and damage to the ACM in the Baghran Valley.

The next morning, after a late start because of interdiction patrols conducted during the night, the squadron made its way out of the valley. Progress was faster than anticipated, as the ground was favourable to mobility operations. At 1230 hours, the CANSOF patrol linked up, by happenstance, with a patrol that belonged to the 2-87th Infantry. The CANSOF vehicles then followed the Americans to the Musa Qala regional centre to conduct the necessary BHO that evening. The local atmosphere was tense, with looks of hatred stabbing from the local population as the patrol drove through the town.

The BHO with the 2-87th Infantry went well and took approximately three hours to complete. The night was uneventful, although the CANSOF troops continued to do their own sentry watch since unknown ANP troops were in the shared compound. The Canadian patrol was on the road heading for FOB Price the next morning, June 7, 2006, at 0500 hours. They conducted their BHO with ODA 764 later that day and then imposed forced rest until the next morning.

It took coalition forces another three months before they ventured into the Baghran Valley and even then they stayed for only three weeks. Nonetheless, the CANSOF SR patrol had done its part. On June 8, at 0100 hours, the squadron pulled out of FOB Price and crossed the ANP checkpoint at Gheresk, this time without incident. They rolled into FOB Graceland later that morning without incident.

The mission had clearly been a challenge. Jackson conceded, "It was the toughest operation I have ever done in the ATO [Afghanistan Theatre of Operations]. The patrol was extremely taxing on all members. It was three weeks of continual adrenalin and stress.

"You know they will take you at the first chance they can, therefore, you have to be on your game the whole time," explained Jackson, "you have to sustain that intensity over the long haul."

Similarly, Tim Wilson asserted, "It was very stressful throughout. You had to maintain a 360 degree vigilance wherever you went and the tempo provided minimal time to sleep, eat, or relax."

Rutledge agreed. "Most of the guys were pretty stressed," he acknowledged. "It was a game of cat and mouse," he added, "and most of the time we were the mouse."

Many acknowledged it took a full week on return to the FOB to decompress.

But the CANSOF operators appeared to have made a name for themselves with their enemy. Jackson explained, "When we entered the valley, they called us dogs and infidels. When we left the valley three weeks later, they called us commandos. We earned their respect. They passed on to other groups not to fuck with us. They took heavy casualties every time they tried to take us on."

The almost-three-week-long CANSOF SR patrol had written another significant page in CANSOF history. Their mission was a complete success. They had not only traversed the volatile Baghran Valley and shown the presence of the GoA and coalition, but they also bested the Taliban even with terrain, conditions, and circumstances that favoured the insurgents. They inflicted major casualties, disruption, and dislocation on the enemy, while not suffering any significant casualties themselves due to enemy actions. In addition, reconnaissance information and enemy intelligence they gathered provided an important picture for the coalition forces that were designated to venture into the valley and enable a GoA presence. In the end, the CANSOF operators once again demonstrated that they could go where other men dared not travel.

The terrain south of De Lam Ghar.

X

This Toyota Hilux pickup truck was used by the Taliban to transport supplies into the De Lam Ghar area. The vehicle was later blown up in place on September 4, 2005.

This photo shows the centre of the main Taliban defensive position in the major wadi, September 24, 2005.

A Taliban fighter receiving first aid prior to evacuation from the battlefield.

A UH-160 Blackhawk MEDEVAC (medical evacuation) helicopter hovering over a Taliban defensive position while extracting a wounded Taliban insurgent.

A captured Taliban RPG (rocket-propelled grenade) launcher and rocket.

An artist's conception of the Chinook helicopter after being hit by an RPG at Chenartu.

One of the A-10 Thunderbolt strikes (with 500-lb. bombs) on the far west ridge against insurgent forces that were being pursued, May 22, 2005.

Moonscape. The extremely difficult terrain encountered by the CANSOF patrol as it moved north on the west side of the Baghran Valley.

This photo shows the terrain that had to be negotiated on the west flank of the Baghran Valley as the squadron made its way down to the main valley floor.

The barren, rolling hills west of the Baghran River wadi, heading toward the village of Syahcaw.

The terrain as seen looking east across the Baghran River wadi toward Baghran City.

The Baghran Bazaar, on the north side of Baghran City.

This photograph shows the group of elders who shadowed the patrol, wanting to negotiate the release of the two rebels the patrol had detained because they had been following the squadron and, when stopped, were found to be in possession of IED (improvised electronic device) components, June 5, 2005.

Artist's conception of the ambush of the CANSOF squadron in the Baghran Valley.

Transiting Musa Qala through the bazaar to the centre of the town, where the regional centre was located

CHAPTER 5

NO ROOM FOR ERROR:
DESPERATE FIGHT FOR SURVIVAL IN TARIN KOWT

The machine-gun bullets stitched a pattern across the mud wall perilously close to the SOF operators, who were stacked up, ready to make entry into the compound. They were showered with dirt, but no one noticed as the explosive charge blew a man-sized hole into the thick, imposing compound wall. The large orange firewall created a spectacular, albeit momentary, light show in the Afghan darkness. Before the smoke had even cleared, the SOF soldiers poured through the breach and began clearing the enemy compound.

SOF snipers occupying dominating terrain engaged targets both within the compound and outside of it. The enemy had reacted to the coalition intrusion with a fury and tenacity never seen before. The JTF 2 soldiers of the CANSOF task force had been engaged by insurgent fire the moment they stepped off the CH-47 Chinook medium-lift helicopters. The night sky was filled with different colours as tracer rounds flew back and forth in a light show of reds and greens, punctuated by yellowy-orange fireballs, rocket back blasts, and explosions. The din of combat seemed to drown out all other sounds.

The CANSOF troops focused on their mission and penetrated the compound belonging to an important Taliban tactical and operational-level leader. As they fought their way into the compound, few imagined that they would soon have to fight their way out. Despite the accuracy of the SOF snipers and the lethality of the AC-130 Spectre gunship, the enemy was still able to mass on the outskirts of the objective area and move towards the coalition force with the speed and destructive power of a runaway locomotive. There was absolutely no room for error. The CANSOF operators were now in a race against time to clear the compound, accomplish the mission, and withdraw from the area before the developing tide of Taliban fighters surged and crashed over them like a rogue wave. It became a desperate fight for survival.

The latest CANSOF mission, which ran from July 9 to July 10, 2006, was to capture or kill Osami Bari, a Taliban commander at his compound in the Tarin Kowt district.

The importance of the target was indisputable. Bari was a key member in the village of Dehjawz-e-Hasenzay in the Sorkh Morghab region of Tarin Kowt district. He provided assistance to local villagers, and was a critical element of the Taliban command structure in the area. The subordinate to Dost Agha, the divisional Taliban commander who controlled all Taliban forces in the Tarin Kowt to Baluchi Pass region, Bari was also, himself, a Taliban commander and controlled at least thirty fighters. Moreover, he had participated in combat only three weeks prior, against Australian coalition forces.

Bari was known to deploy two or three fighters with him in his home compound at night for protection. He was also frequently visited by other Taliban commanders in the area, who normally visited with their personal security detachments (PSD) and stayed overnight in his compound or the adjacent mosque.

In addition to his normal PSD, Bari could also count on thirty to sixty Taliban fighters in the immediate area who could respond and be at his compound within thirty minutes. In particular, Bari could count on his own group of fifteen to thirty gunmen in the village of Khurma, two kilometres to the west. As well, coalition sources also believed that a minimum of at least fifteen to thirty armed villagers could also respond within five to fifteen minutes. Added to these numbers would be the PSDs of visiting Taliban commanders that could range from four to twelve individuals for each leader. Along with the significant number of ACM forces, there was supposedly a substantial cache of weapons available to them. This included, ominously, RPG launchers, recoilless rifles, and 107mm rockets.

Not only did Bari have a substantial number of well-equipped fighters to help protect him, he also had the clear support of the village. Due to Bari's stature, as well as the benefits that accrued to the villagers as a result of his presence there, he was strongly supported by the village. Quite simply, he was a trusted elder and held in extremely high regard. As a result, coalition analysts believed that the villagers would resist any attempt by the coalition to capture him. As a result, Bari considered himself to be in very safe territory there.

As a consequence of all this, analysts believed that the capture or death of Bari would severely damage the Taliban network in the Tarin Kowt District. Quite simply, his capture would remove an important leader, one who facilitated Taliban command and control (C2) and combat operations in the area. Moreover, an SSE of his compound would likely reveal material of great intelligence value that could lead to follow-on targeting.

In addition, since Bari was perceived by many, particularly the local population, as a Taliban commander and facilitator who had been able to participate in attacks on ANSF and coalition troops with impunity, the coalition felt it was crucial to demonstrate that this was not the case. It was important for the Government of Afghanistan and the coalition to demonstrate that anyone who participated in attacks became a legitimate target.

There was one other reason that Bari was considered such an important target. Given his specialist skills, he would be very difficult for the Taliban to replace. Removing him would seriously injure the Taliban's ability to function, the coalition believed.

The operation would not be an easy one, though. After sustained surveillance, it became evident that Bari stayed continually at his compound overnight. In fact, he rarely moved from his home, even during the day. As a consequence, coalition planners believed that he was vulnerable and that a target of opportunity was at hand.

Bari, located in Uruzgan Province, had in fact been the target of an allied nation once before. They had ramped up a potential CONOP to conduct a DA raid in early June; however, that failed to launch because they could not get the necessary air assets required. Timing once again seemed perfect, but, the allied SOF now lacked the gunfighters to prosecute the mission. At the time, they were preparing for Operation Perth, an offensive action aimed at conducting decisive operations (search/ attack/clear) against ACM in the vicinity of the Baluchi Pass and Chora District of Uruzgan Province in order to degrade ACM capability and enable coalition freedom of movement as part of Operation Mountain Thrust.[1] As such, their SOF assets were allocated to other missions. Therefore, they asked the Canadians if they would take on the target — because of its importance and because of its potential for disrupting the Taliban as they prepared to launch their own operation.

Based on an earlier request by allied SOF to assist with the prosecution of some of their processed targets and on the importance of coalition partnerships, the CANSOF task force commander, Colonel Phil Cameron, was amenable to the idea of conducting operations in Uruzgan Province.

"They truly want[ed] these targets taken care of, [and] they [were] pretty high up the list, and at least one [was] critical to their scheme of manoeuvre," he assessed.

However, Cameron laid out his conditions fairly plainly for them. He stipulated a number of concerns and constraints. First, he emphasized that CANSOF were "not going to do an economy of effort operation [i.e., create a diversion] in support of Operation Perth." Second, the allied nation would be responsible for providing the necessary enablers, such as aviation lift and escort. CANSOF would provide the requisite assault force for any mission. Finally, any target the allied nation wanted CANSOF to prosecute would require a comprehensive and well-developed target intelligence package (TIP) so that the CANSOF analysts and planners could take it and expend energy only on monitoring and providing support planning without distracting from their own special operations intelligence cell (SOIC) with additional target development work. As it was, the SOIC was busy focusing on Canadian national interests, specifically the disruption of threats to Canadian Armed Forces in the Kandahar City/Zhari/Panjwayi sectors. This intelligence nexus was critical for precision SOF operations, which are by nature intelligence driven. Only with the most exact information can a SOF element prosecute a

NO ROOM FOR ERROR

DA that achieves its aim of capturing a high-value target without causing collateral damage.

In the end, the allied nation accepted the caveats and passed on a comprehensive TIP on Bari to the CANSOF task force. It was immediately accepted as a target to prosecute. Colonel Cameron's intent was to respond to the actionable intelligence given on Bari so that a CANSOF and ANSF assault force could move directly to his compound and execute a capture/kill mission followed by an SSE operation. His aim was to disrupt the ACM's ability to react to the upcoming preliminary moves of the Australian's Operation Perth.

Jack Rutledge, the JTF 2 squadron commander assigned to the CANSOF task force, attacked the mission with his characteristic energy and professionalism. "I intend to capture or kill Osami Bari in the vicinity Dehjawz-e-Hasenzay," he stated, "in order to disrupt the Tarin Kowt/Chora ACM network." He planned to use speed and surprise to infiltrate the area, and then assault, secure, and search the subject compound of interest (COI). Due to the threat of Bari's PSD, as well as the potential for a large enemy reinforcement component, he deduced that the insertion of his assault force would have to be done under the cover of darkness.

Rutledge developed a simple scheme of manoeuvre. He planned to use two CH-47 Chinooks to land in two separate helicopter landing zones close to the objective. The accompanying ANSF would be used to create an outer cordon around Bari's compound. This would allow the CANSOF assault force to clear the target area and conduct a hasty SSE. Meanwhile, the Chinooks would return to Tarin Kowt, refuel, and prepare to return to extract the coalition forces. A Predator unmanned aerial vehicle and an AC-130 Spectre gunship would provide ISR (intelligence, surveillance, and reconnaissance) and fire support. In addition, an allied SOF commando platoon in armoured vehicles was on standby to act as a quick reaction force (QRF).

Jackson, the troop commander, was responsible for the ground tactical plan and deciding who would fight the close battle, explained the plan further. "CANSOF will conduct a hard-knock, direct-action assault on the compound of interest," he asserted, "in order to capture/kill Osami Bari and set the conditions for success in the region."

Jackson planned to use speed, surprise, and shock action to aggressively breach (hard knock) and assault Bari's compound. Upon insertion into HLZs "Alpha" and "Bravo," he planned for four CANSOF detachments to move tactically toward the compound and, under sniper over-watch, conduct simultaneous assaults from the east and from the south, with both groups converging toward sector "C" inside the compound itself. Once the compound was secure, a hasty SSE would be conducted and preparations made for the assault on any other subsequent compounds on order from the squadron commander.

In total, the mission was truly a "coalition" endeavour. Beyond the American ISR and fires assets (AC-130), the mission was made up of Canadian gunfighters, Afghan and American outer security, Australian CH-47 Chinook tactical lift, and Dutch AH-64 Apache flight escort. The aviation package was actually the product of the efforts of the CANSOF air liaison officer (ALO) in KAF. Once he determined that the U.S. conventional aviation, which was in high demand, were unavailable, he worked his magic and convinced the Australian aviation commander to request their participation in the mission. This meant that aviation commander had to seek authority from his Australian chain of command. Although the Australian Chinooks had never been utilized for such operations before, Canberra quickly signed off on the operation.

However, with no experience in such combat situations under their belt, both Rutledge and the aviation lift commander agreed that they would conduct a full rehearsal beforehand in the area of FOB Graceland so all parties could get the feel of working together. Doing so also provided the Canadians with an appreciation of the flying capabilities of the Australian pilots.

The assault force conducted daylight and night iterations of the mission profile. The skills of the pilots quickly impressed the ground force leadership. In addition, the menacing-looking mini-guns hanging out of the door gunner windows always made an impression with the SOF operators.

The operation seemed straightforward. It would be a one hour in-and-out mission. At sunset on July 9, 2006, multi-source resources indicated that Bari was present at the compound and all was normal. There were no Taliban checkpoints in the area and the nearest Taliban fighters were to the west. The mission was a go.

The Australian Chinooks picked up the Canadian and ANSF elements at FOB Graceland at 2321 hours, July 9, 2006, and flew to FOB Davis in Tarin Kowt, escorted by the Dutch Apache helicopters. Delays in ISR coverage delayed the H-Hour by sixty minutes, to 0100 hours, July, 10, which gave enough time for the respective liaison teams to be exchanged between the main assault force and the QRF. Rutledge, who was up in the front of the Chinook speaking to the aviation force commander, would have to wait to meet the Australian liaison team sergeant until he got off the helicopter on the objective. Subsequently, the assault force departed for the mission at 0055 hours.

En route, the Chinook pilots observed flashing lights "to their seven o'clock at an unknown distance as they headed north." However, the flashing lights were not an uncommon event. They were part of the ACM early warning system.

Once the AC-130 gunship was in position, the Australian CH-47s began their run-in on the target. Spectre provided objective sparkle to help guide the Chinooks in on their landing zones, which were located immediately adjacent to the target compound. The Dutch Apache helicopters flying escort declared the HLZs clear for landing; however, the AC-130, immediately cut-in "all excited," recalled Rutledge and informed the Chinook pilots, "negative, the HLZ is 'hot.' You have guys all over the place!" The AC-130 specifically identified at least six to twelve individuals at each landing site. Rutledge "could clearly see guys running across the landing zone." He looked over and saw that his squadron sergeant major's chalk going into HLZ "Alpha" was about to hit the deck. The ground force commander then reinforced to the lead pilot to put the bird down — the assault force was getting out despite the hot landing zone.

At 0101 hours, with mini-guns blasting non-stop, the Chinooks flared in preparation for touch down. As they neared the ground, one of the CH-47s observed two fighting-age males run from just outside the objective and into the compound. The two men were not observed to have weapons and were most likely spotters, providing compound security. The rotor wash of the large machines created huge amounts of dust, which prevented the aircrew from viewing the area and resulted in no visual of ACM activity. However, on departure, the helicopters noticed fighting-age males running into neighbouring compounds to the north and east. The Dutch Apache helicopters provided overhead security; however, they did not engage any ACM or target area due to their poor visibility.

Two factors provided the CANSOF and ANSF assault force a fighting chance as they unloaded on the hot HLZ. First, landing close to the objective minimized the amount of time the assault force was in the open, something which ended up saving lives. Second, the "brown out" created by the rotor wash was actually fortuitous. The ACM were not able to zero in on the aircraft or the coalition soldiers in the first few minutes of the insertion. By 0110 hours, the SOF operators were on the ground and moving.

Jean Demercier, one of the CANSOF snipers recalled, "The Australian Chinook landed us fifty metres from our compound under fire — no one else would do that." He added, "the dust cloud was so bad guys were hanging on to the guy in front of them so not to get lost."

Despite the close distance to the target, they were still under constant fire from the insurgents. The JTF 2 linguist remembered, "As soon as you got out of the chopper, you could hear the splatters — the rounds hitting the ground all around you."

Rutledge recalled:

> Bullets [were] popping by as I got off the helicopter and walked over and introduced myself to the two Australian QRF liaison team members. They just looked at me and were taking in the chaos of the dust and noise. I think they were relieved when I told them to follow me and we moved with the squadron headquarters to a position to return fire.

CANSOF declared troops in contact (TIC) immediately. They were now under fire from insurgents from the wood lines and compounds to the north and northeast, as well as from those to the south and southwest. To the west, the ACM engaged the ANSF troops as they approached the mosque. Amazingly, from the moment the coalition forces stepped off the aircraft to the time they finally extracted, they would be under constant fire.

The enemy in the area was very well organized. They had established defensive positions and a high amount of radio traffic indicated that the attack on the CANSOF assault force was well controlled. Its intensity was increased on order, as was the engagement of the heavier weapon systems. The Australian SOF liaison team also reported that "the ACM were pushing families out of their houses to use them as cover."

The rapid movement of ACM elements at the objective area, and the ensuing firefight with the coalition ground forces indicated a strong Taliban presence in the area. The assault force estimated that there were easily over one hundred Taliban rapidly massing in the area. The "big unknown," as Jackson later revealed, was that there was a large *shura* (leadership engagement) consisting of four to six Taliban leaders and their PSDs in a compound approximately five hundred metres to the southeast of the target of interest. Not surprisingly, the Taliban leaders and their fighters quickly reacted to the assault on Bari.

Despite the less than friendly welcome, the assault force quickly moved to their target area, returning fire at the same time. Blocking forces made their way to their positions and began to take casualties. The AC-130 immediately began pounding the enemy wherever they seemed to be massing, which apparently was everywhere.

The ANSF soldiers moved to a block position to the east of the compound, at the end of an alley, when they were engaged by ten to fifteen Taliban firing from behind a low orchard wall. As the ANSF forces continued along the alley between compounds, an insurgent on the other side of the wall fired a full burst from his AK-47, emptying his entire magazine of 7.62mm rounds and killing one Afghan soldier and wounding three others, including Stan, the American mentor. All were immediately evacuated into the main compound.[2] The Taliban continued to engage the ANSF troops as they held their blocks at both ends of the alley.

Meanwhile, the snipers had adopted their positions of observation and fire. They had become accustomed to being the first in and the last out. They ruthlessly applied their skills to buy time for the assault force to breach the compound, ironically placing themselves in greater danger so that the assault force could attain a position of greater safety — inside the defended target. In the short time they were on the ground, the snipers had already attained seven to ten confirmed kills.

Concurrently, call signs (C/S) 11 and 13 and the troop commander, who disembarked at HLZ "Alpha," moved east towards their designated breach point. At the same time, C/Ss 12 and 14 and the troop warrant officer, who landed at HLZ Bravo twenty-five metres from the compound, moved south towards their entry point. Mark Rogers, the detachment commander responsible for the initial break-in, had already been assembling his breaching charge as he was disembarking from the Chinook on the LZ. His detachment, C/S 14, quickly began to place it against the southwest corner of the target. Chaos seemed just one bound away as the enemy kept a continuous stream of fire aimed at the coalition forces. Regardless, the CANSOF assault force split up into its multitude of groups, each with their own specific task.

An RPG slammed into the north wall, barely missing the snipers. One of those was Tim Wilson. He was physically rocked when the rocket exploded literally five feet from him. At first he thought it was the assault force breaching the compound, but he was then told it was a near-miss RPG. On top of the explosions, tracer streamed in from the south and more RPGs were fired at CANSOF troops as they were preparing to breach the compound in the south.

"It was unreal," said Demercier, "it was like in a movie, tracer all around you. At one point I had a stoppage and I yelled out stoppage!" He smiled, "We laughed [at] how we reverted to training as this huge battle was going on. It's amazing how calm you really are because of training and selection."

Throughout, the enemy radio chatter betrayed not the slightest hint of panic from the Taliban command structure. One assaulter stated of the enemy, "They are slick, They have shitty weapons, very few radios, crappy ammo, yet they put up a good fight." He was not far off. If anything, the radio traffic underlined that the enemy was determined to fight.

Within two minutes of landing, the assault elements made their way to their breaching points. There was no natural entry point in the south so an explosive breach was made in the southwest portion of the compound wall by C/S 14. Luckily, a natural entry was found in the eastern sector of the objective.

Before the smoke could clear from the resounding boom that somehow drowned out the other noises in the battle zone, C/S 12 moved in to secure sector "E." As they entered the compound, enemy was immediately encountered. The first individual was carrying two AK-47s; the next was both carrying an AK-47 and attempting to load an RPG. The third was also armed with an AK-47. All were engaged and killed by precision fire. There was no collateral damage. It was later determined that the individual with the RPG was in fact Osami Bari. He was identified by distinguishable tattoos and a unique ring he was known to wear.

"This was the first compound we ever hit where everyone fought to the death," reflected Rutledge. "At all the others, the Taliban usually gave up once you breached the compound."

With the squadron headquarters moving into the relative cover of the compound, Shawn, the American joint terminal air controller, joined the snipers in their position so that he could get the best observation on the enemy and effectively call in the life-saving fire of the AC-130.[3] Throughout the entire engagement, Shawn would often remain standing, exposed, directing assets through the hail of Taliban fire.

At the same time, C/S 11 made entry and secured sector "D." Subsequently, C/S 13, reinforced by C/S 14, assaulted and secured sector "C." Upon completion, C/S 11 moved through and secured sector "A." By now sectors "C," "D" and "E" were locked down. Therefore, C/S 11 moved through to secure sector "A" while C/S 14 searched sector "B."

During the clearing of the compound, three males (as already described) were killed and four other males were detained and safeguarded at a central location, separate from, but in proximity to, the women and children, who were collected and moved to a central zone where they would be protected from the continuing insurgent fire.

Amazingly, by 0118 hours, the Taliban had amassed a large number of fighters and were engaging coalition forces from all directions. The AC-130 identified groups moving through orchards from the north, south, and east towards the objective area. Specifically, Spectre reported that a group of at least fifty Taliban were moving from the south, another group of at least fifty were moving from the north, and a group of enemy "too many to count" were massing for an to attack to the east. In addition, the observer noted that the insurgents demonstrated fairly sophisticated fire and movement tactics as they advanced towards the objective.

At 0127 hours, with the situation potentially getting unmanageable — too much even for the AC-130 to subdue — Rutledge decided to call the Australian QRF forward from their staging area, which was supposed to be approximately fifteen minutes away to the southwest. He had assessed that the enemy forces arrayed against him were substantial and, more important, they were determined. Significantly, they were not deterred at all by the close air support (CAS), despite the pounding they were taking from the AC-130 gunship. Equally as influential in Rutledge's decision was the fact that Spectre, in many ways their lifeline, was running out of ammunition. In addition, the large amount of radio traffic indicated that the Taliban command structure had directed its fighters to continue with their attacks and fight on and engage whatever enemy (i.e., coalition forces) they observed. The insurgents were also told by their leaders that they would be reinforced shortly. As a result, Rutledge decided he would call the QRF, who could create a strong point to which the assault force could withdraw.

The decision to call the QRF appeared timely. Initially, the Australians had assigned an attached Dutch platoon, which had little experience in theatre, to the task. The ground force commander had discussed this with the Australians, who had then, fortunately as it was to work out, assigned a commando platoon to the task. In the end, they would be instrumental in providing a screen and fire support for the CANSOF assault force to withdraw from the compound and extract by helicopter.

At 0135 hours, Bari's compound was finally secured. The hasty SSE uncovered a veritable insurgent warehouse. A cache of weapons, ammunition, and military equipment was found in the largest building in sector "A." One of the small rooms contained one RPG, three RPG rounds, PK and AK ammunition, still in the Soviet boxes/packaging, as well as bandoliers and improvised or village-made blue denim chest rigs containing AK magazines. It must be noted that a large amount of additional weapons were located throughout the compound. In addition, a non-clinical pharmacy within the compound revealed prescription medication, pharmaceutical equipment, needles, bags of human hair, and six RPGs. Moreover, poppy stalks, bulbs, and possibly raw opium were also found.

Within the compound were also a total of seven women and twenty-one children. They were safeguarded in a central collection point in sector "C" so that they would not be inadvertently injured during the clearance of the compound and would be protected from the incoming Taliban rifle and rocket fire. There were also four detained fighting-age males — one was found dressed in woman's clothing, while another was found hiding under blankets behind a woman and children. They were also moved to a protective location close to, but separate from, the women and children.[4]

At 0149 hours, the QRF, which was now approximately one kilometre from the objective, came under enemy fire. The Taliban unleashed a volley of RPGs and hosed the convoy with PKM machine gun fire. The Australian commandos fought their way through the ambush and took up their positions four hundred metres to the west of the compound to cover the withdrawal and extraction of the CANSOF and ANSF assault force. They immediately attracted the wrath of the Taliban. The JTF 2 linguist recalled, "seeing a shit load of RPGs hitting the Australian vehicles all at once." As a result of drawing so much enemy fire, they also drew a great deal of pressure off the assault force.

Back in the compound, once it was confirmed that no women and children were in the building or in sector "A," all military materials (AKs, RPGs, ammunition, and chest rigs) were placed in the room that housed the weapons cache and were subsequently destroyed in a controlled explosion set by the CANSOF explosive expert at 0245 hours.

Seven minutes later, at 0252 hours, the assault force departed the compound once again, moving out under the protective over-watch of the snipers and the AC-130, which had just called in that he was out of 105mm ammunition.

It was ironic. Initially, the assault force had to fight their way into the compound. At a point in the battle, the compound became argu-ably the safest place and the CANSOF and ANSF elements fended off the Taliban from recapturing it. Now, the coalition forces were in the position of having to fight their way out of the compound and run a four-hundred-metre gauntlet through an orchard and link-up with the Australian QRF.

The CANSOF troops had barely left the objective, when, at 0306 hours, the AC-130 reported insurgents inside and all around the compound. The enemy had taken up better positions from which to continue to engage the withdrawing coalition forces and the incoming helicopters.

Shawn, the attached American JTAC, confirmed all "friendlies" were clear of the compound and heading to their extraction point. He then gave Spectre the clearance to engage the enemy that was pouring in from nearby compounds and fields, to relieve the pressure and assist with the withdrawal under contact of the CANSOF and ANSF assault force. According to the task force commander, the "U.S. JTAC saved the day."

With the assault portion of the operation over, the JTAC attached to CANSOF passed control of the air space to the Australian JTAC who accompanied the QRF. As the last of the Canadians passed through the Australian QRF position toward the new extraction area to the west, Rutledge sought out the Aussie platoon commander and shook his hand. "Sorry we have to leave you hanging," apologized Rutledge, "but it looks like we have to go!" The Australian captain just grinned and both exchanged patches prior to Rutledge moving off to the extraction site.

At 0309 hours, CANSOF requested extraction from what had become a veritable shooting gallery. In the interim, the aircraft had returned to Tarin Kowt to refuel and to await the extraction notice. They immediately lifted off and made their way back to the objective. At approximately five hundred metres southwest of the pick-up zones, one of the escort Apache helicopters received effective small-arms fire, which resulted in two rounds striking the aircraft and damaging hydraulic lines. As a result, it was forced to return independently to Tarin Kowt to set down.

The remainder of the aircraft continued on with the extraction. "The Aussies came into a hot LZ," Demercier said. "We were completely impressed by them." He explained, "You could see tracers flying by and they still came in."

Aaron, one of the CANSOF operators, revealed, "We never thought that with all the contact we had during the insertion they would come back to pick us up, but they did!"

However, dust was once again an issue on the objectives, resulting in severely reduced visibility. The CH-47 door gunners engaged multiple targets with their mini-guns and laid down an impressive suppressive fire to assist with the extraction. As the Chinooks lifted-off, muzzle flashes could be seen coming from compounds around the objective. Nonetheless, by 0345 hours the CANSOF assault group had completed the extraction and were on their way back to their FOB. They arrived at 0502 hours, July 10, 2006. Amazingly, neither of the two CH-47s were hit by a single round. The Dutch Apache escorts, however, were both hit with small-arms fire.

Once the Chinooks had left, the Australian QRF, which had remained under fire for the entire time, began its own exfiltration. And none too soon. Twelve minutes after the CH-47s departed, the AC-130 reported it was out of 40mm ammunition. It had fired its entire load of 105mm and 40mm shells. The QRF were now on their own. Their withdrawal became a harrowing tale of courage and tenacity, as they remained in a running battle, enduring machine gun, small-arms, and RPG fire for the next two hours as they fought their way back to FOB Davis in Tarin Kowt, covered by a sole B-1 bomber.

"It was a mess," acknowledged Craig Steele, who was one of the JTF 2 liaison officers assigned to the Australian QRF platoon. He explained, "Everywhere we went; every time we thought we broke contact, another pocket of enemy would engage us."[5] He added, "We felt that we were trapped in the village. Each time we would try to exit we would be stopped by concentrated enemy fire. We would then have to stop, turn around, and try to find another route." Making the withdrawal even more difficult was the fact that they had no ISR platform in the air informing them where the enemy was massing. "We just [had to drive] into them," remarked Steele. Finally, the Australian QRF commander decided to just "punch through." Steele explained, "We dumped suppressive fire on a localized point and then just crashed through."

The QRF commander also called in additional Australian SOF to assist with their extraction. They finally broke out of the village and continued to fight their way back home. They finally arrived safely at 0745 hours. Amazingly, although the vehicles were riddled with bullet holes, they had suffered no serious casualties. But they were almost completely tapped out. The QRF was out of all .50 calibre and MK19 40mm ammunition and only two vehicles had any 7.62mm machine gun ammunition remaining.[6]

In the aftermath of the mission, few who participated in, or who simply knew about, the mission harboured any doubt that the operation could have had a much different outcome because of the inaccurate picture of the enemy situation on the ground. Quite simply, the enemy dominated the area around the objective within minutes of the arrival of the CANSOF assault force. In the end, it was estimated that there were well in excess of a hundred Taliban in the fight. In fact, the situation differed so much from what the intelligence picture painted, particularly from what was supplied by human intelligence (HUMINT), that the task force commander conceded, "compromise is suspected." It was not until additional information was received from the local sources that the task force discovered that a large *shura*, which was being conducted only five hundred metres away from their objective, had been the source of the bulk of the fighters and leadership during the engagement.

Nonetheless, the CANSOF operators achieved their mission. Colonel Cameron explained that the success of the operation could be attributed to the skill, courage, and fortitude of the CANSOF and ANSF operators, as well as that of the Australian Chinook crews. He also added that success was also due to the precision and effectiveness of the AC-130 aircrew and the JTAC, as well as the determination and courage of the Australian QRF commando platoon.

Remarkably, the coalition forces were engaged continuously from insertion to extraction, with the helicopters engaged in flight at H-30 seconds and until well after they had lifted off on extraction. An investigation following the assault noted that the Taliban tenacity under fire was remarkable. "This was the second time I realized," shared Jackson, the troop commander, "that the fighters in Uruzgan [Province] are amongst the most aggressive in Afghanistan."

But the Taliban lost badly. According to a public statement by the Tarin Kowt national directorate of security (NDS) chief, Abdul Rauf, the official government assessment of damage caused following the DA conducted against Osami Bari on July 9–10, 2006, was fifty-seven Taliban killed and thirty-five wounded. The death toll included Bari himself, as well as two Taliban sub-commanders. Rauf stated that the assault was one of the most successful attacks against the Taliban during his tenure and, as such, thanked the coalition forces for their efforts. The Australians later told the CANSOF commander that "that single action changed the security posture of Uruzgan Province for the next three to four months."

However, the successful DA on Bari created a tempest. In its aftermath, local villagers alleged that there was collateral damage. Ten civilians had died, including women and children. The media went into a frenzy and reported there were one hundred civilians killed. Afghan parliamentarian Abdul Khaliq warned that locals would rise up against the coalition forces as a response to the assault. By July 13, 2006, President Hamid Karzai ordered an investigation into the deaths. He appointed Maulvi Muhayuddin Baluch, his adviser on religious affairs, and four others as part of a five-member team to determine the details of the deaths.[7] In the end, Karzai criticized coalition use of excessive firepower, but also admonished the insurgents for the cowardly use of women and children as human shields.

The CANSOF task force was cleared of any culpability. "Only surgical and discriminate fire was used by the assault force within the compound and we know for certain that the assault force was not responsible for any civilian casualties within the compound," asserted Colonel Cameron. He added, "It is assessed that the only damage to the compound caused by the assault force was the breached wall in sector 'E' and the controlled explosion in sector 'A'." However, he clarified, "Throughout the battle there was considerable exchange of fires between CANSOF/ANSF defending from within or near the target compound, and the estimated one-hundred-plus Taliban engaging CANSOF/ANSF from the orchards, walls, and other compounds surrounding the target compound." He then explained, "This heavy exchange of fires (including virtually the entire AC-130 arsenal) was required to eventually allow CANSOF/ANSF to fight their way to the link-up with the Australian QRF and the extraction HLZ."

Colonel Cameron acknowledged, "There were potentially non-combatants in or near the compounds surrounding the target that may have been killed or wounded in the exchange of fires both before the withdrawal of CANSOF/ANSF, and afterwards, during the lengthy extraction of the ground-based Australian SOF QRF (with CAS fires controlled by the Australian SOF JTAC)." The task force commander concluded, "I firmly believe that CANSOF and QSF took extraordinary measures to prevent collateral damage to non-combatants." He insisted, "CANSOF and attachments conducted this operation appropriately and with extraordinary concern and diligence to prevent non-combatant casualties. That there were non-combatant casualties is tragic but should not be laid upon the conscience of CANSOF."

He was not alone in his judgment. Combined Joint Task Force 76 (CJTF 76), the divisional headquarters responsible for operations in Afghanistan under Operation Enduring Freedom, also launched an investigation. A statement later released indicated, "While civilians may have been killed and wounded, none were injured during the CQB [close quarter battle] inside the compound." The official determination was an adamant "no violations of the law of armed conflict" occurred. Moreover, officials noted that the CANSOF actions to safeguard the women and children were "notable and laudable under these extreme combat conditions." Although the coalition, in response to public outcry, conceded that there may have been some civilians injured in the follow-on fight, they explained that the AC-130 engagement of Taliban, who were continuously in pursuit of coalition forces, was not a violation of the rules of engagement (ROE). In the end, the coalition concluded, "If there were civilian casualties they were accidental and unavoidable and occurred while coalition forces exercised their right to defend themselves against an enemy force actively engaging coalition forces with deadly fire."

Despite the tragic loss of civilian lives, the mission was a complete success. As Sean, one of the CANSOF snipers stated, "We proved SOF skills and training; we can fight big numbers and come out on top." But more than that, the direct action raid had sent a clear message to the enemy — coalition forces could strike with great precision and eliminate Taliban leaders wherever they were and no matter how well they were protected. And, the operation had tremendous impact. The strike created apprehension within the Taliban leadership, who were now afraid the success of the raid would act as a catalyst for others. But it was a near-run thing. Outmanned, outgunned, and in the middle of hostile territory, there was no room for error. A straightforward mission became a desperate fight for survival, and only the courage, tenacity, and skill of those involved turned chaos into a resounding triumph.

X

CHAPTER 6

WHEN THE THUNDER COMES:
THE INVISIBLE HAND OF SOF SHAPING THE BATTLEFIELD

The bright sun shone relentlessly on the hard baked Afghan ground. The countryside seemed tranquil as the convoy of Canadian light-armoured vehicle (LAV) IIIs roared down the highway. Then, suddenly, without warning, the stillness of the morning air was split as a resounding KABOOM reverberated through the air. A colossal orange fireball preceded the actual noise of the explosion and by the time most realized what had happened, a plume of dense, jet-black smoke was already spiralling skyward.

The explosion caught the second LAV III in the convoy in its deadly grip. The eighteen-ton, eight-wheeled behemoth shuddered as it was hit by both the force of the explosion and the torrential shower of hot shrapnel. The vehicle, with its right-side flank armour ripped and peeled and with three of its four tires on that side shorn from their struts, careened to a lumbering halt. Another IED had successfully wounded Canadian soldiers and destroyed another vehicle.

Although the conventional forces had become increasingly successful at counter-IED activities, it was impossible to stop them altogether. The Taliban's focus on non-conventional/asymmetric tactics, such as the combined use of IEDs and suicide bombers, made the fight difficult. The Afghan War was a war fought largely in the shadows; a struggle of hit-and-run attacks facilitated by a network of financiers, bomb makers, and IED cell commanders, who plotted a campaign of terror against ANSF and coalition troops. These savvy individuals operated among the local populace, which, either because of intimidation or because they were sympathetic supporters, helped them to stay underground and develop the necessary production facilities to maintain an output of deadly IEDs.

The latest attack, however, did not pass without notice. Behind a solid wooden door, accessed only by a coded keypad, an integrated team of specialists made up of intelligence analysts from the Canadian Armed Forces (CAF) as well as other government departments pored over all available data to develop the clearest possible picture of the adversary — their leaders, networks, and locations.[1] This group of intelligence analysts was developing the precise intelligence that would allow CANSOF to strike at their seemingly phantom adversaries on the battlefield.

By the fall of 2008, the coalition assessments had begun to paint an ominous picture of a number of Taliban commanders and a major IED network that seemed to be working with impunity in the Zhari district. Specifically, the analysts reported that an insurgent commander, an individual in charge of active patrolling in the Anizai area, which was a recognized Taliban command and control node for the Zhari district, was present with approximately thirty to forty-five fighters. This enemy commander was noted to have links to the Meyer Group, which was an IED network operating in Zhari as well.[2] Surveillance soon identified a series of compounds and associated guest houses and "grape huts" (i.e., large buildings with thick mud walls, used for drying grapes) that were being used by the enemy commander in question, other insurgent commanders, and their fighters, as well as the Meyer Group. Not unusually, the Taliban commander and his group of fighters had seemingly taken up residence in a mosque.[3]

As the coalition gained more insight into the region, it became more and more evident that the area under observation was an anti-Afghan forces (AAF) stronghold. By late November, two other AAF sub-commanders, as well as their twenty to thirty fighters, were also reported to be bedding down in the vicinity of two compounds associated with the main target and the IED-making cell. These two sub-commanders were involved in kidnapping and detaining local nationals who were suspected of being informants for the ANSF and coalition forces. They and their fighters were also actively involved in operations against ANSF and coalition troops in the Pashmul district.

By late 2008, the intelligence picture began to burgeon with targets. Two other important AAF commanders were also reported to have been bedding down in the same compounds in the area in question. One of the targeted compounds was also identified as the property of a named insurgent who was a key member of the Meyer IED Group.

It became evident that the insurgents considered the Zhari district, specifically the Anizai area, was, if not entirely a safe haven for the Taliban, certainly an area in which they could move and act with a great sense of security and a high degree of freedom of movement. Unsurprisingly, it attracted a significant number of Taliban fighters. In fact, intelligence assessments placed a very large number of fighters in reserve in the Anizai area. Moreover, the Taliban maintained an active security posture in the area. They conducted foot patrols at night and had vehicles patrolling the local routes. The vehicles each held between five and seven fighters armed with AK-47 assault rifles and RPGs. In addition, each vehicle also carried an 82mm recoilless rifle. The AAF maintained a very active and well-developed early warning system. Finally, IEDs on the major access routes provided a further impediment to ANSF/coalition operations into this apparent Taliban sanctuary.

In light of the growing intelligence picture of the AAF activities in the area, it became clear that coalition forces would have to act to counter this activity. Accordingly, the 3rd Battalion, The Royal Canadian Regiment (3 RCR) battle group (BG), in coordination with the British 42 Royal Marine (RM) Commandos prepared for an operation in the late fall of 2008. However, with such a heavy enemy presence, particularly with the high number of Taliban commanders in the area, the risk was very high. As a result, CANSOF determined that it was necessary to shape the battlefield to ensure success of the upcoming operation.

Commanders within the region all assessed that the primary effect of exploiting the growing target pack they were building was disruption of a significant command and control node and IED production network for Zhari district. Clearly, the capture/kill of any of the Taliban commanders in the area would have a negative impact on network cohesion, coordination, and operational capability in the district. Moreover, striking the compounds of interest (COI) in an area where numerous insurgent leaders were working and living would also have a wider disruption effect on AAF activities. Specifically, the removal of the main target would significantly degrade the ability of the AAF to operate in Zhari/Panjwayi as it would eliminate a well-connected commander and IED facilitator. In addition, the coalition commanders also believed it would make his superior Taliban commander for the Zhari/Panjwayi districts more vulnerable to targeting. Many in the coalition went so far as to predict that the removal of the main target would likely impact all other AAF commanders in the area.

The mission, however, was not without risk. "The place is a snake pit," confirmed the Canadian special operations task force (SOTF) ground force commander, "still is because we haven't held the ground." There were known Taliban defensive positions, particularly along major routes, supported by IEDs pre-positioned with wires ready for connection. The area was saturated with fighters at any given point in time and the Taliban were known to have good communications and coordination. Actual response times by Taliban reinforcements were not known, but the presence of roads made it possible to move fighters by vehicle quickly throughout the area. Moreover, the AAF located in the compounds of interest were interrelated and could draw on reinforcements from across the region. The ground force commander explained, "It's very AAF-friendly and we [SOF] can only go in at night when they can't see us."

With this in mind, CANSOF decided to strike. The timing seemed to be fortuitous, as in addition to the main target, three other insurgent leaders and members of the Meyer Group were in the area. "My intent," stated the CANSOF SOTF commander, describing his strategy,

[was] to use CANSOF elements to inhibit the AAF capacity to organize, plan, and act, in order to increase the freedom of manoeuvre for ANSF and coalition forces. The precision capabilities of the CANSOF SOTF [were to] be focused against intelligence-driven targets operating in and transiting through Zhari/Panjwayi.

He elaborated, "The intent [was] to capture the primary target and clear compounds of interest in order to disrupt insurgent IED networks and shape the battle space ahead of Canadian BG operations." To achieve this goal, he gave his ground commander a seemingly simple, yet very dangerous mission: The CANSOF SOTF "[was to] capture/kill the Taliban commander in question [in the designated] compounds of interest [COI] 09 and 04 in order to disrupt AAF IED command and control node activities in the vicinity of Anizai."

The mission was planned and set to go prior to the commencement of the conventional operation. Once all the requisite approvals and intelligence triggers were in place, the task force was ready to launch. The fact that the 3 RCR BG was already in its staging area, prepared to cross the start line at first light, necessitated CANSOF action. "We knew," explained the task force commander, "that we were now at our last executable window."

His ground force commander agreed. "We knew we had to go in," he echoed, "we assessed a lot of Canadians could die if we didn't strike."

The CANSOF soldiers were under no illusions. They knew they were heading deep into the enemy's lair. "We fully expected a gunfight," acknowledged Williams, one of the detachment commanders. In fact, they assumed they would be engaged during the infiltration itself. As a result, they were heavily weighted down with ammunition.

The beefed-up CANSOF assault force departed their forward operating base rotary wing. Knowing the density of enemy in the area, the task force commander realized he needed to reinforce his normal assault package. So, he pulled a precision assault detachment from another location and elicited the assistance of coalition SOF.

As always in combat operations, "friction" was not long in coming. Just shortly after stepping off the ground, the force commander received word that the mission had lost a component of its aerial support. The aircraft had engine problems and was unable to lift off. After a brief radio conversation with the task force commander, the mission continued. Both the task force and ground force commanders agreed that they still had the necessary assets to conduct the mission. It was what the ground force commander described as "modern blitzkrieg — air support with SOF on the ground."

Although the route was carefully chosen and stealth was used to maximum advantage, it appeared that a very small element of the local nationals attempted to warn the Taliban of the approach of the assault force. The CANSOF soldiers witnessed flares, some distant and some from closer, being fired off into the pitch-black night. Whether this was coincidence or direct targeting of their approach was not known. Luckily, the inky-black darkness with no moon and little ambient light in the countryside turned the SOF assault force into virtual apparitions as they moved toward their target.

As the assault force neared their objective, they were warned of sentries surrounding the compounds of interest. The ground force commander sent a few individuals forward to quietly eliminate the sentries if necessary. Their cautious approach allowed them to actually close with the first objective compound, COI 9, without being seen. This was surprising since the approach was exceptionally noisy due to extremely dry leaves and underbrush that crackled and crunched as SOF operators advanced. As a result, the ground force commander decided to push his forces out to take up their designated spots around the compound of interest. Simultaneously, to save time, he moved his precision assault element up slowly so that they could breach the compound the moment the external cordon was in position. Call Sign (C/S) 11 was responsible for clearing the centre (i.e., main) part of COI 9; C/S 12 was tasked with clearing the northern portion; and C/S 15 was given the northwest piece of the compound.

As the detachment responsible for a portion of external cordon (BP) 1 approached its location, they could hear a PKM machine gun being cocked. Then the night was split by a gunshot. With that shot, controlled chaos erupted. The BP 1 operators reacted instantly. The pin was removed from a grenade and tossed over the wall where the enemy sentry had revealed himself. The loud guttural "crump" ended any resistance from that PKM-wielding insurgent. At the same time, two individuals exited the southernmost building of the compound and were quickly engaged by BP 1. The detachment commander recalled, "it seemed like forever but the whole action took place in about thirty seconds."

The shot and subsequent explosion from the grenade were heard by all. With the stealthy approach compromised, the ground force commander quickly ordered everyone to "go" on his radio, setting in motion the immediate attack of the compound by all the precision assault teams.

"When that first grenade went off," smiled one assaulter, "it got real, really fast."

Everything now happened at once. The block force commander quickly moved with a group of special operators to reinforce BP 1. As he passed within two feet of a large grape hut on the exterior of the compound (known as Building 97), another PKM machine gun opened up. The bright red flames that shot out of the muzzle of the chattering weapon seemed to reach out in an attempt to grab him. "I had the distinct feeling of everything slowing down," he remembered, "the auditory exclusion was surreal." The enemy tried to track the block force commander and tried to fire through the thick mud walls, which in turn propelled chunks of rock-hard mud flying out with such force that it threw the block force commander against a nearby wall and knocked his weapon from his hand. He quickly picked himself up and flung a grenade into the grape hut.

Not far away, C/S 11 began their assault into the main compound. Two assaulters moved into position when suddenly the PKM machine gun in the grape hut (i.e., Building 97) opened up. Inside that virtually impregnable fortress were a large number of insurgents who, although unable to clearly see the CANSOF troops outside, poured a withering fire throughout the area as they sprayed all likely approaches and wherever they suspected the Canadian troops might be.

Elsewhere, the enemy acted equally as quickly. Ed Simmons recalled, "As that first grenade went off, suddenly four enemy with RPGs on their shoulders burst out of the compound and ran toward us." Although the enemy was engaged, they were so fast and unexpected that they escaped into the surroundings. Simmons and fellow assaulters now took up dominating fire positions and began to engage targets of opportunity both inside and outside the compound.

Simmons next focused on providing intimate support to his assigned assaulting detachment (C/S 11). However, now fully exposed, he came almost instantly under severe machine gun fire from Building 97. "We were right in their beaten zone," said Simmons.

Exacerbating the problem was the fact that simultaneously C/S 11, which had now breached the COI, was also heavily engaged in a close quarter battle (CQB) inside the main compound. Simmons was now faced with a dilemma. Although under heavy enemy fire that turned his current position into a boiling cauldron as the surface around him was ripped apart as the machine-gun rounds hammered in, tearing apart everything in their path, he knew that C/S 11 required him in his position to assist with their CQB. Yet, to avoid the incoming fire he would have to seek cover and leave his preferred position of observation and fire. Faced with these two alternatives, he ignored the enemy fire that shredded the surface all around him and instead coolly engaged multiple enemy insurgent fighters inside and outside the main compound. In an amazing display of courage, Simmons selflessly disregarded his own safety and placed himself in the direct line of fire so that he could better assist his comrades.

As C/S 11 entered the compound, it was as if someone had lifted a rock. Enemy fighters scattered in all directions like insects. Five enemy, armed with RPGs and AK-47s, poured from the grape hut, while other insurgents exited from a buildings in the centre of the compound. The detachment cleared the main building in the central core of the compound and then moved to clear the adjacent building. At that point, they were quickly fired on by an insurgent who had surrounded himself with women and children. Four other fighting-age males were found, all of whom, despite the chaos and roaring din of battle, were feigning sleep. They were taken under control.

Concurrently, the BP 4 detachment set off at a run for their position. Since they had the furthest distance to go, they decided to trade some security for speed so that they could slam shut the exit route they were to block. As always, it was mission first — they knew they had to seal the perimeter.

The moment they arrived, rounds began to whine all around them. They could even feel the spray off the mud walls as the rounds tore into the concrete-hard surface. It took a while for them to locate the insurgent who was firing at them, eventually locating him on a roof in the main compound where he was shooting through a firing port in the wall. Louis Gagme recalled, "Rounds started flying over our heads, which at first I thought were the enemy from a position farther out. But," he explained, "it was from an embedded shooter in the 97 building." Luckily, the insurgent was firing at noise and could not see the blocking force in the oily-black night.

Unexpectedly, that same insurgent dropped from the roof. He was stunned to find himself confronted by the Canadian soldiers. The insurgent was challenged and told to stop and raise his arms. His baggy clothes made it difficult to ascertain whether or not he was still armed. However, upon being challenged he raised an AK-47 and was immediately engaged and killed.

Simultaneously, C/S 12 began the clearance of their portion of the COI. As they entered the compound, they quickly cleared two rooms. Upon exiting, they discovered three heavily armed insurgents running out of the buildings in the northern end of the compound. They were engaged; however, they escaped. They were later killed by the external cordon force when the insurgents opened fire on them.

Vigilance and skill also prevented C/S 12 from walking into a trap. As they prepared to move from a building in the centre of the compound to assist in clearing buildings in the northern sector of the objective, an insurgent was waiting in ambush behind a small outbuilding to catch them as they prepared to enter the nearest structure. Fortuitously, one of the coalition SOF members scanning the compound spotted the danger and quickly neutralized the threat.

C/S 12 also rapidly cleared a building in the northwest part of the compound. They were moving to the furthest northern building. All was going without incident when they encountered two fighting-age males and a woman. One of the males suddenly pulled a weapon and fired on the assaulting force. He was quickly killed and the other male was taken under control.

Meanwhile, Building 97, the mud-hardened grape hut that had the characteristics of a reinforced concrete bunker, was proving extremely troublesome. It could not be silenced. The barricaded machine-gun nest inside was pouring a constant rain of fire throughout the entire compound. The ground force second-in-command conceded, "The barricaded shooter was holding up progress into the main compound." He added, "It took a considerable amount of time to deal with that."

The ground force commander now redirected Michel Lafleur, the detachment commander for C/S 15, who had finished their original clearance task, to assist with the silencing of the grape hut. In support was "Rat," the detachment commander of the coalition SOF team, who had made his way toward the grape hut as soon as it had opened fire. Both tossed in grenades, to no apparent effect. To add to the immediate concerns, the Taliban kept sending fighters to outflank the assault force and a battle within a battle soon developed for control of the grape hut that housed the machine-gun bunker. Lafleur and Rat soon ran out of grenades as they tried to deal with both the machine gun and the Taliban trying to reinforce their position.

The ground force commander was attempting to get a better perspective on the battle when a heavy burst of fire drove him into the ground. The Taliban flanking party had turned the corner and one insurgent pointed an RPG at a group of friendly forces. Rat threw a grenade and killed the lead enemy in the group. The ground force commander engaged the next enemy, who was armed with an AK-47 assault rifle, with a body shot. He then took out the RPG. The brief drama all transpired in about five seconds.

Meanwhile, BPs 2 and 3 had nothing significant to report and monitored their sectors. However, BP 4 suddenly had three armed insurgents emerge over the compound walls, moving in an attempt to escape. They were ordered to stop and get down. The enemy initially complied but then pulled out weapons and started to shoot, at which point they were engaged. Tim recalled, "The first guy had an AK and as he turned I saw it and shot the first guy in the chest."

As the fighting raged on all around him and tracers and debris seemed to fill the night air, one special operator couldn't help but be "amazed at the composure of the guys on the ground." He remembered, "They were very relaxed, after all there is nothing you can do but maintain your situational awareness and deal with the situation the best you can."

Back at the grape hut (Building 97), Lafleur and Rat were still attempting to deal with the machine gun that was firing from within, without getting themselves killed. Once the enemy reinforcements were dealt with, they were able to focus exclusively on the bunker. "Lafleur and Rat were fighting like demons to neutralize the machine-gun nest," recalled the ground force commander, who himself was moving back and forth along the axis of assault trying to control the entire battle and ensure there was a link maintained between the various detachments fighting within and outside the compound. At this point, additional grenades were thrown in to the grape hut.

Amazingly the insurgents inside the grape hut were still alive. However, the explosives that had been tossed in had by now created a hole in the corner of the building. Lafleur and Rat crawled in and were immediately confronted by four insurgents. Lafleur tossed a grenade. The resultant explosion silenced the enemy but also caused the ceiling to collapse. "You couldn't see anything," he recalled, "you couldn't breathe; the air was really thick."

It quickly became evident why the Taliban machine gun was so difficult to silence. Inside the building was a secondary chamber. Lafleur and Rat crawled along the floor and approached the final hold-out. Luckily, the back wall of the interior room was already breached with a hole. Grenades were lobbed inside; these were followed up by four magazines that Lafleur quickly emptied into the room. Two other assaulters swept through and cleared the position. The stubborn and tenacious enemy stronghold was finally silenced.

After being in contact for approximately two hours, the compound was finally secured. A quick SSE was conducted and the search produced a cache of weapons and communications equipment, which were destroyed.

The march to their pick-up zone went extremely quickly and the last members of the assault force loaded on to the helicopters and lifted off as the first signs of dawn slowly began to creep over the horizon.

In the end, a total of fifteen insurgents were killed in action and six detainees were removed from the objective. The enemy had been willing to fight and had fought hard. "One enemy was wounded," recalled George Williams, "but he didn't stop fighting and he never asked anyone for help."

Similarly, another SOF operator observed, "Even though the enemy were told to stop, they still always attempted to fire at us." He shook his head, "They were clearly willing to die for their cause."

Of the six detainees taken, two were later identified as Taliban commanders. The first reportedly controlled twelve fighters and had conducted ambushes against ANSF and coalition forces. He was responsible for the death of several Canadian soldiers. The second enemy was described as an IED expert and a member of the Meyer IED Group. He had been previously captured and imprisoned in connection with a suicide vehicle IED attack but had escaped from Saraposa prison during the Taliban operation of June 13, 2008.[4] He was responsible for the death of at least seventeen ISAF personnel, including Canadian and U.S. soldiers.

The operation had been an enormous success. Just as the CANSOF soldiers were winging their way back to their FOB, the conventional forces were beginning their operation. However, by this time the Taliban leadership throughout the entire area had scattered and was unable to return to provide the necessary command and control to resist the coalition offensive. As a result, the 3 RCR BG and 42 RM Commandos were able to conduct their operation virtually unopposed.

This is not surprising. Aside from the two Taliban commanders captured, the task force discovered that they had also killed two AAF sub-commanders and human intelligence sources reported that several members of the Meyer Group were dead as well. Coalition analysts noted:

> Given the resistance that CANSOF received while conducting its operation in the vicinity of Anizai and the lack of resistance that 42 RM Commando received as part of the Canadian Battle Group operation, it is assessed that the initial effect of the CANSOF operation was to disrupt AAF command and control (C2) in the vicinity of Anizai providing the battle group freedom of movement.

The coalition assessment added, "The comfort and sense of security that they [Taliban] might have felt in Anizai has been undermined, and this will have caused them to focus on their personal security and possibly disrupt their operational focus for at least the near term." Commanders and staff from the battle groups and brigade headquarters were effusive in their praise. Collectively, they concluded that the Anizai area was clearly disorganized and that there was little evidence of their command and control organization. Although they acknowledged that some fighters remained it the area, they believed most fighters were caching their weapons and blending in with the local population until the AAF could rebuild their command and control structure.

The task force commander explained, "We disrupted a C2 [command and control] node; captured and killed a number of Taliban leaders and IED specialists, and, most important, set the conditions for Canadian conventional operations with no casualties." He continued, "We never gave up [on conducting the operation] because we realized the harmonizing effect the task force can have." As a result, he concluded, "Despite the risk, we set the conditions for the battle group operation."

Once again, the CANSOF Task Force that reached out, unseen by friend and foe alike, to protect Canadian, coalition, and Afghan forces, as well as the local population. Utilizing stealth and precision, they were once again able to remove Taliban commanders, facilitators, bomb makers, and fighters from the fight with no collateral damage. In doing so, once again the invisible hand of SOF directly saved lives.

Artist's conception of the gunfight at Tarin Kowt.

CANSOF SOTF training in Afghanistan.

CANSOF operations in Afghanistan.

Difficult terrain, similar to that which the CANSOF personnel had to traverse during the night of November 25–26, 2008.

Typical farmland in Pasmul, showing the lush foliage, the fields with mud walls, and formidable and dominating grape-drying huts.

Typical compounds in Afghanistan.

Courtesy Silvia Pecota.

The 3 RCR BG (Royal Canadian Regiment, 3rd Battalion) in coordination with the ANA (Afghan National Army) and 42 Royal Marine Commandos launched Operation Array into Anizai on the heels of the SOF operation. They suffered no casualties and met little or no resistance.

P02905364/Canadian Press (Allaudon Khan).

Building 4 in Kandahar City.

Different perspectives on Building 4 and surrounding area after the Taliban attack.

Some of the captured munitions.

CHAPTER 7

CHAOS IN KANDAHAR:
THE BATTLE FOR BUILDING 4

The hot Afghan sun poured down on the forward operating base on the edge of Kandahar City with a relentless tenacity. Even shade provided but a temporary respite. However, for the Canadian special operations forces deployed in FOB Graceland, the heat, much like the complex, ambiguous, and ever-changing environment they worked in, was taken in stride. Then, single shots cracked in the distance, piercing the relative midday tranquility of the FOB. Like a faltering engine, the shots started in spurts and soon increased in frequency, until there was a consistent rhythm. At one point, tracer arced over the FOB, prompting some to believe their camp was under attack.

The commander of Special Operations Task Force (SOTF) 58 and his ground force commander (GFC), Captain Grant Morrison, quickly moved to the tactical operations centre (TOC) to discern what was transpiring in the city. Hearing shots fired within the environs of the sprawling urban mass was not unusual, particularly as a result of the insurgency, but clearly something significant was occurring. The volume and pattern of the exchange of fire, which was punctuated by sporadic explosions, clearly indicated trouble. Moreover, the widespread and persisting nature of the violence seemed to indicate it was not localized to one specific area.

As the CANSOF officers and their staff were busy contacting higher headquarters and other sources to determine what exactly was occurring, a runner from the Afghan Provincial Response Company — Kandahar (PRC-K) arrived with a message from his commander. The PRC-K, which was co-located with the CANSOF forces at FOB Graceland, had been called out by their Afghan National Police (ANP) chain of command. In fact, they were told to get the PRC-K downtown to the governor's palace as quickly as possible. The Canadians were now intimately drawn into the drama unravelling in Kandahar City on May 7, 2011. With no information, but with indications that an attack was occurring close to their FOB and with the knowledge that the current fighting season had already proven to be one of the most violent of the insurgency, SOTF 58 was rapidly being pulled into the chaos and crisis that had arguably began to grip the city.

The hook dragging SOTF 58 into the fray was the PRC-K. It was an Afghan National Special Police unit consisting of 105 personnel, organized in three special response teams (SRT), roughly platoon size, of thirty-five personnel each. It was SOTF 58's Canadian Special Operations Regiment that had been responsible for both training and mentoring their Afghan partners. CANSOF had attempted to assign a readiness cycle to the three SRTs to allow for stability in training, operations, and personnel management. As such, the three SRTs would be in one of the three designated cycles: Green (ready to deploy on operations); Amber (reinforcement if required but undergoing training); and Red (on leave and/or out of area courses).[1]

However, when the Ministry of the Interior (MoI) or ANP chain of command called for the PRC-K, they expected all available troops to respond. Moreover, there was an implicit understanding that the PRC-K, and its mentors, would deploy immediately, much akin to a quick reaction unit. This, however, was problematic for CANSOF, who preferred to deal with any request for deployment more like the model used by a domestic counterterrorist (CT) unit, which allowed for a more thorough assessment of the situation, a leader reconnaissance to determine a plan,

and then a deliberate execution of that plan. Rushing to the sound of gunfire was always fraught with risk. The SOTF-58 commander explained:

> Our concern was that we would get sucked into something
> we didn't want to be part of; that we would get hit and get
> sucked in with the PRC. Specifically, that they would run to
> the sound of gunfire and we would get drawn in and not have
> the opportunity to adhere to our tactics — our TTPs [tac-
> tics, techniques, and procedures]. We wanted to examine the
> actual situation with the mentors and the SOTF and deter-
> mine whether this should be a mentor assist or whether we
> would just make the situation worse (e.g., during the riots in
> the aftermath of the Koran burning).

CANSOF's concerns in this regard had been borne out in February
2011, when an insurgent attack on ANP headquarters in the city
prompted the chief of police (CoP) to call out the PRC-K. SOTF 58 held
them back until they could better define the threat, confirm friend or foe
identification, and plan out the required response. However, the ANP
rushed in to respond, and as they did the Taliban detonated an IED. The
worst was yet to come. As the ANP and other first responders assembled
outside the objective after the attack, a vehicle IED (VIED) cut down
the assembled government forces much like a scythe in a field of wheat.
Casualties were horrific.

Although CANSOF had been vindicated by the February events,
the Afghan officials' desired outcome thereafter was no different. They
still wanted the PRC-K available when they called for them. In addition, the perceived slow response by the PRC-K and their mentors
during the February incident had created inevitable tension between
the Afghans and the coalition. As a result of this incident, SOTF 58
and NATO's International Security Assistance Force (ISAF) Regional
Command–South (RC(S)), in coordination with the Afghan government, established Operation (OP) Response, which laid out the contingency plan, responsibilities, and process for calling out the PRC-K.[2]
The deputy commander of RC(S) directed that the PRC-K must be able

to respond to their national chain of command. He also stated they must go with mentors.[3]

Complicating matters was the fact that when SOTF 58 took on the responsibility for training and mentoring the PRC-K it was not yet at initial operating capability (IOC). In fact, many personnel had not been trained. Some were still missing basic ANP qualifications and the basic PRC training. Captain Morrison, the GFC and officer commanding (OC) the CSOR element, was specifically responsible for developing and executing a training plan that would take the PRC from IOC to full operating capability (FOC) in four months. His team was also responsible for mentoring the PRC-K on operations, as well as conducting liaison with ANP intelligence organizations. This entailed a weekly coordination with senior Afghan officials and senior coalition military personnel to enhance situational awareness and develop an Afghan employment mechanism (i.e., analysis of intelligence, development of the necessary warrants issued by legitimate Afghan authorities, and execution of subject warrant within a framework of the "rule of law") for the PRC-K.[4]

In any case, since the PRC-K was co-located in a tented camp in FOB Graceland, the activation of the PRC-K was fairly simple. Normally, the provincial chief of police (PCoP) and/or the Kandahar chief of security (KCoS) would task the PRC-K. The ANP liaison officer at FOB Graceland would receive the call by cell phone and this would trigger OP Response, the mutually agreed contingency plan to activate the PRC-K and mentors for an operation. On notification, the CSOR element would prepare the PRC-K, as well as themselves, to deploy, while SOTF 58 headquarters would immediately coordinate battlefield deconfliction with the battle space owners (BSO) and notify its chain of command (Joint Task Force — Afghanistan (JTF-A)) and RC(S) that OP Response was being executed.

Notwithstanding the significant gap in training, the PCoP insisted on employing the PRC-K on security operations within Kandahar City. For the Afghans, the PRC-K, regardless of their state of readiness, were an integral part of the Kandahar City security plan. This was not hard to understand. The SOTF 58 commander explained, "Although we thought they required additional training, they were competent and capable. They were the best of the Afghan units."[5]

And so, despite the complete absence of information on the events that had seized the city, SOTF 58 prepared to deploy the PRC-K. The SOTF commander acknowledged, "The Afghans were upset the PRC-K wasn't sent out [in February], so we knew we had to go out. We followed as close[ly] as possible."

The SOTF commander was clearly between a rock and a hard place. He understood the Afghan concern and dependence on PRC-K and their mentors. However, he also shouldered the burden of command. He was responsible for ensuring that Canadian lives were not recklessly put at risk. His dilemma was at the heart of the myriad challenges that leaders at the tactical level face in counter-insurgency operations. What made the situation worse was the fact that, as the SOTF commander, a veteran of multiple Afghan tours, observed, "Spring 2011 was markedly different than other tours [he had] served in Afghanistan."

He was not mistaken. Strategic analysts stated violence in Afghanistan in 2010 had reached its worst levels since 2001. With the end of the poppy season, the 2011 fighting season continued the trend. Significantly, much of the insurgent focus appeared to be in Kandahar City itself. Haji Atta Mohammad, a former police general who was the head of the Kandahar council of former mujahedeen commanders, commented, "The Taliban are more active in the city than at any time since 2001. They've taken the war inside Kandahar."[6]

His assessment was not hard to understand. On April 2 and 3, the Taliban joined protests over the burning of a Koran by Pastor Terry Jones in Florida and attacked the governor's compound. The protests left nine dead and more than ninety injured.[7] Less than a week later, on April 7, the Taliban attacked a police training centre, leaving six dead. On April 15, they infiltrated ANP headquarters and killed the chief of police, and nine days later, on April 24, the Taliban tunnelled four hundred militants out of Saraposa prison. Significantly, the last two operations were accomplished with support from the inside.[8] This only perpetuated the growing vulnerability of government and coalition forces, as insurgents increasingly committed attacks and ambushes dressed in ANP and Afghan National Army (ANA) uniforms. Moreover, the Taliban had vowed to kill anyone working for the government. As a result, the Kandahar municipal administration was able to fill only 52 out of 119 budgeted positions at the time.[9]

Not surprisingly, the chaos and turmoil impacted everyone in the city. Increasing attacks and social unrest within the city made normal operations exponentially more demanding. Exacerbating the already difficult and complex urban operations was the fact that it was becoming increasingly hard to tell friend from foe. Between Taliban fighters dressed in government uniforms, and sympathizers and active "agents" ready to turn on their former colleagues and allies, the battlespace was as complicated as it gets.

This was the situation when, at approximately 1230 hours on May 7 2011, Taliban insurgents conducted a massive coordinated attack in the city. They hit multiple objectives, including the governor's palace; the old ANA Corps headquarters; a police substation (close to FOB Graceland) as well as three other police sub-stations, ANP headquarters; the mayor's office; and two high schools. The attacks involved direct fire from small arms, machine guns, rocket-propelled grenades, as well as suicide vehicle IEDs and VIEDs. Taliban forces also attempted to block major roads leading into the city.

The Taliban offensive was a major operation. Insurgent commanders declared their objective was nothing short of "taking control of the city."[10] The attack was part of the Taliban spring offensive, which they code-named Operation Badar. It was intended to turn Kandahar City into a "scene of bloody fighting."[11] As always, estimates of the numbers involved vary. NATO's assessment was that sixty insurgents participated in the attacks; the Taliban claimed that one hundred fighters were involved. In addition, there were reports that the Taliban also deployed up to twenty suicide bombers.[12] Significantly, some insurgents were in ANP uniforms.

The attack on Kandahar City and its estimated one million people was part of a deliberate strategy to give the insurgency in the Kandahar region more of an urban focus, as the American surge in the rural regions had pushed the Taliban out of their strongholds in the surrounding districts. American officials confirmed the trend. U.S. Army Major-General James Terry, the commander of coalition forces in the south of Afghanistan and commander of the 10th Mountain Division at the time, confirmed,

"Whereas last year it was worse in the districts than it was in the city … the paradigm has reversed now. Now we have to put more effort in the city."[13] Haji Toorjan, a former senior Taliban commander who reconciled with the government, revealed, "The Taliban have made a deliberate decision to center their war effort on Kandahar City after finding it hard to counter the U.S. military onslaught in the rural districts."[14]

Having learned from years of fighting, the Taliban carefully chose their tactics. The Taliban commander responsible for attacking the governor's compound claimed forty men were assigned to the task. He also acknowledged that the plan to attack multiple targets was designed to overwhelm security forces. "We know," he explained, "that if we attack one place, all the security people will come and surround us; this way they can't stop us."[15]

The devious strategy held some truth. The battle opened with an explosion outside the provincial governor's compound, followed by gunfire from the upper levels of a multi-storey commercial shopping centre. Interior ministry spokesman Zemari Bashary stated eight suicide bombers had blown themselves up during the simultaneous attacks on the governor's compound, an office of Afghanistan's intelligence agency, and police outposts.[16] Haji Pacha, an influential elder from the Alokozai tribe said Kandahar was "completely empty. There is still fighting going on in at least three districts of the city and all the shops are closed, the people completely terrified."[17]

And so, at 1330 hours, May 7, 2011, the Afghan authorities activated OP Response. With one insurgent attack a mere four hundred metres from FOB Graceland, the commander of SOTF 58 had some major decisions to make. He remembered:

> We heard shots. They sounded like they were coming right into camp. It was evident things were going on in the city. We were trying to figure out what was going on. So was the battlespace owner. In the northern part of [FOB] Graceland, we could see … where the canal and school were situated. Insurgents were holed up there. We watched the drama unfold on the Graceland cameras. With the multiple attacks

in the city, I ratcheted up the camp to full stand-to as we tried to figure out what was going on. It was very chaotic. We figured the PRC-K would be called out so we increased our notice-to-move (NTM). No one knew what was going on. Between the BSO and us, no one knew. Shortly thereafter the PRC-K was called out to defend the governor's palace. Initially I figured Graceland was the only safe stronghold so we didn't send mentors.

With that decision, Morrison and his CSOR element, which was on a perpetual thirty minutes notice-to-move, focused on assisting the PRC-K in getting out the door. However, they, too, began to prepare to deploy, knowing the inevitable call would be made. The PRC-K were eager as they drew their weapons, stored their ammunition, and marshalled their vehicles. Once assembled, all, with the exception of one section kept back in reserve, quickly raced off to the sound of gunfire only a short distance away.[18]

The PRC-K arrived shortly at the governor's palace, and the senior ANP commander on the ground quickly put them to use. Initially, they were deployed as part of the cordon around the palace compound. However, insurgents had seized the two-storey "Blue Building" north of the palace grounds and were firing at the governor's residence and surrounding buildings with small arms and RPGs. The PCoP and KCoS quickly employed the PRC-K in the attack. A prolonged firefight and assault ensued and the PRC-K requested an ammo resupply of AK-47 ammunition and RPG rounds at approximately 1505 hours. The CSOR element mentors then dispatched the PRC-K reserve section, which had been left at FOB Graceland, to deliver the ammunition so that the assault against the Blue Building could continue.

CANSOF personnel at FOB Graceland were on a 100 percent "stand-to." Fortuitously, some information began to dribble in from JTF-A headquarters as the situation began to crystallize. By now the Taliban objectives had been identified and mostly isolated. One of the major targets was a large three-storey commercial shopping complex (designated as Building 4) south of the governor's palace. Insurgents had barricaded themselves inside and were pouring fire into the governor's compound and adjacent buildings. Even before the PRC-K had completed their assault on the Blue Building to the north, the Afghan MoI demanded they attack the new objective.

Consequently, at 1700 hours, the BSO, an American battle group under Combined Task Force (CTF) Raider, codenamed Phoenix 6, requested that SOTF-58's CSOR element and their mentored PRC-K begin planning for a deliberate assault on the shopping mall complex. This was a big and dangerous undertaking — the mall contained in excess of one hundred different rooms. Knowing the complexity of the task was beyond the PRC-K, Captain Morrison and his men left FOB Graceland to link-up with Chantu, the PRC-K commander, and the BSO, to begin conducting planning for a deliberate assault on the new objective.[19]

The drive to the governor's palace seemed surreal. "[The] city overall was eerily calm," voiced Warrant Officer (WO) Jerry Gervais, the ground force warrant officer (GFWO), who was on his third Afghan tour. Nevertheless, he stressed, "we were hyper vigilant, because we knew the whole city was under attack." In the distance could be heard gunfire and the occasional explosion.

As they neared the rendezvous point (RV), Morrison tried to establish communications with Phoenix 6 but was unable to. Then, suddenly, as they rounded the corner to pull up to the RV they were met by a scene of devastation. In the midst of all the destruction, an American mine-resistant ambush-protected (MRAP) vehicle, which had just hit an IED, was limping backward. "That whole area was obliterated," said Sergeant Harry St-George, describing the scene. "You could tell a lot of bombs had gone off. The entire area was a complete mess"

Sergeant Al Taylor recalled, "the governor's palace was shot to shit."

Warned that there were additional IEDs planted in the road ahead, the CSOR element convoy backed up and established an alternate vehicle drop-off point (VDO).

WO Gervais noted, "everything became extremely real."

Captain Morrison and his team arrived at the RV point at approximately 1800 hours. By this time, the PRC-K had just secured the Blue Building. Their successful assault netted two insurgents killed, as well as one of their own wounded. Although tired, the PRC-K soon appeared at the RV, prepared to take on their second assault of the day.

The objective had been cordoned off by the American battle group, who provided force protection by keeping any new insurgents approaching from different areas from attacking the assembled PRC-K and mentors. However, the Americans were clearly played out. They had been stretched thin throughout the city with multiple incidents throughout the day. Moreover, the threat of suicide bombers and IEDs remained extremely high. Everyone was on edge.

Phoenix 6 now provided guides to take the PRC-K and their mentors through the palace grounds to allow them to reach the objective building from a less exposed approach. Exiting the governor's residence, they were able to move to a low concrete wall that stood between the palace grounds and the target building. Morrison used this as his assembly area. From here, he conducted a leader's recce to confirm the point of entry. Meanwhile, his snipers and joint terminal air controller (JTAC) moved into an adjacent building to the west of the objective, where the Americans and ANP had already established a vantage point. The snipers quickly established themselves and began to observe the objective for movement.

The task before the CSOR element and their assigned PRC-K was daunting. The building was massive in scale. Adding to this was its complexity. It was a kaleidoscope of shops and bazaars, each one more overflowing with goods and wares than the last. Rugs, tapestries, burlap bags full of goods of every description littered the shops, hallways, and entrances. Anyone and anything could be hidden from view. It was nothing short of a death trap.

The challenge and risk did not escape the CANSOF personnel. "I was immediately struck by the size of the building," conceded Captain Morrison.

Sergeant J.F. Giguard assessed immediately, "We don't have enough guys."

Sergeant Taylor gasped, "It was huge — a CQB [close quarter battle] nightmare."

The SOTF 58 commander exclaimed, "The building was one large danger area. There were no hard walls within the building. Someone could fire from one floor to the next."[20]

Despite the scale and scope of the objective, which would easily be able to suck in a number of highly trained conventional infantry companies, Morrison had only twenty-five SOTF 58 personnel, as well as approximately fifty-five members of the PRC-K to conduct his assault. However, with a plan in place, and after notifying his chain of command and allowing the team leaders to brief their respective detachments, Morrison commenced the clearance operation at 1830 hours.[21]

The U.S. cordon force indicated that the enemy was last seen in the building ten minutes earlier. However, they had no idea how many insurgents occupied the building or where they might be now. Up until this juncture, the Americans and the Afghan ANSF had only exchanged fire with the building occupants. No one had dared to enter the gigantic complex. The assault group were now ready to begin their search, commencing in the basement since it was the safest point to start. The OC reasoned that the building was so large and his force so small that he had to keep the plan simple. Moreover, he was concerned about separation and the risk of "blue-on-blue" engagements. At every control point (i.e., at each floor, at one of the three stairwells), the mentors were to leave a PRC-K member.[22] Morrison also tried to leave one of his CSOR personnel at strategic points so that they could control a number of PRC-K members, who, as a general rule, tended to be easily distracted and prone to leaving their posts if not carefully supervised.[23]

With approval in hand, and night rapidly descending, the assault detachments rushed across the open ground and raced to the entry point. As they moved into the open, they observed a number of civilians on a balcony.[24] The Afghan civilians were ordered to come down and were taken into custody.

Sergeant Denis Charron, who was on his fourth combat tour in Afghanistan, remembered, "It surprised us. We weren't expecting to see that many 'friendlies' still there."

This now raised the potential level of complexity. The squadron wondered if there were additional non-combatant civilians still in the building.

With this concern in their minds, Sergeant St-George and his team secured the entry point and north staircase. He quickly realized that the south stairs also allowed access to the basement, so he was forced to "lock them down as well, eating up the limited, valuable manpower before the clearance actually began."

Sergeant Charron and his assault detachment then proceeded to clear the basement. The shopping complex was the nightmare the CANSOF operators dreaded it would be. There were gaps in the floor that allowed one to see into the basement, or, conversely, see up. The PRC-K and mentors began the clearance of the basement, using a clockwise, zig-zag methodology.[25] It was huge, with many locked doors. It took considerable time and effort. As the mission was to find the insurgents, the search was not overly detailed. Doors locked from the outside were left for a later, follow-on search. Nonetheless, it was far from simple. The large, dark, garbage-strewn basement was also cluttered with a large number of big bags of powder and various boxes.

When the basement was finally cleared, Sergeant St-George leap-frogged his assault detachment through that of Sergeant Charron and cleared the first floor. Once again, there was no contact. Sergeant Charron's detachment now moved to the second floor. They quickly found an individual and took him under control. However, he was slowing down the search, so Charron passed him to Sergeant St-George's team to escort him down to the "persons under control" (PUC) holding area.[26] During the remainder of the sweep, they found an additional four people, one of them wounded. As there was no way at that point to determine their status (i.e., combatant or non-combatant), they too were taken into custody and temporarily "controlled" by the PRC-K. However, the necessity of manning a PUC guard detail, as well as the requirement to post sentries on all the stairwells, ate into the number of troops St-George had available for clearance operations. As a result, Charron's assault detachment pushed through and carried on to clear the third and final floor.

By the time the assault force reached the third floor, the mission seemed to be anticlimactic. Complacency began to set in with the PRC-K. Despite the fact that Sergeant Charron warned his Afghan PRC-K troops "to keep their eyes open," since any remaining insurgents had to be on the third floor, the Afghans began to simply trail their weapons, and their attention to the task became lackadaisical. It became increasingly difficult for the mentors to focus their Afghan partners.

The final level appeared to be just more of the same. The third floor, similar to the others had a bank of shops, one running into the next, along the exterior wall. Some doors were locked, others were not. In the centre was a large atrium, which appeared to simply house another solid block of shops. Cut through each level were empty columns that ran from open skylights in the roof to the first floor. Connecting everything was a corridor or walkway that ran like a race track around the entire floor, connecting the staircases and inner atrium to the bank of shops on the exterior wall.

As Sergeant Wayne Cook ran up the staircase to join his detachment commander on the third floor, he emerged on the landing just in time to meet some of the PRC-K personnel who had just begun sweeping the upper floor. Sergeant Charron, who was leading the PRC-K through the clearance of the shopping mall building, also appeared. Then, without warning, shots that sounded like miniature explosions in the confined space, rang out. Immediately, the mentors and some of the PRC-K members returned fire, turning the narrow walkway into a virtual shooting gallery. Shots thudded into beams and supports and splintered the thin walls. One Afghan was shot in the hand through his pistol grip. He was left with a finger dangling, held only by tissue.

Charron now pulled everyone back so they could assess the situation. It appeared that a number of insurgents were barricaded in a series of shops at the corner of the atrium. With night setting in, it was difficult to see the exact location of the shooters, or, in fact the layout of the actual block of shops. What did appear evident was that they had selected their barricaded position very carefully. The storefront they were holed up in was encased in a series of iron bars with glass, which not only made it difficult to approach without actually being seen but also made it nearly impossible to determine where the door was actually located. Moreover, the metal grill exterior made it difficult to enter, since it would require an explosive breach or a power saw. But most important, the shooters had a dominating position of fire. From their den, they could sweep the walkway with a deadly fire that would make approaching from any direction a virtual death-wish.

Charron posted security on the barricaded shooters and ensured the wounded PRC-K member was moved to the casualty collection point at the entrance of the building. After discussing the situation with the OC, he then attempted to manoeuvre around the third floor from the opposite direction, in an attempt to better define and engage the threat.[27] The snipers had been cleared to fire into the shooter's den if they detected movement.

Charron now looked for an alternate approach. As they skirted some shops, they came across a number of wounded fighting-age males (FAM) in adjacent shops. They were evacuated to the CCP. Having verified the ground, Charron's group was now in a position to attempt a second assault. This time he decided to try an approach from the opposite direction. He told his interpreter to stay close behind him so that he could pass instruction to his PRC-K assault force. A major concern was the fact that the PRC-K preferred not to use night vision goggles, had no lasers, and relied on flashlights. Not surprisingly, as the assault force stepped off, the crunching glass and bobbing flashlights warned off the insurgents, who reacted violently and unleashed a torrent of fire.

Sergeant Charron went to turn back and fell over the interpreter who was literally directly behind him. Charron fell to the ground. As he crawled back to cover, the concrete wall directly above him was shot up by machine gun fire, spraying him with shards of metal and concrete. Some bullets actually passed through his uniform.[28] The close combat quarters and heavy enemy fire now caused the Afghan PRC-K members to scatter in panic.

All of this made clearer to Charron how well-chosen the barricaded position was. It commanded a dominating position of observation and fire that swept with all approaches with deadly fire. The nature of the building was such that it did not allow easy access to the barricaded shooter's den. Moreover, it funnelled anyone attempting to assault the position into a deadly killing zone.

The second attempt had failed. Captain Morrison revealed the complexity he had to deal with. "It was not just the enemy," he explained.

> We had to spend time confirming where the Afghan PRC-K members were. Some went to the stairway and others to the entry point. We had to send guys looking for them to confirm whether there were any wounded or missing. We also had to

get flashlights for them since they didn't like using their night vision goggles (NVGs). As a result, we lost a lot of time.

In the end, Sergeant Charron managed to reassemble a force and imbue them with a will to fight. He then led yet a third attempt against the insurgents.[29] The detachment commander now planned to hug the wall of stores and attempt a stealthy approach to the target area. Charron fired two 40 mm rounds from a stand-alone M203 into the insurgent's position. He then led his assault team forward. Once again, their movement was given away by the sound as they crunched through the glass and debris, and the moment the PRC-K troops turned on their flashlights, the insurgents opened up a deluge of fire. The Afghans panicked and immediately scattered. Very quickly the CSOR mentors found themselves caught in a vicious crossfire.

During the latest attempt, one Afghan soldier was wounded in the eye by shrapnel. He was evacuated to the CCP. Time was lost as the mentors accounted for all their PRC-K charges, many of whom simply decided they were done for the day.

Charron realized there was no way they could stack-up by the door because of the layout of the objective. After discussing the next approach with the OC, they decided on an "old-school" assault using covering fire as they moved down along the frontage of the shops. Sergeant Todd Wallace recalled, "It was surreal going up and down the stairs, hearing shots and grenades going off, hoping it was not one of our guys who [was] hit."

As they were discussing the next assault, Sergeant Pascal Collette, positioned in the VDO, informed the OC that they had eyes on and could use the .50 heavy machine gun (HMG) to pound the shooters' den. Collette then used his laser to paint the target. The snipers then "walked" him directly onto the insurgents' barricaded location. The air quickly vibrated with the staccato of the "boom, boom, boom" as the HMG pounded the insurgent lair. However, it would later be determined that the angle from the VDO to the target was too great and the rounds impacted high in the actual shop occupied by the insurgents. Fatefully, however, the tracer rounds ignited a fire in an adjacent shop that quickly grew in intensity and created a witch's brew of black, toxic smoke.

Captain Morrison ordered the VDO to cease fire and then, in coordination with his snipers in the adjacent building, he laid down covering fire for the fourth assault as Charron and his team began to move down the atrium, clearing shops on the way to their target. With thick, black smoke billowing along the ceiling like angry clouds rolling in warning of an impending storm, the assault group inched forward, posting grenades into each room as they slowly moved down toward the objective. Repeatedly, Charron was forced to step into the open to lead and mentor his Afghan charges, as well as his own men. Although this meant exposing himself to the deadly enemy fire, he felt compelled to take the risk to spur the PRC-K members into action.

His continued bravery impressed Captain Morrison. "Sergeant Charron never hesitated to lead the assault against insurgents and exposed himself to intense close-range fire each time," lauded the OC, "He showed incredible skill in his ability to motivate his wavering Afghan force for each assault."

Sergeant Cook, the detachment second-in-command (2IC) commented, "I witnessed Sergeant Charron lead the assaults, placing himself under large amounts of small-arms fire while maintaining coherent, concise control and leadership with our Afghan partner force."

Yet another detachment member, Corporal Darryl Adams, stated, "After many attempts on the assault of the barricaded insurgents, Sergeant Charron would re-motivate and reassure the PRC, keeping them calm." His courageous action and continual verbal communications kept his PRC personnel engaged.

Progress was slow, but the assault force made headway. Charron detonated two distraction devices (DD) to signal the firebases to stop their covering fire. As they prepared to close with the objective, one of Charron's biggest concerns was that the gunmen would likely be rigged with explosives and would blow themselves up once the assault force was close. Despite his trepidation, he pushed forward. However, as they neared the den, one of the Afghan police continued on past the safe area and into the actual target frontage. The insurgents came to life once again and showered the hallway with lead, hitting the unfortunate PRC-K member in the throat.

It was 2305 hours, and the building clearance had to this point taken four and one half hours. The majority of the PRC-K members now attempted to break contact on their own; however, Corporal Spike Smith, who was positioned at the back of the assault group, held them in place. Meanwhile, Charron and an Afghan crawled out to rescue their wounded colleague. They crawled as far as possible under a stream of gunfire. Stretching out their hands, they were able to lock onto the wounded policeman and drag him back to cover. "CSOR pulled a wounded Afghan out of line of fire," recounted the SOTF 58 commander, "that built credibility — shoulder to shoulder — the relationship was solid after that."

Charron realized the wound was bad. Corporal Smith, the detachment's tactical care provider, who had himself to this point constantly put himself in danger to mentor, encourage, and lead PRC-K personnel, now quickly came to the aid of the seriously wounded policeman.[30] He ignored the hail of gunfire perforating the walls all around him and provided immediate medical care, which saved the life of his Afghan colleague. He then assisted in the evacuation of the wounded individual to the CCP.

Captain Morrison revealed that "other PRC were visibly shaken by the wound and the wounded PRC member was initially noncompliant with treatment."

In the CCP, Sergeant Sandy Lewis, assisted by Master Corporal Jeremy Bing, worked hard at controlling the bleeding and stabilizing the patient. Sergeant Lewis recalled, "The patient became combative, his face and lips turned white and his eyes began to bulge." The patient could not breathe. Sergeant Lewis now performed a battlefield tracheotomy under very dire conditions. They then called for an immediate CASEVAC. Amazingly, all the wounded during the operation were saved.[31]

The process had been draining. Sergeant Taylor explained, "We tried to ensure they did their drills, but it was a nightmarish situation."

Sergeant St-George noted it was extremely chaotic. "We were constantly trying to figure out where our people were," he explained, "because we were concerned someone could be hurt, lying unknown somewhere." Almost blind to the myriad dangers in the smouldering death trap, the CSOR mentors focused on the mission and their Afghan charges.

COLONEL BERND HORN

Undeterred by fatigue, or the extended close combat, and with the fire in the adjacent room raging out of control, the heat searing anything and anyone in the area, Charron now led a fifth attack. This time he placed himself and two mentors at the very front of the assault. Using a firebase for covering fire and hugging the wall of shops, they once again moved forward. Once they reached the target area, Sergeant St-George posted a grenade and Corporal Smith tossed in a DD. As the PRC-K detachment approached, however, incredibly, the insurgents sprang to life again and opened fire. Chaos ensued. The PRC-K police broke and withdrew to safety, jeopardizing the lives of the mentors who were once again caught in the middle of hail of fire.

Charron conceded, "I really thought we would make entry [that] time, but when I looked around it was only Canadians up there."

To this point, it had been a constantly increasing mix of fatigue and stress with a constant rotation of assault, regrouping, new plan, and back into the fray. While the fifth attempt had again ended in failure, Charron was able to conclude that it was impossible to make entry from the front, due to the metal bars and, more important, due to the fact that in order to stack by the door the detachment would have to expose themselves a mere metre or two from the shooters.[32] The CANSOF command chief warrant officer commented, "The substantial enemy lanes of fire turned the normal high risk of the assault into just plain dangerous; it wasn't even calculated risk anymore."

The risk, however, was shared by all. Throughout the ordeal, Sergeant Taylor held a tenuous position at the northern stairwell for an extended period of time within the arcs of insurgent fire. However, Taylor, remaining calm and committed, ignored the enemy fusillade and supported each assault with well-aimed covering fire and target definition. As one point, a large fire, spewing a witch's brew of toxic smoke and incredible heat ignited in a room a mere ten to fifteen metres from his position. Shortly after that, a large explosion rocked the building. Undeterred by the fire or the subsequent explosion, Taylor continued to provide covering fire and security for the assault element.

Captain Morrison described Taylor's actions, "Sergeant Taylor was unfazed by this detonation and continued to provide effective covering fire throughout." It was not until the OC pulled back all his assets to allow for a heavy ordnance strike on the stronghold that Sergeant Taylor was able to withdraw from his position.

Sergeant Giguard was in a similar position at the southern stairwell. With the PRC-K disappearing in large numbers, Giguard passed his Afghan partners off to assist with assaults, leaving himself in a very tenuous position, one with virtually no support.

Following the latest attempt, fatigued by the extended period of combat, including their previous action at the governor's palace and now distracted by the casualties they had taken, the PRC-K became increasingly unreliable and difficult to mobilize. Many suffered from dehydration, as they had a tendency not to bring water on operations. Many simply returned to the CCP, or VDO, and completely shut down and went to sleep.

"The PRC-K was extremely fatigued," noted the SOTF 58 commander. "They had been fighting since early afternoon. Our guys got frustrated because the Afghans ran out of steam. The mentors were no longer coordinating and coaching the Afghans — they were leading them and in some cases dragging them forward." For example, for the fifth assault, the mentors were able to assemble only six PRC-K members to participate. After that effort, Sergeant Charron revealed, "it was impossible to get any PRC to assist."

With the fire raging out of control and the PRC-K played out, Captain Morrison now called a pause in the action and gathered his detachment commanders to discuss alternate solutions. He was "shocked at how much ammunition we put into the room and they were still firing back." They would later discover that the insurgents had planned and staged the attack carefully, pre-positioning weapons, explosives, and equipment. In addition, they had created "mouse holes" between some of the walls, which allowed them to retreat deeper into the atrium, hiding behind protective barriers and only coming out once the assault force came close to their barred stronghold. In any case, the OC kept the insurgents under observation and pulled back to reconsider options. He called back to FOB Graceland for a resupply, specifically ammunition, demolitions, water, and rockets. Based on the current state of the PRC-K, he also requested reinforcements, specifically the Black Team, which referred to the SOTF 58 integral JTF 2 detachment.

The Black Team assault element leader was Conrad Pascal. In order to deploy his team, he had to borrow vehicles from a neighbouring group of Americans, since there were no military pattern armoured/protected vehicles left in FOB Graceland. They arrived at approximately midnight. After a briefing, Pascoe, Morrison, and their detachment commanders conducted another leader's recce to reassess the situation. Then, suddenly, at 0055 hours, the darkness was transformed into day as a huge orange fireball erupted, followed almost immediately by a huge reverberating boom as a VBIED, assessed as being on a timer, detonated inside the cordon, almost directly beneath the position being used by the snipers in the adjacent building.

The enormous explosion rocked both buildings and knocked down a large number of individuals. "All of a sudden it was loud and orange," recalled WO Gervais, "I remember an orange flash and then it was all black and I was on the ground and I could hear someone saying, 'stay down, stay down.'" Gervais had been slammed into the wall by the explosion. For the next thirty minutes he remained dizzy and groggy.

He was not the only one to suffer injury. In the adjacent building, a wall partially collapsed on the JTAC. The SOTF commander observed, "The Taliban picked the site carefully. It showed the amount of preparation [they had done]. They had pre-positioned [the] vehicle IED where they expected first responders to be." In fact, the VIED was in the proximity of the originally planned VDO.

With the stubborn defence ongoing, RC(S) headquarters had authorized AH 64 attack helicopter gun runs on the target. However, Morrison had resisted, for fear of excessive collateral damage. But, the idea of utilizing overwhelming precision firepower to hit the insurgent stronghold had taken root with the Canadians. At 0207 hours, with the fire dying down, Morrison now took another approach. Using an external firebase, he coordinated a volley fire of 66mm M72 rocket launchers in a precision strike against the barricade. An M48 grenade launcher was used to punch a hole in the wall, which provided a direct line of fire into the insurgent barricade. It allowed the more effective use of 7.62mm and .50 calibre fire as well.

The tactic had great effect and hit the enemy den. However, it ignited yet another fire. Thick, black, toxic smoke soon billowed from the doomed shopping mall as building materials and plastics melted in the intense heat. Stockpiled insurgent ammunition stocks began to cook off and visibility within the building became extremely limited. Sergeant St-George reasoned, "Unleash Hell on that room and let it burn until morning."

The American BSO, Phoenix 6, was kept apprised throughout. He was vocally thankful that they did not have to do the task. WO Gervais remembered, "The American colonel came over and said, 'We can hear it; we know what's going on and we appreciate it.'"

Between 0215 and 0230, the snipers believed that they saw movement inside the barricaded stronghold and they unleashed a second volley into the insurgent position. At 0300, the fire was still burning.

The danger and stress to this point had been unending for the OC, who by that point had been under the gun for over eight hours. One report noted, "Captain Morrison was instrumental in providing calm and professional leadership to motivate both his own personnel and the PRC-K in attempting to clear the barricaded shooters." Throughout, Major Morrison supervised the escalation of engagements in an attempt to neutralize the insurgents. His resources, however, were limited, as he had only a few SOTF 58 and PRC-K members to conduct the assault since others were tied down securing vital points of the building that had been cleared.

Moreover, Morrison himself was immersed in the close fight. Repeatedly, he exposed himself to enemy fire to provide covering fire to manoeuvring forces and to provide target indication in the confined cordite-filled hallway using white light. Sergeant Taylor noted, "As I was preparing 40mm grenade rounds, he provided me with the white light needed to place the munitions into the correct room, thereby seriously divulging his position to the insurgents."

Sergeant Charron lauded, "I witnessed Captain Morrison exposing himself to small-arms fire on many occasions to provide suppressing fire support, enabling my section to close in with the enemy. Even with the intense firefight, IEDs exploding , the proximity of the enemy, and the multiple casualties, Captain Morrison demonstrated on many occasions his leadership and warrior skills by making quick, rational, and aggressive decisions while always adapting quickly to the ever-changing situation."

The brief respite was welcomed. By 0343 hours, the fire was almost out and David, guided by advice from the SOTF 58 commander decided to reassess the situation. Extreme fatigue within the small team now started to show itself. Members of the PRC-K had been fighting since early afternoon in oppressive heat. The mentors, had also been on stand-by since early afternoon, had not eaten since that time as they had been caught up in deploying the PRC-K and then preparing themselves. Moreover, they had been immersed in extremely stressful circumstances, leading and supervising their partner force, who increasingly began to pull out of the fight, thereby placing not only the burden of leadership and command on the mentors but also the actual fighting. Added to this, the extreme heat, exacerbated by raging fires, darkness, an enveloping smoke, and tenacious insurgents all fuelled an extremely dangerous situation. Not surprisingly, Captain Morrison now decided to contain the situation and to allow for some rest and regrouping.

Throughout, the personnel at FOB Graceland remained on heightened alert status. Everyone left at the camp, from intelligence operators, cooks, to material technicians, was on a rotation to take positions on the walls to augment the guard force manning the observation towers. Quite simply, the situation in the city still remained tenuous.

As light began to sneak across the Afghan horizon, the ground force commander was ready to renew the operation. At 0515 hours, Morrison issued orders for the final clearance. Once again, the assault force began from the basement. Reinforced with the Black Team, who had not yet been engaged in direct clearance operations, Morrison designated them to lead the PRC-K in the renewed assault. Once again, they commenced at the basement and quickly swept up through the first and second floors, to ensure the insurgents had not relocated during the night.

Then, they emerged on the third floor and pushed through the labyrinth of destroyed shops. This time there was no resistance. In the enemy position they found the badly charred remains of two dead insurgents, along with several weapons, ammunition, and IED components. They also discovered that the insurgents had burrowed through the walls to connect several stores to their main position. This accounted for how the insurgents could have survived the barrage of fire. The mentors surmised that the shooters would retreat to the protection of the other rooms and only appear when they heard or saw the approach of another assault.

Amazingly, they also found an old man, who was wounded in the leg, covered by rugs in a room close by. How he had survived surprised everyone. In any case, the objective was secured at 0612 hours.

Captain Morrison then conducted a physical battle space hand-over (BSH) with Phoenix 6, at which time all fighting-age males who had been detained were handed-over from the PRC-K to the BSO. Final resolution was thus achieved at 0747 hours, May 8, 2011.

On completion of the BSH, the ground force redeployed to FOB Graceland, arriving without incident at 1000 hours. In the end, the results were two enemy killed in action; one enemy wounded; six FAMs detained and passed to the BSO; as well as four PRC wounded. Reviewing the mission, Captain Morrison acknowledged, "It boggles the mind how difficult it can be to deal with a few bad guys."[33]

SOTF 58 and their Afghan partners had earned a well-deserved rest. However, it was not in the cards. One of the other major attacks that was part of the Taliban Operation Badar was the Kandahar Hotel. The attack began at 1309 hours, May 7, 2011. The BSO and ANP cordoned the site and returned fire. For the next forty-one hours, the ANP and insurgents battled for control of the hotel, exchanging fire for protracted periods of time. At one point, the coalition forces brought U.S. SEALs and Afghan commandos, who used AH 64 attack helicopter 30 mm gun runs and other ground level strikes with heavy precision ordnance to subdue the enemy. However, they failed to reduce the insurgents inside, and at the end of May 8, the SEALs and their Afghan commando partner force left.

The ANSF, who were leading the assault on the building, were able to clear the first floor and portions of the second, but were unable to advance any further through the building. As a result, with the battle still ongoing on the morning of May 9, 2011, the ANP chain of command once again called on the PRC-K and its mentors to assist with the resolution of the problem.

With OP Response activated, the SOTF 58 commander issued a simple mission statement: "PRC-K partnered with SOTF 58 will conduct crisis response to assist BSO with clearance of insurgents at the Kandahar Hotel, in Sub-district Two." The news was not uplifting.

Sergeant Charron admitted, "It was stressful just thinking of doing that all over again."

Based on the previous day and the enormity of the new task, the SOTF commander decided, even though FOB Graceland was still on 100 percent stand-to, to send the mentors, both Green and Black teams, to accompany PRC-K. However, this time they would do so in a deliberate manner. First, they sent an advance party at 0500 hours, May 9, 2011, consisting of one PRC-K officer and twenty SOTF 58 personnel, in two HMMVW and three Low Visibility vehicles. The main body, consisting of forty-five PRC-K personnel, twenty-nine SOTF-58 members, and two canine units, in three HMMVW, five Low Visibility, and three PRC-K Ford Rangers were ready to depart on call.

On arrival, the PRC-K and mentor command element met with the KCoS and the Afghan Border Police commander, who were both on the scene. The SOTF 58 commander revealed, "It was very awkward for my subordinate commanders on the ground with so much Afghan brass present. When the PRC-K showed up, it created some shame with the other Afghans."

Nonetheless, the advance party began deliberate planning with the on-scene commander. At least the building was not as complex as the shopping mall the day prior.

As the PRC-K and the Green and Black Team commanders went to give orders to their men, the SOTF 58 snipers who had deployed and had the objective under surveillance noted movement and requested permission to engage. The ground force commander then confirmed with the on-site commander the location of friendly troops only to find out that unbeknownst to them, Afghan Border troops had gone in to clear the rest of the Kandahar Hotel. Apparently, spurred on by the arrival of the PRC-K, the ANSF units originally on scene were able to gain enough momentum to complete the clearance of the building. The SOTF 58 personnel felt that either the arrival of the PRC-K had shamed the other Afghans into action, or the Afghan commanders wanted to ensure they and their organizations received the glory for resolving the event. In any case, the PRC-K was dismissed from duty without any involvement in the incident and returned to FOB Graceland at 0710 hours, May 9, 2011, without incident.

With the resolution of the Kandahar Hotel attack, the city could now begin the cleaning-up process. Like a tornado, the Taliban had exploded onto the city in a swirl of death and destruction. Ahmed Wali Karzai, the head of Kandahar's provincial council, stated, "Everyone know that these types of attacks, with suicide bombers and a few people hiding and shooting, are difficult to stop and can happen anywhere." He insisted, "The Taliban are desperate. They cannot do anything else but try to create news."[34]

However, the impact had been significant. The Taliban had once again paralyzed and traumatized the city's population. In the end, NATO spokesman Major-General James Laster described the Kandahar raid as a "spring offensive spectacular attack which was thwarted."[35] In its wake, a minimum of eighteen fighters, many of them suicide bombers, were killed and four insurgents were captured. Another forty people were wounded, including fourteen ANP policemen.[36]

Emerging from the chaos and crisis, however, was the great efforts of the PRC-K and SOTF 58. CANSOF made a conscious decision to ensure that the accolades for the hard-won fight went to the PRC-K. In turn, the Afghan partner force was duly recognized by both their own government and ISAF. In fact, General David Petraeus, the ISAF commander at the time, noted on May 10, 2011, "It is too bad they [Afghans] don't have the equivalent of the Presidential Unit Citation for Afghan Police units because that PRC down there [Kandahar] probably deserves it."[37] The PRC-K was later awarded a Medal of Recognition by the National Government of the Islamic Republic of Afghanistan.

GLOSSARY OF ABBREVIATIONS

AAF	anti-Afghan forces
ACM	anti-coalition militia
AGL	above ground level
ALO	air liaison officer
ANA	Afghan National Army
ANP	Afghan National Police
ANSF	Afghan National Security Forces
AO	area of operations
AQ	al-Qaeda
ARF	air reaction force
ATO	Afghan theatre of operations
ATV	all terrain vehicle
BG	battle group
BGS	brigadier-general (staff)
BHO	battle handover
BSO	battle space owner
BSP	basic security plan

C2	command and control
CAF	Canadian Armed Forces
CANSOF	Canadian Special Operations Forces
CANSOFCOM	Canadian Special Operations Forces Command
CAS	close air support
CASEVAC	casualty evacuation
CCP	casualty collection point
Cdn AB Regt	Canadian Airborne Regiment
Cdn SAS Coy	Canadian Special Air Service Company
CDS	Chief of the Defence Staff
CENTCOM	[U.S.] Central Command
CFOO	Canadian Forces organizational order
CGS	Chief of the General Staff
CJATC	Canadian Joint Air Training Centre
CJSOTF-A	Combined Joint Special Operations Task Force — Afghanistan
CJTF 76	Combined Joint Task Force 76
CMO	civil military operations
CO	commanding officer
COHQ	combined operations headquarters
COI	compound of interest
CONOP	concept of operations
CoP	chief of police
CP	counter proliferation
CPAT	contingency planning assistance team
CPP	close protection party
CQB	close quarter battle
C/S	call sign
CSOR	Canadian Special Operations Regiment
CT	counterterrorism
CTF	combined task force
DA	direct action
DD	distraction device
DDMA	defence, diplomacy, and military assistance

DND	Department of National Defence
ERT	emergency response team
ETT	embedded training team
EWS	early warning system
FAM	fighting-age male
FID	foreign internal defence
FMC	Force Mobile Command
FOB	forward operating base
FOC	full operating capability
Frag O	fragmentary orders
FSSF	First Special Service Force
GFC	ground force commander
GFWO	ground force warrant officer
GoA	Government of Afghanistan
GPMG	general purpose machine gun
HALO	high altitude low opening
HARP	Hostage and Rescue Program
HLZ	helicopter landing zone
HMG	heavy machine gun
HMMVW	high mobility multipurpose vehicle wheeled
HQ	headquarters
HR	hostage rescue
HUMINT	human intelligence
HVT	high value tasks
IED	improvised explosive device
IFF	identification friend or foe
IOC	initial operating capability
ISAF	International Security Assistance Force
ISR	intelligence, surveillance, reconnaissance

JAS	Joint Air School
JDAM	joint direct attack munitions
JLT-A	Joint Liaison Team — Afghanistan
JTAC	joint terminal air controller
JTF 2	Joint Task Force 2
JSOA	joint special operations area
KAF	Kandahar Airfield
KCoS	Kandahar chief of security
LAV III	light armoured vehicle III
LUP	laying-up position
LZ	landing zone
MANPADS	man portable air defence system
MCT	maritime counterterrorism
MEDEVAC	medical evacuation
MK	Mark
MND	minister of national defence
MRAP	mine-resistant, ambush-protected
MSF	Mobile Striking Force
MVT	medium value target
NAI	named area of interest
NAVSOF	Navy SOF
NCO	non-commissioned officers
NDHQ	National Defence Headquarters
NDS	National Directorate of Security
NEO	non-combatant evacuation operation
NGO	non-governmental organization
NTM	notice to move
NVG	night vision goggles
ODA	Operational Detachment Alpha
OEF	Operation Enduring Freedom

OGD	other governmental department
OP	observation post or operation (dependent on context)
PCoP	provincial chief of police
PPCLI	Princess Patricia's Canadian Light Infantry
PRC-K	Provincial Response Company — Kandahar
PSD	personal security detachment
QRF	quick reaction force
R22R	Royal 22nd Regiment
RAF	Royal Air Force
RCAF	Royal Canadian Air Force
RCN	Royal Canadian Navy
RCR	Royal Canadian Regiment
RC(S)	Regional Command — South
Recce	reconnaissance
RM	Royal Marines
RN	Royal Navy
ROC	review of concept
ROE	rules of engagement
RPG	rocket-propelled grenade
RRB	radio rebroadcast
RV	rendezvous
SAB	student assessment board
SAS	Special Air Service
SEAL	Sea, Land, Air
SERT	Special Emergency Response Team
SF	special forces
SITREP	situation report
SOAC	special operations assaulter course
SOE	Special Operations Executive
SOF	special operations forces
SOIC	Special Operations Intelligence Centre

SOTF	special operations task force
SR	strategic reconnaissance
SRT	special response team
SSE	sensitive site exploitation
SSF	special service force
STS	special training school
SUV	suburban utility vehicle
TF	task force
TIC	troops in contact
TIP	target intelligence package
TOC	tactical operations centre
TTPs	tactics, techniques, and procedures
TU	tactical unit
UAV	unmanned aerial vehicle
US	United States
VCP	vehicle control point
VDO	vehicle drop off [point]
VIED	vehicle improvised explosive device
WO	warrant officer
WTC	World Trade Center
WWII	World War II
1 Cdn Para Bn	1st Canadian Parachute Battalion
2 Cdn Para Bn	2nd Canadian Parachute Battalion
9/11	September 11, 2001

NOTES

Introduction

1   Tom Clancy, *Special Forces* (New York: Berkley, 2001), 3.

2.   Canada, *Canadian Special Operations Forces Command: An Overview* (Ottawa: DND, 2008), 7.

3.   Canada, CANSOFCOM Capstone Concept for Special Operations 2009 (Ottawa: DND, 2009), 4.

4.   The original author of the SOF Truths was Colonel John M. Collins. He noted the "fifth" SOF Truth had been completely ignored by the international SOF community for a long time. It was just recently resurrected by the SOF community.

5.   Canada, CANSOFCOM Capstone Concept for Special Operations, 2009, 6–7.

6.   Ibid., 8–10.

Chapter 1

1.   This chapter is a variation of other works by the author, specifically Bernd Horn, "The Canadian SOF Legacy," in *Special Operations Forces: A National Capability*, ed., Emily Spencer (Kingston, ON: CDA Press, 2011); and Bernd Horn, *We Will Find a Way: Understanding Canadian Special Operations Forces* (Tampa, FL: Joint Special Operations University, 2012).

2.　　See Bernd Horn, "La Petite Guerre: A Strategy of Survival," in *The Canadian Way of War. Serving the National Interest*, ed., Bernd Horn (Toronto: Dundurn, 2006), 21–56; Bernd Horn, "Marin and Langy — Master Practitioners of *la petite guerre*," in *Loyal Service: Perspectives of French-Canadian Military Leaders*, eds., Bernd Horn and Roch Legault (Toronto: Dundurn, 2007), 53–86; Bernd Horn, "Only for the Strong of Heart: Ranging and the Practice of La Petite Guerre During the Struggle for North America," in *Show No Fear: Daring Actions in Canadian Military History*, ed., Bernd Horn (Toronto: Dundurn, 2008), 17–64; and Bernd Horn, "Terror on the Frontier: The Role of the Indians in the Struggle for North America," in *Forging a Nation: Perspectives on the Canadian Military Experience*, ed. Bernd Horn (St. Catharines, ON: Vanwell, 2002), 43–64.

3.　　With a population of only sixty thousand, New France faced the danger of being engulfed by its larger neighbour to the south, namely the English colonies, which numbered approximately 1.5 million. The scale of the threat was enormous. During the French and Indian War, the English colonies outnumbered New France in manpower by nearly twenty-five to one. George F. Stanley, *Canada's Soldiers. The Military History of an Unmilitary People* (Toronto: Macmillan Canada, 1960), 61; W.J. Eccles, "The French Forces in North America during the Seven Years' War," in *Dictionary of Canadian Biography* [henceforth *DCB*], vol. 3, 1741-1770 (Toronto: University of Toronto Press, 1974), xx; Robert Leckie, *A Few Acres of Snow — The Saga of the French and Indian Wars* (Toronto: John Wiley & Sons, 1999), 103; and A. Doughty, *The Siege of Quebec and the Battle of the Plains of Abraham* (Quebec: Dussault & Proulx, 1901), I: 158.

4.　　"Impartial Hand," *The Contest in America Between Great Britain and France with Its Consequences and Importance* (London: Strand, 1757), 128. The writer also notes that the Indians and Canadians who travelled without baggage, supporting themselves with stores and magazines and who maintained themselves in the woods "[did] more execution … than four or five time their number of our men."; Ibid., 138. See also W.J. Eccles, *The French in North America 1500–1783* (Markham, ON: Fitzhenry & Whiteside, 1998), 208; Edward P. Hamilton, ed., *Adventures in the Wilderness. The American Journals of Louis Antoine de Bougainville, 1756–1760* (Norman, OK: University of Oklahoma Press, 1990), 333; and M. Pouchot, *Memoirs on the Late War in North America between France and England* (Yverdon, 1781; reprinted, Youngstown, NY: Old Fort Niagara Association, 1994), 78.

5.　　Walter O'Meara, *Guns at the Forks* (Pittsburgh: University of Pittsburgh Press, 1965), 85. See also Stephen Brumwell, *Redcoats. British Soldiers and War in the Americas, 1755–63* (Cambridge: University of Cambridge, 2002);

and Ian K. Steele, *Guerillas and Grenadiers* (Toronto: Ryerson Press, 1969).

6. "Memoir on the Defense of the Fort of Carillon," *The Bulletin of the Fort Ticonderoga Museum* 13, no. 3 (1972): 200–01; Ian K. Steele, *Betrayals. Fort William Henry & the Massacre* (New York: Oxford University Press, 1990), 96; and Fred Anderson, *Crucible of War* (New York: Vintage Books, 2001), 187.

7. The deep strikes into English territory during the Seven Years' War consistently disrupted British campaign plans and kept them on the defensive from the summer of 1755 until 1758. Moreover, they ravaged frontier settlements, economies, and public morale. The raids terrorized the frontier and tied down large numbers of troops. The plight of the English colonists could not be ignored by their political leaders. The incursions into Virginia alone caused the governor there to raise ten militia companies, a total of one thousand men, for internal defence. Similarly, Pennsylvania raised 1,500 provincial troops and built a string of forts extending from New Jersey to Maryland in an attempt to try and impede the raiders. See General William Shirley, letter to Major-General James Abercromby, June 27, 1756, National Archives (NA), War Office (WO) 1/4, Correspondence, 1755–1763. See also Robert C. Alberts, *The Most Extraordinary Adventures of Major Robert Stobo* (Boston: Houghton Mifflin, 1965), 152; Anderson, 637; Leckie, 101; General William Shirley (New York), letter to Principal Secretary of War," December 20, 1755, PRO, WO 1/4, Correspondence, 1755–1763; H.R. Casgrain, ed., *Lettres du Chevalier De Lévis concernant La Guerre du Canada 1756–1760* (Montreal: C.O. Beauchemin & Fils, 1889), 75; Steele, *Guerillas and Grenadiers,* 24; Le Comte Gabriel de Maurès de Malartic, *Journal des Campagnes au Canada de 1755 à 1760* (Paris: Librairie Plon, 1902), 52–53, 232; and O'Meara, 161.

8. *DCB,* 3:260.

9. Ibid., 261.

10. *DCB,* vol. 4, 1771–1800, 308.

11. Rogers was a smuggler prior to the war. On Robert Rogers and his rangers the definitive works are Burt G. Loescher, *The History of Rogers Rangers, Volume 1 — The Beginnings, January 1755–April 6, 1758* (Bowie, ML: Heritage Books, (1946); reprint, 2001); and Loescher, *Genesis Rogers Rangers. Volume 2 — The First Green Berets:The Corps & the Revivals, April 6, 1758–December, 24, 1783* (San Mateo, CA, 1969; reprint, Bowie, ML: Heritage Books, 2000). *See also,* John R. Cuneo, *Robert Rogers of the Rangers* (New York: Oxford University Press, 1959); *DCB,* 4: 679–82; Timothy J. Todish, *The Annotated and Illustrated Journals of Major Robert Rogers* (Fleischmanns, NY: Purple Mountain Press, 2002); and *Warfare*

on the Colonial American Frontier: The Journals of Major Robert Rogers [*Journals of Major Robert Rogers*] *& An Historical Account of the Expedition Against the Ohio Indians in the year 1764, Under the Command of Henry Bouquet, Esq.* (1769; reprint, Bargersville, IN: Dreslar Publishing, 2001).

12. Cuneo, 33.

13. See *Rogers's Journal*, 13–14; Loescher, 1: 63–64, 87; Brumwell, 213; and Cuneo, 32–33.

14. Quoted in René Chartrand, *Canadian Military Heritage, vol. 2, 1000–1754* (Montreal: Art Global, 1993), 49; and Thomas Gage, letter to General Amherst, Albany, February 18, 1759. NA, WO 34/46A, Amherst Papers.

15. See *DCB*, 4: 308; and Chartrand, *Canadian Military Heritage*, 2: 49.

16. Ironically, despite the apparent utility and arguable success of rangers, as well as the constant calls for their employment, they never became fully accepted by their professional counterparts. During the war, they were never taken on to the official strength of the British Army. Moreover, their lax discipline, dishevelled appearance, unruly behaviour, as well as their manner of war-making was simply unacceptable to most British officers. "I am afraid," lamented Lord Loudoun, "[that] I shall be blamed for the ranging companies." Quoted in Loescher, 1: 164.

17. The last of the British troops were evacuated from the beaches of Dunkirk on June 2, 1940. Fifty-three thousand French troops were evacuated June 3–4. The British Admiralty estimated that approximately 338,226 men were evacuated between May 26 and June 3. The British left behind 2,000 guns, 60,000 trucks, 76,000 tons of ammunition and 600,000 tons of fuel and supplies: Cesare Salmaggi and Alfredo Pallavisini, *2194 Days of War: An Illustrated Chronology of the Second World War* (New York: Gallery Books, 1988); and I.C.R. Dear, ed., *The Oxford Companion to World War II* (Oxford: Oxford University Press, 1995), 312–13. Another account gives the losses as 475 tanks, 38,000 vehicles, 12,000 motorcycles, 8,000 telephones, 1,855 wireless sets, 7,000 tonnes of ammunition, 90,000 rifles, 1,000 heavy guns, 2,000 tractors, 8,000 Bren guns, and 400 anti-tank guns. Yet another source gives the losses as: stores and equipment for 500,000 men, about 100 tanks, 2,000 other vehicles, 600 guns, and large stocks of ammunition: A.J. Barker, *Dunkirk: The Great Escape* (London: J.M. Dent & Sons, 1977), 224. A major problem with determining numbers is the actual categorization of equipments. Whatever the exact number of losses, on June 6 the War Cabinet was informed that there were fewer than 600,000 rifles and only 12,000 Bren guns in the whole of the United Kingdom: John Parker, *Commandos. The Inside Story of Britain's Most Elite Fighting Force* (London: Headline, 2000), 15.

18. Cecil Aspinall-Oglander, *Roger Keyes. Being the Biography of Admiral of the Fleet Lord Keyes of Zeebrugge and Dover* (London: Hogarth Press, 1951), 380.
19. Ibid., 380.
20. Quoted in John Terraine, *The Life and Times of Lord Mountbatten* (London: Arrow Books, 1980), 83.
21. Hilary St. George Saunders, *The Green Beret. The Story of the Commandos* (London: Michael Joseph, 1956), 118.
22. Winston S. Churchill, *The Second World War. Their Finest Hour* (Boston: Houghton Mifflin, 1949), 246–47. See also Colonel J.W. Hackett, "The Employment of Special Forces," *Royal United Services Institute (RUSI)* 97, no. 585 (February 1952): 28. Churchill later penned a note to President Franklin D. Roosevelt that revealed his mindset. "[The] essence of defence," he asserted, "is to attack the enemy upon us — leap at his throat and keep the grip until the life is out of him." Quoted in William Stevenson, *A Man Called Intrepid* (Guilford, CT: Lyons Press, 2000), 131.
23. William Mackenzie, *The Secret History of SOE* (London: St Ermin's Press, 2000), xvii. *See also* Colonel Bernd Horn, *A Very Ungentlemanly Way of War: The SOE and the Canadian Connection* (Toronto: Dundurn, 2016).
24. Ibid., 754. The SOE operated worldwide, with the exception of the Soviet Union. It consisted of two branches — one to provide facilities (i.e., money, clothing, forged papers, training, weapons, ciphers, and signals); the other to execute missions.
25. "Outline Plan of SO 2 Operations from September 1st, 1941 to October 1st 1942," Policy and Planning of SOE Activities in Denmark, ND. NA, HS2/79.
26. Denis Riggin, *SOE Syllabus. Lessons in Ungentlemanly Warfare, WWII* (London: Public Records Office, 2001), 1.
27. Ibid., 11. Once the United States was in the war, the second function (i.e., executing missions) became the SOE's most important one. Camp X and its staff assisted large numbers of Americans from the Office of Strategic Services (OSS) and the Office of War Information to set up their own schools and train their own staff. The OSS was created in June 1942. It functioned as the principal U.S. intelligence organization in all theatres for the remainder of World War II. It was the counterpart to the British intelligence service MI6 and the SOE. *See* Lynn-Philip Hodgson, *Inside Camp X* (Port Perry, ON: Blake Book Distribution, 2000).
28. Roy Maclaren, *Canadians Behind Enemy Lines, 1939–1945* (Vancouver: UBC Press, 2004), 150, 172. 199–200. A total of 3,226 personnel, including all services and civilian employees, were employed in the SOE by 1942. By April 30, 1944, the total strength had risen to 11,752. Mackenzie, 717–19.

29. Quoted in Peter Wilkinson and Joan Bright Astley, *Gubbins & SOE* (London: Leo Cooper, 1997), i. The SOE was disbanded in January 1946.

30. Lord Louis Mountbatten, *Combined Operations. The Official Story of the Commandos* (New York: Macmillan, 1943), 16; and Aspinall-Oglander, 381.

31. "Hand-out to Press Party Visiting the Commando Depot, Achnacarry, 9–12 January 1943," 2, War Diary, COC, NA, DEFE 2/5. Interestingly, commandos in training were shown the 1940 film *Northwest Passage*, with Spencer Tracy, about Major Robert Rogers and his rangers.

32. Brigadier T.B.L. Churchill, "The Value of Commandos," *RUSI* 65, no. 577 (February 1950): 85.

33. Charles Messenger, *The Commandos 1940-1946* (London: William Kimber, 1985), 411. For a detailed account of the British raiding policy and the creation of the commandos, see Bernd Horn, "Strength Born from Weakness: The Establishment of the Raiding Concept and the British Commandos," *Canadian Military Journal* 6, no. 3 (Autumn 2005): 59–68.

34. George Kerr, "Viking Force. Canada's Unknown Commandos," *Canadian Military History* 9, no. 4 (Autumn 2000): 28.

35. Ibid., 29.

36. In December 1940, the commandos were renamed special service units. However, by February 1941 these special service units were split up, and commandos, as independent units, emerged once again. This was a result of the decision to deploy a number of commandos to the Middle East. Nonetheless, the eleven existing commandos were grouped in a special service (SS) brigade.

    The SS brigade's primary mission remained that of carrying out raids. However, it was also given the secondary tasks of acting as an elite or shock assault brigade to seize and hold a bridgehead to cover a landing in force, as well as providing especially trained covering forces for any operation. "Organization and Training of British Commandos," *Intelligence Training Bulletin* No. 3, November 11, 1942, 2, file 145.3009 (D5), Organization and Instructions for the 1st Canadian Special Service Battalion, July 1944–December 1944, Department of Defence (DND), Directorate of History and Heritage (DHH).

37. Kerr, 30.

38. Ibid., 33.

39. The ill-fated Dieppe raid led to recriminations of callousness, incompetence, negligence, and security violations. The original raid, code-named Rutter, was cancelled on July 7, 1942, because of bad weather. Mountbatten later resurrected it, under questionable authority,

under the code name "Jubilee" on August 19. In total, 4,963 Canadians, 1,075 British, and 50 American Rangers took part. In short, a lack of adequate air support and naval gunfire (due to the absence of battleships), as well as the failure of the armour to gain lodgement, compounded by communication errors, the extreme narrowness in the approaches, lack of cover for the assaulting forces, and the strong German fortifications, led to an unmitigated disaster. The Canadians suffered 3,367 (killed, wounded, or captured) casualties of the 4,963 that participated. The British casualties amounted to 275. The Royal Navy lost one destroyer and 33 landing craft, and the RAF lost 106 aircraft. See Brian Loring Villa, *Mountbatten and the Dieppe Raid* (Don Mills, ON: Oxford University Press, 1994); Brigadier-General Denis Whitaker and Shelagh Whitaker, *Dieppe — Tragedy to Triumph* (Toronto: McGraw-Hill Ryerson, 1992); and Will Fowler, *The Commandos At Dieppe: Rehearsal for D-Day* (London: HarperCollins, 2002).

40. E.G. Finley, *RCN Beach Commando "W"* (Ottawa: Gilmour Reproductions, 1994), 1.

41. Ibid., 2. The beach was divided into three beach parties, each commanded by a beach master. Due to the arduous requirements of employment, special medical requirements (relative to those imposed on other RCN volunteers) were imposed on the volunteers. It was declared that the volunteers must be:

a) under 35 years of age;
b) mentally stable, with no family history of mental disease or disorder;
c) without any history of chronic illness (e.g., bronchitis, asthma, TB, rheumatism, arthritis, heart disease, ear diseases);
d) able to pass standard tests for visual acuity and hearing; and
e) free from VD.

Ibid., 10.

42. Ibid., viii–5.

43. The conceptual model for selection was such that one journalist quipped, "You've practically got to be Superman's 2IC in order to get in." "Canada's Jumping Jacks!" *Khaki. The Army Bulletin* 1, no. 22 (September 29, 1943): 1. For a detailed examination of 1 Cdn Para Bn, see Bernd Horn and Michel Wyczynski, *Canadian Airborne Forces since 1942* (London: Osprey, 2006); Bernd Horn and Michel Wycyznski, *Paras Versus the Reich. Canada's Paratroopers at War, 1942–1945* (Toronto: Dundurn Press, 2003); Bernd

Horn and Michel Wyczynski, *Tip of the Spear — An Intimate Portrait of the First Canadian Parachute Battalion, 1942–1945* (Toronto: Dundurn, 2002); and Bernd Horn and Michel Wyczynski, *In Search of Pegasus — The Canadian Airborne Experience, 1942–1999* (St. Catharines, ON: Vanwell, 2000).

44. Robert Taylor, "Paratroop Van Eager to be Tip of Army 'Dagger,'" *Toronto Star,* August 12, 1942.

45. James C. Anderson, "Tough, Hard-As-Nails Paratroopers Arrive to Open Shilo School," September 22, 1942, 1; "Toughest in Canada's Army Back for Paratroop Course," *Toronto Star,* September 21, 1942, 1; and Ronald K Keith, "Sky Troops," *Maclean's Magazine,* August 1, 1943, 18–20, 28. This is simply a representative sample. Virtually every article in newspapers nationwide used similar adjectives to describe Canada's "newest corps elite." See also "Assembling Paratroopers At Calgary," *Globe and Mail,* August 18, 1942, 13; and Taylor, "Paratroop Van Eager to be Tip of Army 'Dagger.'"

46. "Assembling Paratroopers At Calgary," *Globe and Mail*; and Taylor, "Paratroop Van Eager to be Tip of Army 'Dagger.'"

47. "Assembling Paratroopers At Calgary," *Globe and Mail.*

48. James C. Anderson, "Canada's Paratroopers Don't Have Stage Fright," *Saturday Night,* December 12, 1942.

49. 2 Cdn Para Bn was the higher priority of the two units. National Defence Headquarters (NDHQ) directed the commanding officer of 1 Cdn Para Bn to transfer all jump-qualified personnel who volunteered to 2 Cdn Para Bn. The rumour that 1 Cdn Para Bn's supposed sister unit would see action before 1 Cdn Para Bn would, quickly circulated through the ranks of 1 Cdn Para Bn. Predictably, many of the aggressive and action-seeking paratroopers transferred to 2 Cdn Para Bn.

50. The definitive history of the FSSF is Colonel Bernd Horn and Michael Wyczynski, *Of Courage and Determination: The First Special Service Force, "The Devil's Brigade" 1942–1944* (Toronto: Dundurn Press, 2013). See also D. Burhans's *The First Special Service Force. A War History of the North Americans 1942–1944* (Nashville: Battery Press, 1996); Major J.W. Ostiguy, "The First Special Service Force," March 14, 1951, 1, file 145.3003 (D1), DND, Directorate of History and Heritage (DHH), Army Historical Section; Joseph A. Springer, *The Black Devil Brigade. The True Story of the First Special Service Force in World War II* (Pacifica, CA: Military History, 2001); Robert Todd Ross, *The Supercommandos. First Special Service Force — 1942–1944* (Atglen, PA: Schiffer Military History, 2000); Colonel George Walton, *The Devil's Brigade* (Philadelphia: Chilton Books, 1966); and James A. Wood, *We Move Only Forward. Canada, the United States and the First Special Service Force, 1942–1944* (St. Catharines, ON: Vanwell, 2006).

51. Norway represented an important source of scarce ores vital to the war effort. For example, Norwegian molybdenum was an important steel-hardening alloy and it represented 70 percent of the German supply, 95 percent of which came from deposits from the Knaben mine in the south of Norway. In addition, Finnish nickel, refined in Norway, represented 70 percent of the German intake; Norwegian aluminum and copper 8 percent respectively. Burhans, 33.

52. The Romanian and Italian missions were quickly ruled out.

    In the case of Romania, the country supplied approximately three million tons of oil to the Axis powers annually. The oil was derived from approximately five thousand oil wells, clustered in various fields within a fifty-mile radius of Ploesti. The magnitude of the objective and the manpower that would be required to effectively neutralize the target (i.e., thousands of wells), particularly in light of the heavy defences in the area, convinced planners that a ground assault would be no less resource intensive than would a strategic bombing campaign. This, combined with the fact that there was no reasonable extraction plan for the raiding force, caused planners to drop it as a possible target.

    The Italian option was no less problematic. The hydroelectric capacity there was concentrated in only twelve power stations, but they extended along the northern Po River watershed from the French border across Italy. More important, the actual impact of a temporary stoppage on the German war effort would be minimal. Burhans, 30–33.

53. The actual breakdown of the 697 was: colonels (2i/c) — 1; lieutenant-colonels or majors — 4; majors or captains — 6; lieutenants — 36; other ranks — 650. Canadian military attaché, message to Defensor, Washington, July 16, 1942, Library and Archives Canada [hereafter, LAC], RG 24, file HQS 20-4-32, Mobilization and Organization (Vol. 1), Plough Project, 1st Canadian Special Service Battalion (hereafter, 1 CSSBN), Microfilm reel C-5436.

54. Lieutenant-Colonel C.M. Drury, assistant military attaché, Canadian legation, Washington, D.C., letter to the Directorate of Military Operations & Intelligence, NDHQ, Washington, D.C., July 7, 1942, LAC, RG 24, Vol. 15301, 1 CSSBN War Diary, August 1942.

55. The average age of the Forcemen between July 1942 and December 1943 was twenty-six years old. This was considerably higher that of other U.S. Army units. Lieutenant-Colonel Paul Adams, the Force's executive officer, later pointed out that this was a very important factor in the Force's cohesion and maturity. Major Scott R. McMichael, "The First Special Service Force," in *A Historical Perspective on Light Infantry*, Research Survey No. 6 (Fort

Leavenworth, KS: Combat Studies Institute, U.S. Army Command and General Staff College, 1987), 172.

56. Ross Munro, "Albertan Second in Command of Allies' Super-Commandos," unidentified Canadian newspaper clipping, August 6, 1942, LAC, RG 24, Vol. 15301, 1 CSSBN War Diary, Serial 1354, August 1942.

57. CCO, "Plough Scheme" memorandum to CCHQ, January 19, 1943, NA, DEFE 2/6, COC War Diary.

58. Don Mason, "'Air Commandos' Will Strike Hard at Axis," unknown publication, LAC, RG 24, Vol. 15301, 2nd Canadian Parachute Battalion [hereafter, 2 CSSBN], War Diary, August 1942.

59. Horn and Wyczynski, *Of Courage and Determination*, 123. See also: McQueen, memorandum to CGS, October 8, 1942, LAC, RG 24, HQS 20-4-32, "Mobilization Organization" (1 CSSBN), Reel C-5436; Canmilitry, message to Defensor (Stuart to Murchie), GSD 2088, October 8, 1942, LAC, RG 24, CMHQ, Vol. 12,305, File 3/Plough/1 "Organization and Operation of Proposed Plough Project."

60. McQueen, memorandum to CGS, October 8, 1942, LAC, RG 24, HQS 20-4-32, "Mobilization Organization" (1 CSSBN), Reel C-5436. See also, Canmilitry, message to Defensor (Stuart to Murchie), GSD 2088, October 8, 1942, LAC, RG 24, CMHQ, Vol. 12,305, File 3/Plough/1 "Organization and Operation of Proposed Plough Project"; James Wood, "'Matters Canadian'" and the Problem with Being Special: Robert T. Frederick on the First Special Service Force," *Canadian Military History* 12, no. 4 (Autumn 2003): 21.

61. See Military attaché, message to Defensor, Ottawa, MA1286 16/7, July 12, 1942, LAC, RG 24, HQS 20-4-32, Mobilization Organization, Plough Project (1 CSSBN), Reel C-5436; "Minutes of Meeting Held at C.O.H.Q. On 4.1.43 To Discuss Long — and Short — Term Policy Regarding Norwegian Operations," para 4., "Cobblestone Operations," NA, DEFE 2/6, COC War Diary; Peter Layton Cottingham, "Once Upon A Wartime. A Canadian Who Survived the Devil's Brigade" (Private Printing, 1996), 49; and Burhans, 36.

62. Horn and Wyczynski, *Of Courage and Determination*, 123; Marshall, letter to Pope, "Second Canadian Parachute Battalion," October 17, 1942, LAC, RG 24, HQS-2-32, Employment and Movement Operations, 1 CSSBN, Reel C-5489.

63. Defensor, telegram to Canmilitry, No. G.S.D. 2088, October 8, 1942. LAC, RG 24, HQS-2-32, Employment and Movement Operations, 1 CSSBN.

64. Ibid. Not surprisingly the CGS suggested that McNaughton determine whether the British would welcome the 2nd Parachute Battalion in their Airborne Division, or if he would consider adding it to the First Canadian Army so as to develop options in the event the Americans cancelled their participation.

65. Marshall, letter to Pope, "Second Canadian Parachute Battalion," October 17, 1942, LAC, RG 24, HQS-2-32, Employment and Movement Operations, 1 CSSBN, Reel C-5489.

66. Pope, letter to CGS, "Second Canadian Parachute Battalion," October 20, 1942, LAC, RG 24, HQS-2-32, Employment and Movement Operations, 1 CSSBN, Reel C-5489. See also Defensor, telegram to Canmilitry, No. G.S.D. 2088, October 8, 1942, LAC, RG 24, HQS-2-32, Employment and Movement Operations, 1 CSSBN.

67. "Minutes of the War Cabinet Committee," October 28, 1942, LAC, RG 2, Series A-5-B, Cabinet War Committee, Minutes and Documents of the Cabinet War Committee, Vol. 11, Meeting no. 201, October 28, 1942, Reel C-4874.

68. The success of the various SOF raids at the onset of the war drove Hitler to extreme reaction. On October 18, 1942, he issued his famous "Commando Order," which directed that "all men operating against German troops in so-called commando raids in Europe or in Africa are to be annihilated to the last man." Enemy intelligence summaries bluntly acknowledged that "men selected for this sort of commando [mission] by the enemy are well-trained and equipped for their task." So incensed was the German dictator by their constant attacks that he ordered them killed, "whether they be soldiers in uniform ... whether fighting or seeking to escape ... even if these individuals on discovery make obvious their intention of giving themselves up as prisoners." He insisted that "no pardon is on any account to be given." See 10 Pz Div Circular, "Sabotage and Commando Operations," January 10, 1943, NA, DEFE 2/6, War Diary, COC; John Parker, *Commandos. The Inside Story of Britain's Most Elite Fighting Force* (London: Headline, 2000), 2–3; and Julian Thompson, *War Behind Enemy Lines* (Washington D.C.: Brassey's, 2001), 127.

69. Lieutenant-General McNaughton, letter to Major-General Crerar, August 19, 1941, LAC, RG 24, Vol. 12260, File 1, Para Tps/1, Message (G.S. 1647).

70. The school itself faced a tenuous future. Its survival hung in the air pending the final decision on the structure of the post-war army.

71. The JAS/CJATC mission included:

   a) research in air-portability of army personnel and equipment;
   b) user trials of equipment, especially under cold weather conditions;
   c) limited development and assessment of airborne equipment; and
   d) training of paratroop volunteers; training in air-portability of personnel and equipment; training in maintenance of air; advanced training of glider pilots in exercises with troops; training in some of the uses of light aircraft.

See "The Organization of an Army Air Centre in Canada," November 29 and December 27, 1945, DHH 168.009 (D45).

72. For a detailed history of the Canadian Special Air Service Company, see Bernd Horn, "A Military Enigma: The Canadian Special Air Service Company, 1948–49," *Canadian Military History* 10, no. 1 (Winter 2001): 21–30.

73. "SAS Company — JAS (Army)," June 13, 1947, LAC, RG 24, Reel C-8255, File HQS 88-60-2.

74. "SAS Company," October 30, 1947, 4, and "Requested Amendment to Interim Plan — SAR," September 11, 1947, LAC, RG 24, Reel C-8255, File HQS 88-60-2.

75. "SAS Company — JAS (Army)," Appendix A, June 13, 1947.

76. "Special Air Service Company — Implementation Policy," September 12, 1947, LAC, RG 24, Reel C-8255, File HQS 88-60-2.

77. "SAS Company," (Air S94), October 30, 1947, LAC, RG 24, Reel C-8255, File HQS 88-60-2.

78. "SAS Terms of Reference," April 16, 1948; "Duties of the SAS Coy," January 29, 1948; SAS Coy — Air Training Directive," December 1948, LAC, RG 24, Reel C-8255, File HQS 88-60-2.

79. "SAS Company," October 27, 1948. LAC, RG 24, Reel C-8255, File HQS 88-60-2.

80. Luc Charron, "Loss of a Canadian Hero," *The Maroon Beret* 4, no. 2 (August 1999): 28.

81. Interviews of former serving members by author. See endnote 73 for additional details.

82. See Bernd Horn, *Bastard Sons: A Critical Examination of the Canadian Airborne Experience, 1942–1995* (St. Catharines, ON: Vanwell, 2001); George Kitching, *Mud and Green Fields. The Memoirs of Major-General George Kitching* (St. Catharines, ON: Vanwell, 1986), 248; "Command, Mobile Striking Force," October 21, 1948, DHH 112.3M2 (D369); and Sean Maloney, "The Mobile Striking Force and Continental Defence 1948–1955," *Canadian Military History* 2, no. 2 (August 1993): 78.

83. *Special Committee on Defence. Minutes of Proceedings and Evidence*, June 21, 1966, 298–99.

84. Colonel D.H. Rochester, "The Birth of a Regiment," *The Maroon Beret* (1988): 34.

85. For a definitive history of the Canadian Airborne Regiment, see Bernd Horn, *Bastard Sons: A Critical Examination of the Canadian Airborne Experience, 1942–1995* (St. Catharines: Vanwell, 2001).

86. "Formation of the Canadian Airborne Regiment — Activation and Terms of Reference," May 15, 1967, 3.

87. Ibid., 3.

88. Ibid., 2.

89. Cdn AB Regt planning staff, "Canadian Airborne Regiment — Operational Concept, Annex C"; and *CFP 310 (1) — Airborne, Volume 1, The Canadian Airborne Regiment,* Chapter 1, Section 2, "Role, Capabilities and Employment" (N.p.: N.p., 1968).

90. The move and reorganization, however, became a defining moment for the Cdn AB Regt. It signalled nothing short of the organization's eventual demise.

    Also of great importance, and fundamental to the regiment's subsequent decline, was the loss of independent formation status. It was now simply an integral part of the newly created SSF. The Cdn AB Regt became nothing more than just another infantry unit, albeit an airborne one. It lost its special exemption from taskings and was now given assignments in the same manner as the other units within the SSF.

    However, there was a more serious consequence. As the regiment became defined and viewed as just another infantry unit, its claim on seasoned officers and soldiers was dismissed. Tragically, it lost its preferred manning. It was no longer in the enviable position of receiving only experienced and mature leaders and men. Prior to the reorganization all riflemen within the commandos had to be qualified to the rank of corporal. This of course meant that those soldiers were generally more mature and experienced. However, after the move to CFB Petawawa, the former pre-requisite was no longer followed. The resultant influx of younger, immature, and more junior soldiers had an eventual impact on the character and reputation of the Cdn AB Regt. See Horn, *Bastard Sons,* 143–84.

91. The SSF was formerly 2 Canadian Mechanized Brigade Group (CMBG). It reverted back to 2 CMBG in 1995.

92. Incidents included the mistreatment of prisoners on several occasions; the alleged unjustified shooting and resultant death of an intruder; and the torture death of an apprehended thief. These occurrences ultimately defined the Airborne's achievements in the public consciousness. For additional details see Horn, *Bastard Sons,* 185–248.

93. See Horn, *Bastard Sons,* 185–209.

94. Ibid., 217–48.

95. Brigadier-General Jim Cox, interview with author, April 27, 2010.

96. See Peter Harclerode, *Secret Soldiers. Special Forces in the War Against Terrorism* (London: Cassell & Co, 2000); Paul de B. Taillon, *The Evolution of Special Forces in Counter-Terrorism* (Westport: Praeger, 2001); Benjamin Netanyahu, *Fighting Terrorism* (New York: Noonday Press, 1995); Christopher Dobson and

Ronald Payne, *The Terrorists* (New York: Facts on File, 1995); Landau, 187–201; Marquis, 62–65; and Brian MacDonald, ed., *Terror* (Toronto: Canadian Institute of Strategic Studies, 1986).

97. New units were created or existing ones assigned new tasks. For example, the Germans established Grenzschutzgruppe 9 (GSG 9) in September 1972; the British assigned the counterterrorist (CT) role to the SAS that year same year; the French formed the Groupe d'intervention de la gendarmerie nationale (GIGN) two years later; the Belgians created the Escadron spécial d'intervention (ESI) also in 1974; the United States formed its premier CT unit, the 1st Special Forces Operational Detachment (DELTA) in 1977; and the Italians raised the Gruppo di intervento speciale (GIS) in 1978. In the end, most countries developed specialist CT organizations to deal with the problem. See Major-General Ulrich Wegener, "The Evolution of Grenzschutzgruppe 9 and the Lessons of 'Operation Magic Fire' in Mogadishu," in *Force of Choice — Perspectives on Special Operations*, eds. Bernd Horn, David Last, and Paul B. de Taillon, (Montreal: McGill-Queens University Press, 2004); David Miller, *Special Forces*, (London: Salamander Books, 2001), 18–73; Harclerode, 264–85, 411; Adams, 160–62; Marquis, 63–65; Weale, 201–35; Colonel Charlie Beckwith, *Delta Force* (New York: Dell, 1983); Connor, 262–356; Neillands, 204–46; and Leroy Thompson, *The Rescuers. The World's Top Anti-Terrorist Units* (London: A David & Charles Military Books, 1986).

98. Discussion between author and a former lieutenant-governor of Ontario who was a member of the federal government at the time, June 21, 2006. This speaks to the perceptions of many senior conventional leaders with regards to SOF at that point in time.

99. Brigadier-General Ray Romses, the first JTF 2 CO, stated that part of the rationale for the transfer was the government's emphasis on "economizing how it did business." With the Cold War over and DND looking for new roles, the deputy ministers of the various departments rationalized that the seventy-five RCMP officers at SERT, who only trained, would be more beneficial doing actual police work, while DND, which was effective at training and looking for a new role, could do HR/CT. Interview with author, June 21, 2008.

100. DND News Release NR-04.098, dated December 8, 2004, "Joint Task Force 2 Members Receive U.S. Presidential Unit Citation."

Direct action is the term used for short duration strikes and other precise, small-scale offensive actions conducted by special operation forces to seize, destroy, capture, exploit, recover, or damage designated targets. Direct action differs from conventional offensive actions in the level of physical and political risk, operational techniques, and the degree of discriminate and precise use of force to achieve specific objectives.

Special reconnaissance (SR) is the term used to designate missions conducted to collect or verify information of strategic or operational significance. These actions complement and refine other collection methods, but are normally directed upon extremely significant areas of interest.

SSE is a type of direct action operation involving the gathering of intelligence and/or evidence from a specific area or location. SSEs may be conducted in friendly, hostile, denied, or politically sensitive territory. SSEs may include the destruction of weapons, munitions or equipment if the aforementioned items cannot be recovered. If there is no reasonable expectation of encountering enemy or hostile forces, SOF would not be required.

101. CANSOF utilizes an integrated operating concept that is based on SOTFs. The concept is predicated on a broad spectrum of SOF capabilities, which, in the event of a deliberate deployment or crisis, are tailored and scaled into an integrated force package. SOTFs are developed, generated and, where required, force employed in order to achieve tactical, operational, and strategic effects required by the Government of Canada. See Canada, *Canadian Special Operations Command — 2008* (Ottawa: DND, 2008); and Canada, *CANSOFCOM Capstone Concept for Special Operations 2009* (Ottawa: DND, 2009), 11, for additional detail.

102. Allan Woods, "Canada's elite commandos and the invasion of Afghanistan," *Toronto Star*, www.thestar.com/news/canada/afghanmission/article/800296-
-forged-in-the-fire-of-afghanistan, accessed April 25, 2010.

103. "Ottawa: Canadian Commandos Were on Afghan Frontlines," http://circ.jmellon.com/docs/html/jtf2_canada_super_commandos.html, accessed March 12, 2004.

104. Ibid.

105. Martin O'Malley, "JTF 2: Canada's Super-Secret Commandos," *CBC News*, circ.jmellon.com/docs/html/jtf2_canada_super_commandos.html, accessed March 12, 2004.

106. Cited in Woods, "Canada's elite commandos and the invasion of Afghanistan."

107. All non-attributed quotes are based on interviews with author.

108. Day noted, "We went through a pretty low period before Clyde [Russell] came in [as CO]. We started to suffer training fatigue — we were among the best, if not the best in the world at hostage rescue." But the problem was — they were never deployed. Many worried they had inherited some RCMP cultural affectations — a police mentality in many ways. The "two-

way range in Afghanistan forced us to adopt a more warrior mentality."

109. Colonel Mike Day, March 5, 2008. Day became the second commander of Canadian Special Operations Command, in July 2007.

110. The citation package also provided a brief history of CJSOTF (South): CJSOTF(S)/ TF K-Bar.

In October 2001, in response to the terrorist attacks of 9/11, Commander US CENTCOM directed the establishment of a combined joint special operation task force (CJSOTF) to conduct special operations in southern Afghanistan to destroy, degrade, and neutralize Taliban and al-Qaeda forces.

Captain (Navy) Robert Harward, U.S. Navy Commander, Naval Special Warfare Group One/Commander, TF K-Bar, began conducting maritime interception operations in the Arabian Sea. Ground combat operations began on November 22, 2001, when attached units conducted a ninety-six-hour clandestine SR in advance of a United States Marine Corps (USMC) assault on landing zone (LZ) Rhino in southern Afghanistan, while other units conducted advance force operations, reconnaissance, and assessment of alternate landing zones. On November 24, his Naval Special Warfare Task Force provided terminal guidance for the USMC assault on LZ Rhino.

On November 26, after seizure of LZ Rhino, Captain Harward stood up CJSOTF(S) and forces conducted a series of SR, DA, and SSE missions to detect, apprehend, and destroy Taliban and AQ forces. The TF provided critical SR in support of conventional forces during Operation Anaconda in March 2002.

From October 2001 to March 2002, CJSOTF-SOUTH conducted forty-two SR, twenty-three DA and SSE missions, directed 147 close air support missions, intercepted and searched twelve ships, apprehended 112 detainees and inflicted over 115 enemy casualties. All at a cost of three friendly casualties: one dead, two wounded.

111. "Joint Task Force 2 Members Receive U.S. Presidential Unit Citation," DND News Release NR-04.098, December 8, 2004.

112. Six awards (one Meritorious Service Cross (MSC), one Meritorious Service Medal (MSM) and six Mention in Dispatches (MiD)) were eventually given.

113. "Joint Task Force 2 Members Receive U.S. Presidential Unit Citation," DND News Release NR-04.098, December 8, 2004.

114. Canadian Alliance, "Expansion of JTF 2 Dangerous," February 7, 2002, http://circ.jmellon.com/docs/txt/joint_task_force_2_expansion_dangerous.txt, accessed March 12, 2004.

115. Ambassador Paul Cellucci, Conference of Defence Associates Conference, Ottawa, March 7, 2005.

116. General Rick Hillier, *A Soldier First: Bullets, Bureaucrats and the Politics of War* (Toronto: HarperCollins, 2009), 368.

117. David Pugliese, "Canadian Forces Make Mark in Afghanistan," *Defence News*, May 19, 2008, 18.

118. "We can't just take them out. It's tempting to simply fire a missile or sniper bullet and be done with suspected terrorist leaders — but it's a lot more complicated than that," Paul Robinson, *Ottawa Citizen*, May 27, 2008.

119. Lee Winsor, David Charters, and Brent Wilson, *Kandahar Tour: The Turning Point in Canada's Afghan Mission* (Mississauga, ON: John Wiley & Sons Canada, 2008), 167. The term *Tier 1 Taliban* refers to the hard line insurgents who fight for ideological, political, and/or religious reasons, as opposed to Tier 2 insurgents, who are considered guns for hire — young men driven to fight largely because of monetary considerations or coercion.

120. Lieutenant-Colonel Rob Walker, interview with author, October 5, 2008.

121. Pugliese, "Canadian Forces Make Mark in Afghanistan," 18.

122. "Talking Points. CAF Transformation Initiative," CDS GO/FO Symposium, Cornwall, February 2005, 3.

123. *Canadian Special Operations Command — 2008*; and *CANSOFCOM Capstone Concept for Special Operations 2009*, 8.

124. Hillier's desire to transform the CAF was based on his perception that the CAF had to become more responsive, adaptive, and relevant. He declared:

> We need to transform the Canadian Armed Forces completely, from a Cold War–oriented, bureaucratic, process-focused organization into a modern, combat-capable force, where the three elements — navy, army, and air force, enabled by special forces — all work together as one team to protect Canada by conducting operations effectively at home and abroad. I envisioned a flexible, agile, and quick-thinking military that would be able to bring exactly the right kind of forces to accomplish whatever mission they were given, whether it was responding to a natural disaster like a tsunami or an ice storm or fighting a counter-insurgency war in southern Afghanistan.

Hillier, *A Soldier First*, 323.

125. Canada, *Canadian Special Operations Command — 2008* (Ottawa: DND, 2008); and Canada, *CANSOFCOM Capstone Concept for Special Operations 2009* (Ottawa: DND, 2009), 8.

126. The events of September 11, 2001, led to the immediate assignment of the CBRN response capability of the CAF to a new, dedicated high-readiness

unit, the Joint Nuclear, Biological, Chemical Defence Company (JNBCD Company). By June 2002, the MND had approved the project that enabled the creation of the unit as well as a stand-alone CBRN response team (CBRN RT) to form the CAF component of the National CBRN RT with the RCMP and Public Health Canada partners. Since February 1, 2006, the unit has been a part of CANSOFCOM. Its name was officially changed to the CJIRU-CBRN in September 2007.

127. Canada, *Canadian Special Operations Command — 2008*; and Canada, *CANSOFCOM Capstone Concept for Special Operations 2009*.
128. Pugliese, "Canadian Forces Make Mark in Afghanistan," 18.
129. David Pugliese, "Military Forms New Quick Reaction Task Force," *Ottawa Citizen*, www.ottawacitizen.com/news/Military+forms+quick+reaction+task+force/3290244/story.html, accessed July 18, 2010.
130. Ibid.
131. Ibid.
132. CANFORGEN 030/08 CDS 003/08, 041846Z Feb 08.
133. CANFORGEN 029/08 CDS 002/08, 041846Z Feb 08.
134. David Pugliese, "Getting the Drop on Special Ops," *Ottawa Citizen*, July 17, 2010.
135. Ian Elliot, "Special forces different from video game portrayal," [Kingston] *Whig-Standard*, www.thewhig.com/ArticleDisplay.aspx?e=2882136, accessed January 26, 2011.
136. Larry Murray, interview with author and Bill Bentley, October 6, 2010.
137. Cited in Pugliese, "Getting the Drop on Special Ops."
138. Cited in Ibid.

Chapter 2

1. This name, like all other insurgent names used henceforth in the book, unless indicated otherwise, is a pseudonym.
2. Clearly, Mullah Omar is the actual name.
3. The commander CJSOTF-A developed the SOF CTF concept to conduct ATO wide, high-tempo disruption operations against point or area targets in known ACM sanctuaries to disrupt insurgent activities in the lead-up to, duration, and aftermath of the national elections in 2005. A lead nation was designated for each CTF operation. As such the lead nation was responsible for designating the target and taking lead on planning, co-ordination and support plan development. Commander CJSOTF-A believed this would enable concurrent planning and retention of a high operational tempo.
4. SSE is a type of direct action operation involving the gathering of intelligence and/or evidence from a specific area or location. SSEs may be conducted in

friendly, hostile, denied, or politically sensitive territory. SSEs may include the destruction of weapons, munitions or equipment if the aforementioned items cannot be recovered. If there is no reasonable expectation of encountering enemy or hostile forces, SOF would not be required.

5.   This name, like all other CANSOF personnel mentioned and all of the names used henceforth in the book, unless indicated otherwise, is a pseudonym.

6.   The Taliban fighter identified himself as a day labourer in Kandahar. He was alone, walking in the area. He refused to provide any further information.

7.   The term *chalk* is a military designation for a load of soldiers boarding an aircraft. Chalk numbers are allocated to specific aircraft for the sake of organization and identification.

8.   Commander CJSOTF-A promulgated his intent to maintain unrelenting pressure on the ACM leadership in order to preempt, disrupt and defeat ACM attacks and their ability to interfere with the Afghan parliamentary elections that were held in September 2005. As part of this campaign, he created CTF operations throughout the Afghanistan theatre of operations. Within this framework, CJSOTF-A authorized operations that were based on the combined forces of CANSOF and allied SOF. This CTF was specifically responsible for conducting high-tempo disruption operations in the period leading up to, during, and after the national elections that were scheduled for 18 September 2005, to choose the National Assembly.

9.   The conventional TF was comprised of the 3rd Battalion, 319th Airborne Field Artillery Regiment, of the 82nd Airborne Division. They deployed to Afghanistan from 2005–2006. They were assigned a task force role for manoeuvre operations in Kandahar Province under the 173rd Airborne Brigade. They were also responsible for indirect fires and radars in Afghanistan.

10.   Conventional nomenclature for call signs will be used to differentiate elements within the missions for clarity of text. They are based on a universal military system that breaks down the subordinate components of a unit. For example: C/S 1 indicates a sub-unit of a larger organization; C/S 11, 12, 13, etc represents a subordinate organization of the sub-unit, and C/S 11A, 11B, 11C or 12A, 12B, 12C, etc represents a subordinate organization of the sub-sub-unit.

11.   "Squirters" was slang used to denote insurgents that attempted to flee an area on the approach or arrival of coalition forces.

Chapter 3

1. De Chenartu Tangay was effectively two hamlets. Both were frequently visited by Taliban and the northernmost hamlet contained a probable Taliban safe house.
2. CJTF 76 was the higher headquarters to CJSOTF-A. It was a division-level HQ, responsible for fighting the combat brigades in Afghanistan. Its mission was to conduct the full spectrum of operations throughout its operational area, to defeat enemy extremist movements, establish enduring security, and set conditions for long-term stability.
3. Hamid Karzai became the first democratically elected head of state in Afghanistan on December 7, 2004. Elections to choose the National Assembly were scheduled for September 18, 2005.
4. Direct action (DA) is the term used for short-duration strikes and other precise, small-scale offensive actions conducted by special operation forces to seize, destroy, capture, exploit, recover, or damage designated targets. Direct action differs from conventional offensive actions in the level of physical and political risk, the type of operational techniques used, and the degree to which discriminate and precise use of force is used to achieve specific objectives.
5. Review of concept (ROC) drill is the process whereby ever element of the ground force walks through their actions through every phase of the operation to ensure coordination, deconfliction, and total understanding of the entire plan by all.
6. Whether or not the mission was compromised is hard to tell. Intelligence analysts believed surprise was achieved on the objective. However, quick reaction by the enemy after the initial surprise and the error of over-flying the HLZ and flying back along the enemy "gun" line mitigated any advantage that was initially achieved.
7. Code words are fictitious.
8. C-6 refers to a 7.62mm general purpose machine gun (GPMG).
9. Pelletier was seriously wounded. His squadron medic said,

I called for the JTAC to initiate a 9-line MEDEVAC request imme-diately. I continued with the casualty by packing the wound with Kerlix and then got word that we had to get the casualty up the hill if we needed to evacuate him. One member piggy-backed him up the hill because it was putting too much pressure on his belly to do the fireman carry. It was very difficult to get him up the hill and it took approximately five people to assist in that task.

Once at the top, I reassessed him. He was still conscious and responding to verbal stimuli. I started an IV line on him with a 500cc bag of N/S. I kept it at TKVO because I was certain that he was bleeding in his belly and because he still had a strong radial pulse. I was notified that there was another serious casualty so I handed the casualty off to 12A and told him to let me know if his condition changed.

10. The Priority 1 CANSOF and ANA casualties were evacuated to FOB Davis in Tarin Kowt.

11. The term blue-on-blue refers to an engagement between friendly forces. The term is derived from map symbology. The enemy is always marked in red on a map. Friendly forces are always marked in blue.

12. The enemy was always very effective at evacuating their dead and wounded from the battlefield whenever possible. This was done to both deny the ability of coalition forces to determine how many they killed, as well as to ensure the killed jihadists received the necessary last rites in accordance with their religion. Nonetheless, coalition ISR assets were normally able to spot casualties during the battle and the withdrawal.

13. An American JTAC who sat in on the after-action review commented, "You're very rough on yourselves. You planned this in a few hours, launched and still were successful in fighting at the squadron level."

14. David Pugliese, "JTF 2 soldier seriously hurt in firefight," *Ottawa Citizen*, December 8, 2005, A1.

15. For Alain Picard the battle was informative. "What was revealing when we got back," he stated, "was that no one person was real sure what exactly happened. To truly understand the bits and pieces on the ground you had to talk to everyone." The events, Picard stated, "revealed how chaotic things [can get] and how quickly one can lose the broader sense of things around you." Nonetheless, he concluded, "it was a great job by all." Picard did concede, however, "we fooled ourselves into believing that the enemy wouldn't be able to figure out how we do business." He acknowledged, "Anything that could go wrong — did." However, similar to the sentiments of his troop commander, he pointed out, "we got through the situation with no one killed and we had relative success [in] disrupting the enemy in a major way."

Chapter 4

1. SR/DA is the abbreviated form of special reconnaissance/direct action. Special (some nations use the term strategic) reconnaissance missions are missions conducted to collect or verify information of strategic or operational significance. These actions complement and refine other collection methods, but are normally directed upon extremely significant areas of interest. HMMVW translates to High Mobility Multipurpose Vehicle Wheeled.

2. Another key player in the region was a former Afghan militia commander who was paid a large sum of money to defect to the GoA banner. Reporting at the time indicated that despite his public claims of GoA support, he was actively supporting the insurgency and still held a key position in the Hizb-i-Islami Gulbuddin (HiG). He was also reported to have retained access to large cache of weapons in the Baghran district that he established during his time as a militia commander.

3. Insurgents launched an attack against the Musa Qala district centre on the evening of May 17, 2006. A reported 200-350 Taliban fighters participated in the attack under the leadership of a regional Taliban sub-commander. This was the second attack conducted against a district office. On April 30, 2006, fighters under another Taliban sub-commander launched a number of attacks against the Baghran district centre. The centre finally fell under the pressure of a reported one hundred Taliban fighters. The loss of the district centre was soon followed by the Taliban seizing control of Baghran village. The ANP took the brunt of the insurgent attacks. On April 28, 2006, four ANP officers were killed during an ambush while on patrol in Baghran district. Two weeks earlier, Taliban fighters assassinated Baghran district Chief Mullah Abdul Majid Akhund. This left the Baghran police in command. His force was eventually overrun on April 30, 2006.

4. The literacy rate in Afghanistan at the time was approximately 36 percent of the population. The literacy rate for males was estimated at 50 percent and for females 21 percent. Radio is the primary means for mass communication.

5. American Forces Press Service, "Operation Mountain Thrust Continues Momentum," U.S. Department of Defence News, http://www.defense.gov/news/newsar, accessed April 8, 2014.

6. Although on the surface the task seemed simple, the mission carried a number of implied tasks such as: confirm or deny ACM activity in NAIs; disrupt ACM C2 nodes and facilitators in the Baghran Valley; fix ACM for DA strike force; determine blocking position in north portion of Baghran Valley; route recce in Baghran Valley; determine interdiction routes along East edge of Baghran Valley; determine potential HLZs (northern Baghran Valley blocking positions and squirter routes); link-up with allied SOF in north Baghran Valley on June 1, 2006; recce location for forward logistic element in vicinity of Musa Qala and Baghran City for 2-87 Infantry combat service support company; determine population atmospherics; BHO with 2-87 on June 9, 2006; coordinate with CJSOTF-A for tactical reserve/QRF, based on allied SOF element / infantry company; coordinate psychological operations (PSYOPS) team

from 205 Corps (Afghan PSYOPS); coordinate information operations (IO) leaflet drops; coordinate 2-87 Infantry for concept of operations for Phase II; Be prepared to conduct offensive operations; be prepared to conduct sensitive site exploitation (SSE); conduct local indigenous liaison; establish detain detainee control and battlefield screening; reinforce other coalition elements; coordinate with FOB Price for staging on infiltration and exfiltration (e.g. refuelling); coordinate with the allied SOF element from TF-73 for air assault into north Baghran Valley; conduct mobility training and rehearsals for squadron and ANA attachments; coordinate for air resupply; coordinate intelligence, surveillance and reconnaissance (ISR) plans and platforms and fire plan; locate and develop mechanisms to mitigate EWS; conduct special intelligence surveillance; conduct intelligence preparation of the battlefield (IPB) of Baghran Valley; and confirm actionable intelligence.

7. The detainee handling procedure was well articulated prior to the mission. Any individual to be detained was to be initially secured and controlled by CANSOF. Photographs were to be taken along with a voice recording and sent by communication DATA to CANSOF headquarters at the FOB in Kandahar, along with justification for detention. Detainees were to be consolidated and extracted by the rotary wing QRF. Detainees were to be accompanied by a Canadian escort to Kandahar Airfield (KAF) for release or transfer to Afghan authorities as appropriate.

8. The original plan was to have the 2-87 Infantry conduct an air assault into the north end of the valley to create a blocking position.

9. This was not totally unusual and was standard practice for ANP in many areas. It made recognition difficult for coalition forces and resulted in a number of friendly fire incidents. The practice also made the loyalty and motives of the ANP suspect.

10. The enemy was so rattled by the engagement that even hours later, they refused to go back on the ridge line to the OP position to search for a missing comrade.

11. Rutledge actually later identified one of the village "elders" with whom he had spoken the day previously as they were setting up a fire base to cover the obstacle crossing. The indiviual moved into the village, where two local dogs from a compound he walked by, attacked him. In addition, a woman ran over and removed two children who were in his path. If he was truly an elder from the village, this would not have happened.

12. A local stated that all people in the Baghran Valley were sympathetic to the Taliban by either choice or force and that the greatest number of Taliban supporters and Taliban lived to the east of the regional centre. He

disclosed that the Baghran District Centre was heavily infiltrated by the Taliban. He further revealed that he had been forced to help the Taliban in the past. The most recent event happened approximately fifteen days ago when the Taliban forced their way into his home. When he replied that he was unable to help them due to lack of supplies, the Taliban proceeded to beat him with their weapons. He further stated that the local population was indifferent to the situation, they merely wished that all elements, insurgents, GoA, and coalition forces would leave the area.

13. The accusation of collateral damage was immediately reported up the chain-of-command. A review of footage from the strike quickly indicated the accusations were false. However, the truth had little impact in the villages where the rumours continued to spread.

14. The patrol learned that the ACM were having an internal debate whether to engage the patrol or not. Some commanders felt it was best just to let the CANSOF patrol go on their way without engaging them.

15. The next morning the CANSOF members found that the IR glow sticks were broken to activate them but the paper coverings were not properly removed.

Chapter 5

1. Bill Roggio, "The Great Taliban Turkey Shoot," The Long War Journal, September 12, 2006, www.LongWarJournal.org/archiv, accessed April 10, 2014; and Australian Government/Department of Defence, "Sergeant Brett Wood — To be awarded the medal for gallantry," www.defense.gov. au/vale/sgt_v, accessed April 10, 2014.

2. Rutledge later went to check on Stan, a retired allied SOF operator who had participated in a number of seminal SOF missions since 1980 and had never been shot. This time, he was hit by seven 7.62mm rounds, the majority being stopped by his radio, webbing, and rifle. Two, however, hit home, one taking off his thumb and the other hitting him in the thigh. When Rutledge came across him, he was propped up against a wall trying to shoot his rifle through a hole in the wall. His only remark was, "I can't believe I was shot."

3. Shawn was later killed in Iraq.

4. The detainees were left in sector "C" when the assault force extracted to the west because they were assessed to be of insufficient intelligence value to warrant the further risk to the ground force of trying to extract them. As it was, the CANSOF and QSF troops had to fight their way out of the compound through a gauntlet of fire while carrying one dead and three wounded soldiers.

5.   Steele had literally just arrived in theatre. He heard the ground force needed a liaison officer to work with the Australian QRF and he was briefed that the target contained approximately five Taliban. As a result, he thought, *How hard can it be — I'll take this even though I just arrived on the ground.*

6.   The Australians awarded a number of honours and decorations.

7.   Karzai later stated there were sixteen civilian deaths.

Chapter 6

1.   The Harper government directed that the title *Canadian Forces (CF)* revert back to its pre-1968 unification name *Canadian Armed Forces (CAF)* in December 2012.

2.   The Meyer Group (fictitious name) included up to three Chinese nationals who were specialists in IEDs and explosives.

3.   This was not unusual. Reporting by local nationals indicated that insurgents often used mosques to store IED materials and weapons.

4.   The prison break operation was initiated by a suicide bomber who drove a truck laden with explosives into the prison's main entrance and then detonated the lethal cargo. The explosion destroyed the gate and buried the guards under rubble. At that point, motorcycles raced toward the prison, carrying insurgents who breached the prison walls through the destroyed gate and entered the facility firing RPG and AK-47 assault rifles. A second breach was blown in the rear wall of the prison. Hundreds of prisoners, including an estimated four hundred captured Taliban insurgents, escaped during the twenty-minute battle.

Chapter 7

1.   Normally, for crisis rapid reaction–type tasks, SOTF 58 would attempt to deploy the Amber Cycle SRT, thereby leaving the Green Cycle SRT available for more deliberate operations as the Afghan partner force for SOTF 58.

2.   OP Response was in essence a crisis response contingency operation to protect the people of Kandahar City.

3.   The ISAF command chain normally consisted of non-Canadians. As such, the Canadian SOTF commander could play the "national red card." Although the standard operating procedure (SOP) was that the mentors would accompany the PRC-K, he would veto this requirement if he felt that without the necessary intelligence picture, planning, and preparation the situation was too risky to deploy mentors.

4.   By the end of the tour of SOTF 58, the PRC-K had arrested a Taliban assassin and commander in Kandahar City based on Afghan intelligence and in accordance with the rule of law.

5. Commander SOTF 58 explained, "The PRC-K wore special uniforms with special fighting assault gear — old CANSOF tactical vests. They carried AK-47 rifles with modified laser modules and early generation NVGs. They didn't always wear NVGs, due to comfort. In any case, you could clearly differentiate the PRC-K from ANP. However, normally they wore ANP uniforms so they wouldn't stand out and be targeted. During special missions, they would wear their special uniforms."

6. Yaroslav Trofimov, "Taliban Move into Kandahar City," *Wall Street Journal*, http://online.wsj.com/article/SB100014240527023036548045763412713033806658.html, accessed March 23, 2012.

7. Pastor Terry Jones held a mock trial at his Dove World Outreach Center on April 2, 2011, in Gainesville, Florida. He originally intended to burn the Koran on the anniversary of 9/11, in response to plans to develop an Islamic centre near the site of the September 2011 terrorist attack. The act sparked days of deadly protest worldwide. In Afghanistan, protests at the United Nations compound in Mazar-I-Sharif resulted in the killing of seven U.N. employees. As a result of the mock trial, the Church's membership plummeted. In addition, furniture sales, on which the Church relied, also steeply declined. Moreover, the Church's internet and insurance providers cancelled their services. Jones has since launched a new organization, "Stand up America," which plans to protest the Koran, Shariah law, and radical Islam. Kevin Sieff, "Florida pastor Terry Jones's Koran burning has far-reaching effect," *Washington Post*, www.washingtonpost.com/local/education/florida-pastor-terry-joness-koran-burning-has-far-reaching-effect/2011/04/02/AFpiFoQC_story.html, accessed March 23, 2012; and Adelle M. Banks, "Florida pastor oversees Quran burning," *USA Today*, www.usatoday.com/news/religion/2011-03-21-quran-burning-florida_N.htm, accessed March 23, 2012.

8. Trofimov. A government spokesman conceded the escape was a "disaster" for the government. Ismail Sameem, *Reuters*, "Afghan forces battle Kandahar insurgents for 2nd day," www.reuters.com/article/2011/05/08/us-afghanistan-violence-idUSTRE7460Q020110508, accessed March 23, 2012.

9. Trofimov.

10. Jon Boone, "Taliban launch multi-pronged attack on city of Kandahar," *Guardian*, May 8, 2011. www.guardian.co.uk/world/2011/may/08/taliban-launch-attack-kandahar-city, accessed March 23, 2012. Despite Afghanistan president Hamid Karzai's declaration that the attacks in Kandahar were in direct retribution for the American raid that killed Osama bin Laden, Taliban commanders clearly proclaimed the attacks were not in revenge for the killing of the al-Qaeda leader. Sameem, "Afghan forces battle Kandahar insurgents for 2nd day."

11. Boone.

12. As always, numbers vary depending on the source used. See Sameem, "Afghan forces battle Kandahar insurgents for 2nd day." Other sources quoted in this work also have numbers within the range given in the text.

13. Trofimov.

14. Ibid.

15. Boone.

16. Sameem.

17. Boone.

18. Their rush to deploy created one accident. One of the Toyota Hilux pickup trucks rolled when the driver attempted to negotiate a turn approximately two hundred metres outside the rear gate of the FOB at too high a speed. The gravel road had steep embankments and the driver fell prey as he was unable to make the turn safely. CSOR members from the CSOR element scrambled to conduct the vehicle recovery. No one was seriously hurt.

19. Chantu, the Afghan-appointed PRC-K commander, was well connected on a personal basis with some of the higher echelon. The GFC felt he was motivated to accomplish missions, although he was not tactically skilled. As a result, he would always default to the mentors and let them conduct the operations.

20. Many of the mentors shook their heads when they arrived. Ironically, a number of CSOR personnel were sent to the governor's palace the week prior and were told to park their vehicles in the area between the palace and the shopping complex. A number of them immediately noted the massive commercial building and evaluated it as a threat, specifically because it could be used as a strongpoint due to its complexity, strategic location close to the governor's palace, and dominating position for fire and observation. Their concerns were ignored and they were assured by the security detail in the area that the building was kept under a close watch.

21. Complicating matters was the fact that briefing the teams on the plan had to go through a translator. This was ponderous and slow, and increased the risk of misunderstanding or key details not being passed on correctly.

22. Due to the size of the building and the small assault force, Captain Morrison had to be content with leaving only a piquet at the major control points (i.e., stairwell access points at each floor level).

23. PRC-K members apparently did not seem to absorb the importance of securing the stairway access points. Left unsupervised, even for the shortest time period, they would wander off and leave the access points insecure.

24. It is difficult to ascertain exactly the nature of the civilians taken under control. Interview statements describe them as a family: four young males, an old man, and a young child.
25. Normally there would be four to five PRC-K members, followed by two CSOR mentors and then another four to five PRC-K members. This was found to be the optimal stacking to ensure there was the requisite control. Mentors always tried to ensure they were at a minimum in pairs to ensure they had reliable mutual support should the Afghan partners melt away, as happened throughout the assault.
26. Individuals taken under control were later released or transferred to Afghan authorities as appropriate.
27. Chantu, the PRC-K commander, did not participate in the clearance operation. Throughout, he could be found at either the VDO or CCP.
28. At the end of the mission, Sergeant Sebastien noticed a number of bullet holes in his uniform. In addition, he also realized he had taken some small shrapnel fragments in the leg.
29. Adding to the leadership challenge was the fact that for each attack the CSOR mentors had to assemble a new group, as some PRC-K members just disappeared, while others would outright refuse to participate.
30. During the operation, Corporal Smith provided medical care to five wounded Afghans, one wounded insurgent, and two wounded civilians.
31. Sergeant Colin required light to perform the procedure, which took him under three minutes, so he needed the PRC-K members who had sought refuge in the CCP to point their flashlights, which were attached to their weapons, at the site of the procedure. He conceded he was concerned at having all those weapons pointed at him, but he had no choice. Meanwhile, the wounded PRC-K member's fireteam partner was "freaking out" and others had to restrain him from shooting all the PUCs.
32. Sebastien noted, "Mentally, being a few metres away from someone who desperately wanted to kill you was very weird."
33. The OC also noted that Clausewitzian "friction" is always at play, that is, there are always compounding small problems (e.g., fire, darkness, lack of flashlights, accounting for/finding individuals who scatter) making the task more difficult.
34. Boone.
35. "Afghanistan: Kandahar Taliban attackers defeated," *BBC News*, www.bbc.co.uk/news/world-south-asia-13325855, accessed March 23, 2012.
36. Sameem.
37. COMISAF Morning Stand-Up, May 10, 2011.

INDEX

ABOUT THE AUTHOR

Colonel Bernd Horn, OMM, MSM, CD, Ph.D. is a retired Regular Force infantry officer who has held key command and staff appointments in the Canadian Armed Forces, including deputy commander of Canadian Special Operations Forces Command, commanding officer of the 1st Battalion, The Royal Canadian Regiment, and officer commanding (OC) 3 Commando, the Canadian Airborne Regiment. He is currently the director of the Canadian Special Operations Forces Command Professional Development Centre, an appointment he fills as a reservist. Dr. Horn is also an adjunct professor of the Centre for Military and Strategic Studies, University of Calgary, as well as an adjunct professor of history at the Royal Military College of Canada. He is also a Fellow at the Canadian Defence & Foreign Affairs Institute. He has authored, co-authored, edited, or co-edited forty books and well over a hundred monographs/chapters/articles on military history, special operations forces, leadership, and military affairs.

Other Books by Colonel Bernd Horn

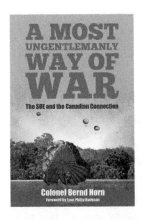

A Most Ungentlemanly Way of War:
The SOE and the Canadian Connection

During the Second World War, British prime minister Winston Churchill created the Special Operations Executive (SOE) to conduct acts of sabotage and subversion, and raise secret armies of partisans in German-occupied Europe. With the directive to "set Europe ablaze," the SOE undertook a dangerous game of cat and mouse with the Nazi Gestapo. An agent's failure could result in indescribable torture, dispatch to a concentration camp, and, often, a death sentence.

While the SOE's contribution to the Allied war effort is still debated, and many of its files remain classified, it was a unique wartime creation that reflected innovation, adventure, and a fanatical devotion on the part of its personnel to the Allied cause.

The SOE has an important Canadian connection: Canadians were among its operatives and agents behind enemy lines. Camp X, in Whitby, Ontario, was a special training school that trained agents for overseas duty, and an infamous Canadian code-named "Intrepid" ran SOE operations in the Americas.

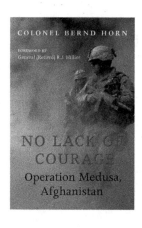

No Lack of Courage:
Operation Medusa, Afghanistan

No Lack of Courage is the story of the North Atlantic Treaty Organization's Operation Medusa, the largely Canadian action in Afghanistan from September 1 to 17, 2006, to dislodge a heavily entrenched Taliban force in the Pashmul district of Afghanistan's Kandahar Province. At stake, according to senior Afghan politicians and NATO military commanders, was nothing less than the very existence of the reconstituted state of Afghanistan, as well as the NATO alliance itself. In a bitterly fought conflict that lasted more than two weeks, Canadian, Afghan, and Coalition troops defeated the dug-in enemy forces and chased them from the Pashmul area.

In the end, the brunt of the fighting fell on the Canadians, and the operation that saved Afghanistan exacted a great cost. However, the battle also demonstrated that Canada had shed its peacekeeping mythology and was once more ready to commit troops deliberately to combat. Moreover, it revealed yet again that Canadian soldiers have no lack of courage.